Rhetoric

THE LANGUAGE LIBRARY

EDITED BY DAVID CRYSTAL

Rhetoric

The Wit of Persuasion

Walter Nash

Basil Blackwell

First published 1989

Basil Blackwell Ltd
108 Cowley Road, Oxford, OX4 1JF, UK

Basil Blackwell Inc.
3 Cambridge Center
Cambridge, MA 02142, USA

British Library Cataloguing in Publication Data

A CIP catalogue record for this Book is available from the British Library.

Library of Congress Cataloging in Publication Data
Nash, Walter.
  Rhetoric: the wit of persuasion / Walter Nash.
     p.   cm.—(The Language Library)
  Bibliography: p.
  Includes index.
  ISBN 0-631-16754-4
  1. Rhetoric.   2. Persuausion (Rhetoric)   I. Title.   II. Series.
PN187.N37   1989
808—dc20   89-986
                                                              CIP

Typeset in 10½ on 12½ Baskerville
by Times Graphics
Printed in Great Britain by
The Camelot Press, Southampton.

Contents

Renaissance Examples – Tropes in Text – The Rhetoric
of Episodes – Where the Author Stands

I have no doubt that I often speak of things better treated, and with more truth, by masters of the craft . . . I may have some objective knowledge one day, or may perhaps have had it in the past, when I happened to come across passages that explained things. But I have forgotten it all; for though I am a man of some reading, I am one who retains nothing.

So I can offer nothing certain, except to account for the extent of my knowledge at the present time.

Michel de Montaigne, Of Books

Preface

It is conventional for authors to say in their Prefaces what their books are about – or what they think they are about. I will be unconventional to the extent of saying what I think my book is *not* about. It is not, I think, about the history of rhetoric, and it is not, I am sure, about the meaning of 'rhetoric' in current literary theory. I am certainly interested in such matters and have inevitably touched upon them here and there in these chapters, but if I were to claim more than a general acquaintance with them the defects of my reading would soon be exposed.

If I have an aim, it is to rehabilitate rhetoric as an ordinary human competence, which, through its power to move and amuse, develops the wit of persuasion. I call it 'ordinary' because that celebrated hero of academic myth, 'the Person on the Clapham Omnibus', makes regular use of it and encounters it every day: in the Press and other news media, in humour, in argument, in popular entertainments, in literary art. It is an ordinary thing with some extraordinary manifestations, some graceful, others less so. There are occasions on which I, like any other critic of language and literature, would question the propriety and indeed the decency of rhetoric. There are, on the other hand, many instances in which I find it appropriate, fair (in two senses) and often highly entertaining; and I do not envy anyone who has never been prompted, by the skill of rhetoric, to applaud a point well made, to feel just a little gooseflesh, to rejoice in beauty, to laugh at the absurd.

As to its plan, the book proceeds, after an introductory discussion, to studies of rhetoric and the emotions, rhetoric as distraction, rhetoric as argument; and so to chapters on rhetoric and language, on rhetorical structures in literature, on rhetoric in comic discourse, and finally on the defence of rhetoric. To list the contents of the book in this way may belie the cumulative purport of what I hope is a cohesive and continuously developing argument. Technical terms are a notorious difficulty, but I hope I have been able to explain these clearly, and that my text is not unduly burdened by them. There is a current revival of interest in the study of rhetoric, and it would be regrettable if an opaque terminology were to make the subject seem inaccessible to all but a philological few. I should be happy to think that my book might remove some of the obstacles to access, and help to persuade university students and others to discover a lively modern appeal in this 2000-year-old discipline.

W.N.
University of Nottingham.

Acknowledgements

The author and publishers wish to thank the following who have kindly given permission for the use of copyright material: Jonathan Cape Ltd and Peters Fraser and Dunlop Ltd on behalf of the Executors of the Estate of C. Day Lewis for 'As one who wanders into old workings' by C. Day Lewis from *Collected Poems 1954*, Jonathan Cape and The Hogarth Press. Faber and Faber Ltd. with Random House, Inc. for an extract from XXIV 'To Christopher Isherwood', a birthday poem by W. H. Auden from *The English Auden: Poems, Essays and Dramatic Writings*; and with Grove Press, Inc. for an extract from *The Real Inspector Hound* by Tom Stoppard. David Higham Associates Ltd on behalf of the estate of the author and New Directions Publishing Corporation for 'A Refusal to Mourn the Death of a Child, By Fire, in London' from *The Poems of Dylan Thomas*; Copyright 1945 by the Trustees for the Copyrights of Dylan Thomas. The *Independent* for material from the 12 January 1988 issue. Methuen, London for material from *The Caretaker* by Harold Pinter, 1960. The *Observer* for 'When the Strain is in Taking the Train', 7 August 1987.

1

'If I Might Claim Your Attention for a Moment...'

I have designs on you, as the tattooist said to his girl friend, thus propounding the scope of rhetoric so adroitly as to make further definition almost unnecessary. For it is indeed the point of rhetoric to have designs on an audience, or a victim; and the purpose of these designs is not wholly to persuade, as may be commonly supposed, but rather to involve the recipient in a conspiracy from which there is no easy withdrawal. In rhetoric there is always an element of complicity; it can be magniloquent, or charming, or forceful, or devious, but whatever its manner it seeks assiduously to involve an accomplice in its designs.

Take, for example, that fateful moment recorded in the Book of Genesis, when the proto-rhetorician, the serpent, practises seductively upon Eve. This is how the story reads in the version of 1611:

> Now the serpent was more subtil than any beast of the field which the Lord God had made. And he said unto the woman, Yea, hath God said, Ye shall not eat of every tree of the garden?
> And the woman said unto the serpent, We may eat of the fruit of the trees of the garden:
> But of the fruit of the tree which is in the midst of the garden, God hath said, Ye shall not eat of it, neither shall ye touch it, lest ye die.
> And the serpent said unto the woman, Ye shall not surely die:
> For God doth know that in the day ye eat thereof, then your eyes shall be opened, and ye shall be as gods, knowing good and evil.
> And when the woman saw that the tree was good for food, and that it was pleasant to the eyes, and a tree to be desired to make one wise, she took the fruit thereof, and did eat, and gave also unto her husband with her; and he did eat.

What the serpent produces here is a sales pitch so transparent as to be almost risible; if we were not aware that the composer of Genesis, describing the villain's designs upon Eve, has ulterior

designs upon *us*, we might well wonder how he could consider this
wormy practice at all 'subtil'. But it is seen to work through the
complicity of the tempter and his victim. It works round a few
emphatically sharp points, represented by the words 'every',
'surely', 'for God doth know', and 'ye shall be'. More precisely, it
works round a pattern of utterances embodying these emphases.
There is, to begin with, a teasing question, 'Hath God said ye shall
not eat of every tree of the garden? (in which, as far as his tenuous
vocal equipment will allow, the reptile lays significant emphasis on
'every'); then there is a robust assurance, 'Ye shall not surely die';
then there is an appeal to authority, 'for God doth know . . . your
eyes shall be opened'; which is followed quickly by the absolute
guarantee, 'ye shall be gods'. Thus the scheme:

1 The Teasing Question	'Hath God Said ye shall not eat of *every* tree?'
2 The Robust Assurance	'Ye shall not surely die'
3 The Authority	'For God doth know . . . '
4 The Guarantee	'Ye shall be gods'

Now is there not something uneasily familiar about these
proceedings? They seem to embody a very durable programme of
seduction, one that has everyday applications in the modern world
of the adman and the punter. For example:

1 The Teasing Question	'Won't your friends look you in the face?'
2 The Robust Assurance	'You needn't suffer from unsightly rashes'
3 The Authority	'MAX PICTOR has the answer'
4 The Guarantee	'Your skin will be the envy of all'

Or possibly:

1 The Teasing Question	'Does your car start at the fifteenth try?'
2 The Robust Assurance	'No call to consult your bank manager'
3 The Authority	'Leading manufacturers recommend our product'
4 The Guarantee	'With WHIZZO you'll *always* start first time'

And if the sales pitch is so obviously resistible, madam, why is it that the bathroom cabinet is crammed to breakout with your lotions, your unguents, your aromatic distillations, your pots and enigmatic tubes? And why is it, sir, that your garage shelves, like mine, are heaped with cobwebbed, rimrusty cans of quickstart and lube-oil and one-shot petrol-miser and scientifically balanced window wash? Were we really persuaded of the necessity of buying these things? Surely someone had designs on us, and we obligingly completed the design.

But to go back to that moment in Genesis. In reading the tale, which is, after all, a very good tale, it is easy to overlook the fact that the subtle tempter is not exactly his own snake. He is a character in a myth, a fictional device; he, the apparent designer, is also a design; he has a creator who has put words into his ophidian mouth, and who has scripted answers for his victim. The Genesis story, like other narratives, incorporates at least two important planes of relationship: an 'inner' relationship, between the characters themselves, and an 'outer' relationship between the author and his audience, or his assumed reader. The 'inner' relationship is what we take for the reality of the text (we speak of fictional characters and judge them as though they were acting in the world of our common acquaintance and experience), but of course it is a 'reality' devised and manipulated by the author, a design effecting a design. Thus the mythographer, having designs on his audience, represents the serpent having designs on the lady:

AUTHOR—Serpent/Rhetorician—Lady/Respondent—READER

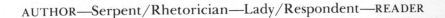

'inner' relationship

'outer' relationship

Ultimately, the author is 'getting at' his reader no less craftily than the serpent is 'getting at' Eve. We have to assume a claim on the readership, a claim that presupposes a cast of mind, a social experience, an emotional or psychological need. The fabulist of Genesis, undertaking to explain the peculiar lucklessness of

humankind, is at pains to impress upon us the effects of herpetolo-
gical wantonness and womanly weakness, with a strong implied
recommendation that if we are to blame someone we must put it
all down to the woman. The fable is designed to support the
ultimate rhetorical claim, which in this instance is a kind of
political act.

THE GENERATION OF ELOQUENCE

The biblical example presents two aspects of the rhetorical act. On
the one hand, we see in it a kind of programme, a set of steps upon
which the design is constructed; and on the other, an aesthetic
form or genre, here taking shape round the designated markers of
the argument; and yet it would be perfectly possible for the same
construction to be incorporated in a different genre. That is to
say, we might take the suggested model – Teasing Question,
Robust Assurance, Authority, Guarantee – and build it into a
different sort of story; into a dialogue set in a supermarket; into a
newspaper editorial on commercial ethics; into a sonnet on love or
democracy or malt whisky; even into a limerick on the art of
composition:

> 'Shall I ever attain the sublime?' –
> 'There's no need to attempt it in rhyme;
> All the Universe knows, from the plod of your prose,
> That it's only a matter of time' –

and so on into any literary variety we may care to attempt. But
note that if we change the genre, we will usually, if not always,
change the kind of claim made on the reader. The rhetorical
construction may remain the same: its development into a
distinctive literary form implies a different author–reader relationship.

This suggests something rather interesting, even disturbing: a
limited, possibly describable, set of basic patterns, or 'constructions', and a virtually infinite variety of possible generic realiza-
tions. It is interesting to the scholarly mind seeking for paradigms
and models, and it is disturbing to those of us – meaning all of us –
who like to see things comfortably posted into social pigeonholes.
It reduces our perception of rhetoric as a species of flashy verbal
behaviour practised by politicians and mountebanks, and implants

the uncomfortable suspicion that for much of the time and in many of our doings and dealings we are ourselves practitioners of this insidious craft. Our workaday purposes generate eloquence.

Roman rhetoricians coped with the awkward ubiquity of rhetoric by ignoring all manifestations unrelated to purposes of value to the state. Then as now, there must have been some quick-witted, quick-tongued people in tavern and market, but the achievements of the natural orator are not recorded. Rhetoric was a curriculum subject, and an important one, highly placed among the *artes liberales*, or acquisitions proper to a free citizen. Roman youths of good family studied it to prepare themselves for public life: to plead cases in the courts, to take part in debate, to deliver speeches on festive or funereal occasions. There were accordingly three conventional divisions of oratory, a *genus iudicium*, a *genus deliberativum* and a *genus demonstrativum*, and these *genera* were determined by the decorum of public occasions. Rhetoric – but perhaps one should qualify – *official* rhetoric – was evidently a gentlemanly ornament, a mark of breeding.

The student in the ancient world was required from time to time to exercise his apprentice skill in *progymnasmata* – which might nowadays be called coursework assignments, or themes, or projects. The subjects of these exercises were such as might typically fall within the scope of the *genera*. (Juvenal mentions in his tenth satire, as a stock subject for schoolboy declamations, the career of Hannibal–an exercise in the *genus demonstrativum*.) The aim was to develop a personable fluency and address, a forensic presence often denoted by the adjective *facundus* and its companion noun *facundia*. Horace, warning his addressee Torquatus that the underworld is quite another country and not at all like Rome, declares:

>   non, Torquate, genus, non te facundia, non te
>   restituet pietas.[1]

('Neither your family connections, nor your eloquence, nor your righteousness will get you out of it.') Horace's trinity of qualifications glances significantly at the required characteristics of a Roman gentleman: to be of good family, to do one's duty, and to be articulate, in pleading or debate. Nothing could be more expressive of public status of rhetoric in Roman times than the poet's single reservation; only when you are dead will it let you down. So honoured in ancient times, the art and practice of rhetoric, especially political rhetoric, is nowadays more ambivalently viewed. Certainly 'good speakers', people who can 'put the message across' are well regarded; but on the other hand, 'windbags' and 'hot air' are routinely denounced. *Facundia* has fallen suspect, like proficiency at games of chance or undue familiarity with the workings of the stock market.

THE TRADITIONAL RULES

What *facundia* required was essentially this: the readiness to seize a discursive structure and adapt it convincingly to a generic form. The structure was in part a predictive facility for the audience, enabling them to follow the argument or the presentation of a case; but the facility was also a trap, a mechanism virtually obliging the addressee to become involved in the addressor's persuasive procedures. The compulsion of structure was disguised, or made acceptable, by graces of language, and in the case of oratory by concomitant graces of gesture and vocal inflexion. Style, in other words, helped both to implement the underlying stratagem and to distract attention from it. In this respect the methods of rhetoric have changed very little since classical times.

The ancient discipline was intended to prepare the novice for tasks that involved speaking in public; the procedures it outlined were therefore connected in part with the psychology of composition and in part with the techniques of performance. The latter are possibly of minor interest to the modern college or university student, who, however, is still deeply involved, know it or not, in compositional aspects of rhetoric. How do you begin an essay? What sort of thing should you write about? What should you concentrate on, dwell on, and what might you pass over lightly, perhaps with some skilful turn that suggests your knowledge of things unspoken? Are there good examples round which you can frame your exposition? And again and again, how do you *begin*, what blessed power will enable you to get through the first paragraph and into the substance of your piece without going disastrously wrong? Such questions in classical times would have been referred to the rhetorical procedure known as *heuresis*, or 'discovery'; in Latin, *inventio*. Our own Augustan writers will occasionally speak of an author's *invention*, but in doing so they do not mean the power to make something up out of nothing.

'Invention' in their sense – and of course in the sense of the Ciceronian *inventio* – meant the capacity to *find*, to rummage through one's personal stock of knowledge and perception, and come up with the right connections.

This is a capacity that can be enhanced by the use of certain instruments that effect an entry or give the writer an initial hold on the subject. Only consider some of the schemes commonly used to enter into academic discourse: devices of interrogation ('What do we mean by X?'); of definition ('X may be described as . . .'); of definition supported by the appeal to authority ('Aristotle has interestingly defined X as . . .'); of comparison ('X is in many ways like Y'); of etymology ('The word X means, by derivation . . .'); even of exemplary anecdote ('Once upon a time . . . which is a pleasant illustration of what we understand by X'). Anyone who has ever listened to a lecture – more desperately speaking, anyone who has ever *composed* a lecture – will recognize these devices and may be able to add others. They are positions from which to manoeuvre dialectically. In Greek, such 'positions' are called *topoi*; in Latin, *loci*. To this day, freshman rhetoric admits the principle of the 'topic sentence', the initial utterance that establishes the ground of the argument. Some of the ancient 'topics', however, were not so much dialectic strategies as images reflecting and appealing to human experience at large. These were the *koinoi topoi*, the 'general topics', which came to be known in Latin as *loci communes*, 'commonplaces'.[2] In modern English, 'commonplace' has become a pejorative term; in past centuries, by contrast, a commonplace was a repository of shared wisdom and experience. The recording of commonplaces, or their collection in 'commonplace books', was once an educational exercise; Hamlet's cry, 'My tables, – meet it is I set it down, / That one may smile, and smile, and be a villain', is an ironic and tortured pretence of wishing to record a *locus communis*.

The heuristic process, the skill of discovery for which we all develop our favoured techniques, is preliminary to, but in some measure also involved with, the planning and ordering of discourse. Of old this planning procedure was known as *taxis* (Latin, *dispositio*). The modern student who dutifully writes out essay headings is engaged in *taxis* of an elementary and indeed rather superficial kind. Some kind of predictive plan is necessary, or one would never begin, but our predictions do not often correspond with the finished form of the work. The process of writing is heuristic in many ways, perhaps most powerfully in revealing to the writer the discursive plan that best represents the material. *Taxis* is therefore not a fixed pattern. It is first predictive, then investigative (as the author experiments with the material), and then, possibly, retrospective, as the work of editing and revising begins. The classical theorists present some general principles of *taxis* (discussed below), but they are no doubt principles permitting of much modification or elaboration.

Lexis (or *elocutio*) was the next stage in the classical programme: the dressing of the topic in appropriately expressive and persuasive language. 'Next stage', however, is misleading. The rhetoricians did not mean that discourse is progressively constructed rather than organically conceived. We must understand a continual interplay between the processes of composition. Just as *heuresis* and *taxis* are interdependent, so there is a creative relationship between *heuresis* and *lexis* ; the style, or diction, begins to be conceived while we are still discovering the substance of our writing. *Heuresis*, *taxis* and *lexis* may indeed be called processes of conception, and any theory of rhetoric, ancient or modern, must concern itself with these processes. For the classical rhetoricians, however, conception had necessarily to be augmented by performance, or delivery. Hence the inclusion, in their view of the art, of the techniques of memorizing (*mneme*, *memoria*) and gesture (*hypocrisis*, *actio*). Even today, a 'good speaker' is one who can perform without frequent and obvious reference to a script, an idiot-board or a teleprompter; and who is able to use physical gesture in expressive or emphatic support of salient points and propositions. (Though it must be said that most of our politicians and trade-union leaders would do better to speak up and stand still; there is a limit to what the clenched fist or the thumb-and-forefinger pinch can communicate.) The forces and graces of gesture are not wholly external to the technique of composition. In composing, gestures of emphasis are often envisaged and are 'scripted in' to the writing, so that a reader can imagine a delivery and a speech style. Equally, it may be argued that composition frequently accommodates some potentially mnemonic elements. It is a psychological necessity, for example, that I should be able to bear in mind the whole of the sentence I am currently writing. If I lose track of the construction I must begin again, casting it in a more compact or at least a more easily memorable form, and so on from sentence to sentence; and in this way my memory controls the ultimate shape of the text. Thus 'gesture' and 'memory' might continue to have a significant place in a theory of composition. On the whole, however, the rhetoric of writing tends to ignore these skills of performance, even though a notion of performance is essential to rhetoric.

THE IMPORTANCE OF STRUCTURE

A notion that has never been ignored is that of discourse structure, the ancient process of *taxis*. The classical view of how to present a case in argument involved a structure of basically five sequent elements. (The scheme could be refined and expanded.)[3]. The speaker would begin with an introduction, or *exordium*, in which he would do his best to make himself agreeable to his audience. The rhetorical manoeuvres this involved are still recognizable by connoisseurs of the after-dinner speech: flattering allusion to the eminence of the auditors ('this distinguished company'), the speaker's confession of his own inadequacy ('ill qualified as I am'), the appeal for goodwill and a fair hearing ('if I may ask you to bear with me'), the identification of the speaker's personality and interests with those of the audience ('we Rotarians'). This ingratiating process, in Latin called *captatio benevolentiae*, is a hardy invention that has survived through centuries in countless speeches, prefaces, prologues, narrative openings.

The *exordium* would be followed by a *narratio* – that is, an outline of the case, or argument, with its contextual circumstances. The case would, of course, call for supporting examples, precedents, analogies and so forth; these were supplied in the phase of discourse known as the *confirmatio*. A prudent speaker, however, would be aware of some of the arguments an opponent might be able to bring against him, and would want to lessen his vulnerability by anticipating and answering these. This was known as the *confutatio* or *refutatio*. Finally there would be a *conclusio* or *peroratio*, a short process of graceful withdrawal, in which the speaker would thank the auditors for their patience and express his confidence in their good sense and goodwill. Such, typically, was the structure of Roman oratory, and it has provided a pattern which we still use in academic debate, in party polemic, in the prosecution or pleading of cases at law, in newspaper editorials. It must be said that this method of construction, so convenient to the

Roman lawyer, is not the only possible kind of textual design. The morning's paper, the day's work, the evening's television will certainly present us with examples of other rhetorical structures. This ancient pattern is none the less a persistent one, and it may be that it is one powerful realization of an archetypal process requiring the imposition of logical form on psychological appeal.

THE IMPORTANCE OF STYLE

The 'discovery' and organization of material were as indeed they must always be – primary tasks; there remained, however, the *lexis*, the patterns of wording that enforced the structures of persuasion. What was important above all else, almost as a voucher of the author's sincerity, was stylistic propriety or decorum, the relevance of the manner to the matter. This is one of the most powerful traditions of classical rhetoric to later ages. One of the best-known reflections of it in literary English is provided by Shakespeare in *Julius Caesar*. Brutus and Mark Anthony both make speeches over Caesar's body, and both are rhetorically accomplished to the point of providing copybook examples of traditional conventions of language and structure. Brutus, however, is the less effective, and his failure is essentially stylistic. He addresses himself to a task fraught with moral burdens, a speech in defence of a political assassination, in a dandified progression of figures:

> Romans, countrymen, and lovers! hear me for my cause; and be silent that you may hear: believe me for mine honour; and have respect to mine honour, that you may believe; censure me in your wisdom; and awake your senses, that you may better judge.

Brutus' opening combines the figures of speech known as *epistrophe*, as when a construction begins and ends with the same word ('hear me for my cause, and be silent that ye may hear') and *antimetabole*, in which significant lexical items are reiterated in the order a . . . b . . . b . . . a ('believe' . . . 'honour' . . . 'honour' . . . 'believe'). Compare this ornate exordium with Anthony's simple – disingenuously simple, designedly plain-spoken – beginning[4]:

> Friends, Romans, countrymen, lend me your ears.

Brutus is sincere, a wholly honest man, anxious to justify to a rational audience the deed of violence he and others have just committed; but his speech is a stylistic disaster. Anthony dissimulates, disclaiming at first any intention to launch into political rhetoric; and then proceeds to a compelling display of the orator's resources of style and devices of performance. 'I am no orator, as Brutus is', he tells the admiring crowd. 'For I have neither wit, nor words, nor worth, / Action, nor utterance, nor the power of speech / To stir men's blood.' But these things are of course just what he *does* have, almost to excess; and the scene is an illustration, mediated to us through Shakespeare's inventive perception, of the importance of style.

The Greek writers on language and composition make recurrent reference to the propriety of stylistic level to generic function. The principle was developed and formalized by the Roman rhetoricians, who distinguish the three levels of the Grand, the Middle and the Plain style. The Plain style was considered most effective in 'proof', or argument; the Middle style most appropriate to the task of pleasing an auditor or a reader; and the Grand style best adapted to the purpose of stirring the profounder emotions of one's audience. Each of these styles had potential defects for the inattentive or unskilled practitioner. The attendant danger of the Grand style was that it might become turgid and inflated (*sufflatus* is the word Cicero uses); that of the Middle style was a tendency to degrade easiness into the merely flaccid; and that of the Plain style to be *exilis*, to lack colour and vitality.[5]

These ideas dominated rhetorical practice for centuries, and continue to do so. They are the origin of the notion of *decorum*, continually worked and reworked by our own Renaissance writers, and amusingly expounded by the egregious (but highly talented) Dr Goldsmith:

> Sir Joshua Reynolds was in company with them one day, when Goldsmith said, that he thought he could write a good fable, mentioned the simplicity which that kind of composition requires, and observed, that in most fables the animals introduced seldom talk in character. 'For instance', (said he,) 'the fable of the little fishes, who saw birds fly over their heads, and envying them, petitioned Jupiter to be changed into birds. The skill (continued he,) consists in making them talk like little fishes.' While he indulged himself in this fanciful reverie, he observed Johnson shaking his sides, and laughing. Upon which he smartly proceeded, 'Why, Dr Johnson, this is not so easy as you seem to think; for if you were to make little fishes talk, they would talk like WHALES.'[6]

Goldsmith's charge is one often levelled against Johnson: his constant and seemingly uncritical use of the Grand style (a charge which, however, close examination of Johnson's work will not always sustain).

The question of stylistic propriety raised in this anecdote is one to which our authors have addressed themselves since medieval times. Chaucer's *Canterbury Tales* is a striking example of a work in which shifts of stylistic level, and devices of rhetoric generally, are not only exemplified in various narrative types, but also commented on. Thus, the Host asks the Clerk of Oxenford for a plain narrative, without rhetorical embellishment:

> Telle us som murie thyng of aventures,
> Youre termes, youre colours, and youre figures,
> Keepe hem in stoor til so be that ye endite
> Heigh style, as whan that men to kynges write.
> Speketh so pleyn at thys tyme, we yow preye,
> That we may understonde what ye seye.[7]

The function of the 'heigh style' is here well defined: it is to be kept for some important official errand, such as writing to a king. Rhetoric in the Middle Ages preserves its ancient importance as an institution serving the concerns of state.

The 'termes', 'colours' and 'figures' of which the Host speaks so dismissively are the very stuff of the stylistic tradition founded in Classical times.[8] They are what we now call 'figures of speech', though that is an insufficient and indeed misleading name – misleading because the phrase 'figures of speech' too often suggests a usage void of serious reference (for example 'When he said he could kill her, that was just a figure of speech'). Figurative language in rhetorical tradition has a more than decorative purport; it is meant to have an effective power, to raise the emotions associated with a subject and correspondingly to evoke emotional responses from an audience. A distinction is traditionally made between *tropes* and *figures* or *schemes*. (*Schema* was the Greek word, *figura* the Latin; both mean 'form', 'shape'.) A trope is a manipulation of meaning – the word *tropos* denotes 'turning'; thus in metaphor there is a 'turn' by virtue of which an A is expressed in terms of a B. Metonymy, synecdoche and irony are similarly tropes. By contrast, antimetabole ('I like pudding but pudding doesn't like me') and anadiplosis ('he left it with the porter, the porter put it in his box, the box was destroyed in the fire') are in the strict sense figures, that is to say purely patterns or sequences of words. In modern usage, however, 'trope' and 'figure' are not rigorously distinguished (understandably, since figures often accommodate tropes) and the words 'figure' and 'figurative' are commonly used to describe stylistic phenomena in general. The figures have always been a prominent feature of rhetoric; at the same time, it must be said that the intensive cultivation of figurative rhetoric has contributed, paradoxically, to a lapse in respect for the ancient art. When Samuel Butler remarked, in a frequently quoted couplet, that 'All a rhetorician's rules / Teach but the naming of his tools' he was jeering at what had become a plethora of learned words for figures of speech.

THE PERCEPTION OF RHETORIC

By Butler's time rhetoric as a subject for study had enjoyed a very long run and had begun to lose academic face. Its centuries-old status as the informing principle of civilized discourse is none the less remarkable. The conspectus of classical rhetoric presented in the foregoing pages is an attempt, necessarily defective, at summarizing the developing doctrines of hundreds of years, from the teachings of Gorgias in the 5th century BC to what is arguably the master-work of ancient rhetoric, the *Institutio Oratoria* of Quintilian, in the 1st century AD. A master-work indeed, but not rhetoric's final statement. The craft and its theory went on into the Middle Ages and Renaissance, entering afresh into the service of religion and politics, and education, and literature, and inevitably changing somewhat its direction and emphasis.

There is neither place nor occasion here to discuss this lengthy post-classical history, but a few general comments are necessary. One of the facts which even a superficial study will quickly establish is the increasing elaboration of the art, partly by augmenting and complicating elements in the oratorical plan, and partly by adding to the repertoire of figures and tropes. The *topoi* of the older rhetoric are the ground for the ubiquitous *sententiae* (maxims, aphorisms) and *exempla* of medieval discourse, and also for the set pieces of declamation which, almost in the fashion of operatic arias, adorn the Chaucerian tale or the action of the Elizabethan stage: passages of description, accusation, justification, lamentation, invocation, stylistic 'patches' which were to become part of the conventional texture of literary works. (In this sense the *topos* still lives in the rhetoric of film scripts and TV shows. During the war of 1939–45, any American film on a social or political theme was likely to include a highlight speech on 'democracy', or 'the people', or 'the little guy'; a convention which older rhetoricians would certainly have approved as the adroit placing of a *topos* to work with maximum effect on the emotions of an audience.)

The ramification of figures is the most obvious and striking development in the history of rhetoric. Aristotle and Cicero mention a mere handful; the Renaissance theorists deal in dozens. The accretion of schemes was such as to suggest a trivial ingenuity, and, indeed, led to numerous overlaps not convincingly explained away; in many cases the distinctive value of the figure might elude all but the most exacting analyst. It was not simply that the emphasis in rhetorical studies had shifted from structure to style, or had relegated *taxis* to the domain of logic, in order to concentrate on *lexis*. That certainly happened; but what also followed was the consequence, observable in other fields, of developing a meta-language – a terminology – in excess of practical functions, so that the terminology itself displaces the proper concerns of the subject. This was the point of Samuel Butler's sarcasm. The perception of rhetorical 'rules' as a kind of wordy tinkering with words affected the perception of figurative rhetoric itself, as a meaningful practice. Samuel Butler's contemporaries, the members of the newly founded (1660) Royal Society, took a Platonic view of rhetoric as a showy deceiver, an enemy of plain truth. Thus Bishop Sprat, in a frequently quoted passage from his *History of the Royal Society*, describes the stylistic principles of the institution:

> They have therefore been most rigorous in putting in execution the only Remedy that can be found for this *extravagance*, and that has been a constant Resolution to reject all amplifications, digressions, and swellings of style; to return back to the primitive purity and shortness, when men deliver'd so many *things* almost in an equal number of *words*. They have exacted from all their members a close, naked, natural way of speaking, positive expressions, clear senses, a native easiness, bringing all things as near the Mathematical plainness as they can, and preferring the language of Artisans, Countrymen, and Merchants, before that of Wits or Scholars.

In this statement we may clearly discern the scientist's wish for a factual rigour of expression and the deluded hankering after a state that never was, of a language with a consistent and unambiguous fit of symbol and referent (the delivering of so many things almost in an equal number of words). Sprat's statement is important as a mark of attitudes to language current among the 'natural philosophers' of his day. In it we see the stirrings of a belief still widely held, that the language of science is necessarily 'exact' and 'factual', whereas that of literature is diffuse, vague, 'airy-fairy', existing only to construct its own show.

THE TACIT SKILL

But that perception of rhetoric, important as it may have been at that particular point in the development of our vernacular culture, did not disable or invalidate the practice of the art. (Nor, for that matter, did it quite put paid to its status in pedagogic theory, since books on figurative rhetoric went on being published up to and into the Romantic period.) What happened, over a fairly long stretch of time, was that rhetoric became a tacit skill, practised by imitation or intuition, adapting to changing historical circumstances and social or intellectual functions. We may perhaps speak of a 'buried awareness' of rhetoric, in which the most deeply implanted yet least understood element is that of structure – the *taxis* of classical theory. So powerfully has European consciousness been affected by Greek and Roman theories of discourse structure that even today those theories guide the presentation of arguments at law, the writing of scholarly papers and theses, the construction of newspaper editorials. But those genres, significantly, are in one way or another associated with the 'official' rhetoric, the rhetoric of the state or its institutions. It is really not very surprising if legal or academic argument at the present day is discernibly similar in its modelling and structural procedures to the recommended patterns of argument in classical times. It would be surprising indeed if those patterns could be easily related to some of the 'unofficial' rhetorics of the salesman, of the adman, of the newspaper reporter, of the video, of the narrator bent on subverting the expectations of narrative. Such 'unofficial' rhetorics, it may be argued, have always existed; when the serpent tempted Eve he followed a plan of his own, without consulting a manual. In any case, they are not always structured in accordance with the old forensic pattern. Diverse functions call for diverse structures, and the study of these would be a primary task for anyone wishing to rehabilitate rhetoric as a modern discipline.

A CLASSICAL CONSTRUCTION

But let us consider some examples of post-seventeenth-century English rhetoric, beginning with a text that answers fairly well to traditional principles of *taxis*. It is taken from Boswell's *Life of Johnson*, and describes a part of the talk among a company gathered at the Mitre Tavern on the evening of Wednesday 3 April 1776. Boswell observes:

> I introduced the topick, which is often ignorantly urged, that the Universities of England are too rich; so that learning does not flourish in them as it would do, if those who teach had smaller salaries, and depended on their assiduity for a great part of their income. JOHNSON. 'Sir, the very reverse of this is the truth; the English Universities are not rich enough. Our fellowships are only sufficient to support a man during his studies to fit him for the world, and accordingly in general they are held no longer than till an opportunity offers of getting away. Now and then, perhaps, there is a fellow who grows old in his college; but this is against his will, unless he be a man very indolent indeed. A hundred a year is reckoned a good fellowship, and that is no more than is necessary to keep a man decently as a scholar. We do not allow our fellows to marry, because we consider academical institutions as preparatory to a settlement in the world. It is only by being employed as a tutor, that a fellow can obtain any thing more than a livelihood. To be sure a man, who has enough without teaching, will probably not teach; for we would all be idle if we could. In the same manner, a man who is to get nothing by teaching, will not exert himself. Gresham College was intended as a place of instruction for London; able professors were to read lectures gratis, they contrived to have no scholars; whereas, if they had been allowed to receive but sixpence a lecture from each scholar, they would have been emulous to have had many scholars. Every body will agree that it should be the interest of those who teach to have scholars; and this is the case in our Universities. That they are too rich is certainly not true; for they have nothing good enough to keep a man of eminent learning with them for his life.'

Johnson's impromptu development of this 'topick' proposed by
Boswell (though of course we do not know how much of the
remarkable coherence of the text we owe to Boswell's own tidying)
is the typical performance of a mind profoundly conditioned by
Greek and Roman models. As to style, it may not sound rhetorical
because its language is quite plain (thus countering the widespread
impression, mentioned above, that all Johnson's utterances are
couched in the Grand style). The structure, however, is discernibly modelled on traditional notions of *taxis*. The *exordium* is a little
irregular, in that Boswell introduces a *topos* which is immediately
challenged by Johnson, who revises the statement of the topic and
then develops the counter-argument. The topic-statement leads
into a *narratio*, a statement of the general case:

> Our fellowships are only sufficient to support a man during his
> studies to fit him for the world, and accordingly in general they are
> held no longer till an opportunity offers of getting away.

This is followed by a *confirmatio*, a consideration of particular cases
in corroboration of the central thesis:

> Now and then, perhaps, there is a fellow who grows old in his
> college; but this is against his will, unless he be a man very indolent
> indeed.[*1st case*] A hundred a year is reckoned a good fellowship,
> and that is no more than is necessary to keep a man decently as a
> scholar.[*2nd case*] We do not allow our fellows to marry, because we
> consider academical institutions as preparatory to a settlement in
> the world. [*3rd case*] It is only by being employed as a tutor, that a
> fellow can obtain anything more than a livelihood. [*4th case*]

Now ensues the *confutatio*, anticipating objections and making the
concessions which in effect refute the opposing argument. Johnson's 'to be sure' signals the transition to this phase:

> To be sure, a man, who has enough without teaching will probably
> not teach; for we would all be idle if we could. [*1st concession*; note
> the reasonable appeal to human nature] In the same manner, a man
> who is to get nothing by teaching, will not exert himself. [*2nd,
> analogical, concession*; but what is 'conceded' here in fact tends to
> support Johnson's case and refute the case suggested by Boswell]
> Gresham College was intended as a place of instruction for London
> able professors were to read lectures gratis, they contrived to have
> no scholars; whereas, if they had been allowed to receive but
> sixpence a lecture, they would have been emulous to have many

scholars. [Example in *refutation* of the implied proposition that lower salaries lead to greater efficiency]

To this is now added a form of *conclusio*, appealing to the common sense of the public ('Everybody will agree') and emphatically reiterating the introductory proposition:

> Every body will agree that it should be in the interest of those who teach to have scholars; and this is the case in our Universities. That they are too rich is certainly not true; for they have nothing good enough to keep a man of eminent learning with them for his life.

Assuming that Boswell's reporting is even reasonably accurate, we must admire this impromptu discourse as an example of Johnson's *facundia*, his true power of mind (not properly represented in his notorious outbreaks of orotundity) that enabled him so rapidly to conceive an argument, find a structure for it and present it in appropriate language. As we read the *Life*, we grow accustomed to Johnson's desire for an audience and his formidable ability to make a claim on it. He is never obliged, it seems, to say 'If I may have your attention . . .' or 'Listen to me, everybody! Generally, he appears to have been a counter-attacker, waiting for someone else to supply a theme, as in this example; always he displays the rhetorical adept's ruling power, to compel his audience to go along with him. There is no doubt, however, that much of that power springs from the ability to construct argument readily on an immanent pattern.

A MODERN INSTANCE

The classic structure lingers on in many modern instances, hardly Ciceronian or Johnsonian in the forcefulness of their language, but none the less models of the conventional *taxis*. Thus, the *Independent* newspaper for Tuesday 12 January 1988 contains an editorial article constructed on lines strikingly similar to those of Samuel Johnson's 200-year-old impromptu. It begins, as the Boswell passage began, with a topic stated and revised:

> The proposal by Sir Rhodes Boyson, a Tory MP and formerly an education minister, that children who fail tests at seven, 11 and 14 should have to spend most of their summer holidays in the classroom, at first sight has a joyless, Gradgrind ring to it. On closer investigation it improves.

Note the tactical similarities between the two openings:

Boswell	*Indepedent*
I introduced the topick, which is often ignorantly urged, the Universities of England are too rich . . . [*pseudotopic*]	'The proposal by Sir Rhodes Boyson . . . that children who fail tests . . . should have to spend most of their summer holidays in the classroom, at first sight has a joyless, Gradgrind ring to it. [*pseudotopic*]
JOHNSON: 'Sir, the very reverse of this is true . . . [*topic*]	On closer investigation, it improves [*topic*]

'Pseudotopic' and 'topic' in the two instances are marked by comparable items of wording; by 'ignorantly urged' and 'at first sight', confessing the statement of a false position, and by the corrective phrases 'the very reverse' and 'on closer investigation'.

The remainder of the editorial's first paragraph and the whole of the second paragraph present the *narratio*:

> Sir Rhodes' tests would be pitched at a level which all pupils with IQs of more than 70 (below this a child is labelled educationally subnormal) would be expected to pass. The tests would be sat again in September by those who had failed them, and would have to be passed before they moved to the next stage of schooling.
>
> Because the tests would be pitched so low, they would not be a sort of latter-day 11 plus. They would be minimum standards, which almost everyone who is properly taught would be able to attain. As Sir Rhodes says, every failure should bring a full inquiry to determine the cause. And as he also remarks: 'If a pupil cannot read and write and number at the age of seven, he may never master these skills, and parents have a right to know by national tests whether their offspring are achieving literacy and numeracy or not.'

To say that this is considerably longer than the Johnsonian *narratio* is merely to observe a distinction between the necessary compactness of conversational performance and the more leisurely procedures of writing. A notable linguistic feature accompanying (perhaps even tending to explain) the length of the editorial exposition is that of modality; the modal *would* occurs no less than eight times, *should* once and *may* once, these occurences collectively emphasizing that what the editorialist is presenting as though it were fact, is as yet a non-existent state of affairs. In the *confirmatio* of the subsequent paragraph there is a shift, almost unobtrusive, from the contingency of 'should be' to the actuality of 'is':

> It is in the interests of pupils, parents and schools, and indeed society in general, that failure to achieve an elementary grounding should be recognised, and that remedial work should be put in hand. [*1st supporting observation*] Schools ought not to be able, by oversight or from despair to abandon children who are doing badly to lifetimes of illiteracy and innumeracy. [*2nd support*] People thus handicapped are likely to find it harder to get work and, having got it, to progress towards more responsible positions. [*3rd support.* NB the first indication of a shift out of modality: not 'would find' but 'are likely to find'] Both they and their employers are the worse for this. [*4th support.* NB the shift from 'are likely to' to 'are'] Economic growth depends in education at all levels within enterprises. [*5th support*] And it is far harder for those with no education to participate in politics. [*6th support*]

In this course of this, the ground of the argument has been 'confirmed' in a double sense; supporting statements have been adduced, and the proponent of the case has persuaded us to shift our attentions from the doubtful territory of 'would be' to the solid domain of 'is'. For a moment at least we are on firmer ground; and so the argument moves on into a paragraph and a half of *confutatio*:

> There is always a danger, when minimum standards are set, that these will come to be regarded as maximum standards. The resources of a school may be concentrated on enabling all children to surmount the tests, to the detriment of more advanced work. The avoidance of confusion between maximum and minimum is one reason why the level of tests should be kept low. Poor marks in these tests are a sign that something is very seriously wrong. Poor marks in more advanced examinations admit a wider range of explanation.
>
> Sir Rhodes contends that the new GCSE examination, which all children will sit, will be far more damaging to less academic pupils, who will be bound to attain low grades, than the tests which he proposes, prepared especially with their capabilities in mind. With his taste for homespun analogy, he likens this to amalgamating all the soccer leagues into one, and obliging a humble village team to play Liverpool, with shattering consequences to the former's esteem.

This is the stage at which the rhetorician begins to conceive of possible cases in opposition (compare Johnson's 'To be sure' and this editorialist's 'There is always a danger'). In the case of the newspaper writer, as in the case of Johnson, the envisaged objection is triumphantly enlisted in support of the proponent's own argument: 'You say that the lowest standard may become the school's highest standard? 'Why, that is the very reason for making the tests so easy – so that they could *never* be mistaken for *anyone's* highest standard!' A logician might have a little fun with the 'avoidance of confusion between maximum and minimum' – if you ask for a minimum it may become a maximum – unless what you ask for is so minimally a minimum that it could never be mistaken, even maximally, for a maximum – but we are here concerned only with the rhetorical structure. And if the argument does seem dizzily ingenious, that may be because we are not quite sure whether the editorialist is speaking in his own voice or echoing that of Sir Rhodes, whose *exemplum* (the village team versus Liverpool) he cites with a hint of mockery. The discursive process here resembles a model proposed earlier, on p. 3. In this case:

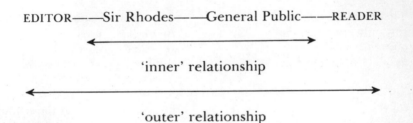

EDITOR——Sir Rhodes——General Public——READER

'inner' relationship

'outer' relationship

This is a complication not encountered in the otherwise analogous pattern of Johson's argument. The editorial writer assumes or discards at his convenience a mask, the mask of Sir Rhodes; his text asserts, in some places, 'this is the case', and in others 'this is what Sir Rhodes says is the case' – so that the writer may designedly influence the reader but at the same time displace responsibility for whatever influence is exerted. What is certainly apparent, whether it be Sir Rhodes or the Editor who speaks, is that this *confutatio* speaks of things as they *are* or *will be*: 'Poor marks in these tests *are* a sign that something *is* very seriously wrong'; 'less academic pupils, who *will be bound* to attain low grades' (italics added). This is a long stride from the modality of the *narratio*, with its proviso that 'Sir Rhodes's tests *would be* pitched at a level which all pupils . . . *would be* expected to pass.' We are now invited to suppose that the provision exists in fact.

And so in the second half of his final paragraph the journalist enters upon his *conclusio*:

> Concern for the weakest pupils is the most creditable part of Sir Rhodes's observations. Far from wishing to punish them by sending them on remedial courses during the summer, he is concerned that the schools they are obliged to attend should send them into the world better able to play a part in it.

This again we may compare with Johnson's impromptu, in the return, with emphasis, to the opening proposition:

Boswell Every body will agree that it should be in the interest of those who teach to have scholars; and this is the case in our Universities [*recapitulation of essential concern*: 'the interest of those who teach']

Concern for the weakest pupils is the most creditable part of Sir Rhodes's observations. [*recapitulation of essential concern*: 'for the weakest pupils]

That they are too rich is certainly not true [*final contradiction of 'pseudo-topic'*: NB 'certainly not']

Far from wishing to punish them by sending them on remedial courses during the summer [*final contradiction of 'pseudo-topic'*: NB 'far from']

for they have nothing good enough to keep a man of eminent learning with them for his life [*summary position*]

he is concerned that the schools they are obliged to attend should send them out into the world better able to play a part in it [*summary position*]

Clearly, Samuel Johnson and the modern journalist draw on a common source for the modelling of their arguments – the ancient tradition of the *genera*, and in particular the *genus iudicium*, the technique of forensic debate. The journalist's written style is not quite as plain as that of Johnson's colloquy. His article is decorated here and there with some of the tricks and graces of his craft. It is entitled 'Sir Rhodes's Poor Scholars' – a playful essay in the trope of *paronomasia* (playing on the names, 'Rhodes Boyson' – 'Cecil Rhodes' – 'Rhodes Scholars'); and in at least one place, a critical point in the *confutatio*, its author uses the figure of *parison* (parallel clause structure) to assert his position: 'Poor marks in these tests are a sign that something is very seriously wrong. Poor marks in more advanced examinations admit a wider range of explanation.' Such small instances illustrate the use of style to catch the attention pleasantly (*delectare*, 'to please', would be the appropriate Ciceronian category) and to enforce points of doctrine (*docere*, 'to teach', a companion category). All in all, what the author of the *Independent* article has wittingly or unwittingly produced is a textbook exercise in persuasion, a *suasoria* composed to the well-tried Roman recipe.

ALTERNATIVE RHETORICS

But there are other rhetorics, conceived in other times and places, serving other masters and other functions; rogue rhetorics, rhetorics revamped, pitches, presentations, hardly to be catalogued except rhetorically. Here is an example of a modern rhetorician at work. His text persuasively recommends to a possible purchaser the latest model of a motor vehicle (the Peugeot 205), and is accompanied by a large photograph drawing attention to a significant new feature in the car's design: the makers have reduced and reshaped the 'spoiler', a kind of coaming fitted to the roof of the car to inhibit aerodynamic lift and improve road-holding at high speed.[9] 'OK, just a little one', says a scribbled and arrowed note, pointing to the redesigned feature; while above the paragraph, in block capitals, are three words: FASTER. SMARTER. SPOILER? Nothing could better exemplify the playful spirit of rhetoric, the enjoyment of language for its own inherently subversive sake, than this impish trope, not readily identifiable with any one of the classical schemes. This is the native tongue begetting a native wit.

It is, however, the continuous text of the advertisement that invites particular notice, as an example of non-classical *taxis*. It reads as follows:

> Take a good look at the 1988 Peugeot 205. Remind you of anything? Of course it does. The 1987 Peugeot 205.
> Now take a drive in it. Something different's going on here. Is it your imagination, or does this 205 seem even nippier than its forerunner?
> 'It does. Because it is.
> Every 205 model up to and including the 1.4 has had its engine

completely re-designed. Every one now has aluminium alloy blocks.
So every one offers more performance.

There's something else. The gearbox was never exactly a slouch,
but was it ever quite this efficient?

No it wasn't.

Because those same models now proudly boast a totally new
gearbox.

Now it's time to take a quick glance round the interior. Yes, it's
definitely smarter than you remember it. And the extra touches of
style about the fascia can't help but bring a smile to your face.

That's it then. You've had your first drive in the 1988 Peugeot
205. And you know how much it stands out, even from last year's
model. But you're only human. And you can't help wanting it to
stand out a little on the outside too.

We understand. Never mind that the Peugeot 205 is regarded by
virtually one and all as a design masterpiece. We've bitten the bullet
for your sake.

Hence the radical, super-duper new aerodynamic lip you see
before you on the left.

Don't say we don't do our best for you.

As the copywriter says, 'Something different's going on here' –
or rather, some old goings-on are going on in new guise. One of
the oldest of these old goings-on is the pretence of an appellative
relationship, the claim of an *I* on a *you*. Thus the serpent to Eve,
'Hath God said, Ye shall not eat of every tree of the garden?'; thus
Mark Anthony to the Roman mob, 'If you have tears, prepare to
shed them now'; thus the copywriter to the wistful motorist,
'Remind you of anything?' Involved in this appeal to *you* – you, my
friend, and you-all, my masters – is the deprecation of self, the pretence of powerlessness, in the cunning old way of the *captatio
benevolentiae*. So Anthony says to the crowd 'You will compel me,
then, to read the will?'– which he had every intention of doing; and
the copywriter humbly states, 'We've bitten on the bullet for your
sake' – as though 'you' had anything to do with it.

Imputing feelings to an audience is a tactic which Shakespeare's
oratorical hero shares with Peugeot's affable salesperson; and this
process is assisted in each case by resorting to the device of the
imagined scene and the shared experience – 'I' and 'you' together
witnessing 'this'. Shakespeare shows Anthony salespitching Caesar
to an audience already on the way to being persuaded:

If you have tears, prepare to shed them now.
You all do know this mantle; I remember
The first time ever Caesar put it on;
'Twas on a summer's evening in his tent
That day he overcame the Nervii: –
Look, in this place ran Cassius' dagger through:
See what a rent the envious Casca made:
Through this the well-beloved Brutus stabb'd;
And, as he pluck'd his cursed steel away,
Mark how the blood of Caesar follow'd it
As rushing out of doors, to be resolved
If Brutus so unkindly knocked, or no;
For Brutus, as you know, was Caesar's angel.

We are all aware – not being innocent Roman citizens – that this is malarkey of a high imaginative order, since Anthony could not possibly know whose dagger made what hole in the well-remembered fabric. No matter; the fancied scene compels the responses of the audience and bonds their relationship with the orator. Now what happens in the advertising copy may be different in kind (no one is inciting us to riot) but it is not too different in method. It, too, sets a scene, not with 'If you have tears, prepare to shed them now', but with 'Take a good look at the 1988 Peugeot 205'; not with 'You all do know this mantle', but with 'Remind you of anything?' Anthony invites his audience to contemplate, in fancy, an act of assassination; the copywriter invites the reader to experience, in fancy, the act of driving a car, and concludes as though the fanciful were the actual: 'That's it then. You've had your first drive in the 1988 Peugeot 205.' And we all know – being, in general, intelligent citizens – that this is high-geared hocus-pocus, but we accept it because, for the moment, we have been caught up in something pleasurable.

What does the catching is the adman's *taxis*, a patterning of the copy (including its sectioning and layout) no more than distantly related to the conventional designs drawn from the old *genera*. The discourse plan of Roman rhetoric, from *introductio* through *narratio* and *confutatio* to *conclusio* makes a poor fit for this text, which nevertheless follows a principle of construction. It is a quite familiar principle to any reader of advertisements, and it is realized in the textual phases *Come-on*, *Pitch*, *Concession*, *Closure*. The formula permits free invention:

Here's a natty hat. ————————————→ *Come-on*
Go on, try it on. ————————————→ *Pitch*
Feel how it sits on your head.
We've designed it not to bend your ears.
Try flopping the brim up and down.
Wear it backwards. it still fits.
Notice?
But you'd probably like a feather in it. ————→ *Concession*
One of those little birdy jobs.
Or a big German shaving brush.
Wouldn't you?
That's all right, you can have that too.
We put one in every hatband.
Now that caps everything, doesn't it? ————→ *Closure*

NAPPER. **The hat that gets you ahead**

This is the 'tactical' shape of the Peugeot advertisement. Its 'come-on' is stated in the first sentence, with 'Take a good look at the 1988 Peugeot 205'; the 'pitch', inviting the putative consumer to make trial of the goods, extends from 'Now take a drive in it' to '. . . can't help but bring a smile to your face'; the 'concession' begins with 'That's it then' and runs to 'We've bitten the bullet for your sake'; and the 'closure' covers the last two sentences. The sectioning of the text on the page helps to make it readable in these terms.

The sectioning helps in fact to present an interior organization, a *microtaxis*, informing each phase of the *macrotaxis*, the larger scheme. For example, the process of making the pitch here involves three subsections ('Now take a drive in it . . .'; 'There's something else . . .'; 'Now it's time to take a quick glance . . .'), two of which have an explicit dialogic structure which becomes implicit in the third. Thus, the first subsection:

> Now take a drive in it. Something different's going on here. Is it your imagination, or does this 205 seem even nippier than its forerunner?
> It does. Because it is.
> Every 205 model up to and including the 1.4 has had its engine completely re-designed. Every one now has aluminium alloy blocks. So every one offers more performance.

The structure is *observation – question – affirmation – explanation* ('I notice this' – 'Is this so?' – 'It is' – 'And this is why'). A parallel structure appears – and is marked by the line-layout – in the second subsection, where, however, 'affirmation' is replaced by *negation*:

> There's something else. [*observation*] The gearbox was never exactly a slouch, but was it ever quite this efficient? [*question*]
> No it wasn't. [*negation*]
> Because those same models now proudly boast a totally new gearbox. [*explanation*]

Between the two subsections there is a slight variation of design, but the reader still responds to the reiterative pattern, as one might respond to matching stanza-patterns in a poem. The third subsection of the 'pitch' procedure is more obviously different:

> Now it's time to take a quick glance round the interior. Yes, it's definitely smarter than you remember it. And the extra touches of style about the fascia can't help but bring a smile to your face.

(Between this subsection and its precedessors, spanning the width of the print-column, is a picture of the fascia.) In spite of the apparent contrast, this is still essentially dialogic, covering the same routine of observation – question – affirmation – explanation. It might have been composed like this:

> Now it's time to take a look around the interior. Doesn't it seem a lot smarter than you remember it?
> It does. Because it is.
> And there are extra touches of style about the fascia that can't help but bring a smile to your face.

This dialogue-pattern, however, is merely implied in a new structure, which we might suppose to be different not only because a third recital of the dialogic routine might be tedious, but also because the writer is looking for a cadence, a way of closing the form and rhythm of his 'pitch' phase.

Modern, 'functional' texts of this kind present the analyst with the need to come to terms – literally, in the sense of finding a descriptive terminology – with kinds of rhetoric either ignored or simply not envisaged by traditional theorists. The Peugeot advertisement has very little resemblance, in its method and in its socio-cultural presuppositions, to a speech of Cicero, a soliloquy in Shakespeare, a sermon by Donne, an essay by Dr Johnson, even a description by Dickens. And yet it *is* rhetoric. It reveals the rhetorician's ancient enthusiasms, for the latent aesthetics of language (note the phonological play with *style – fascia*; *smile – face*), and for the possibility of exercising the power of design. Those who question the claims of rhetoric, those for whom the practice is 'empty' or 'airy fairy' and the practitioners 'windbags', may discount its power, but to do so undiscerningly. They ignore the point that 'empty' rhetoric, which is to say rhetoric that fails to capture its argument and its audience, is obvious in its unsuccess. To say that my rhetoric is empty is merely to say that you have seen what I am up to. But what of the things you do not see so easily, the things that take you by surprise, amuse you, move you, dispose you to be convinced? They also are products of the rhetorical impulse, though you may care to call them by some other name. And you will perhaps consider me insincere, devious even, if I allow you to perceive my rhetorical flourishes while I hide from you my rhetorical method. I am not insincere. I have designs on you, as the tattooist said to his girl friend; and I enjoy making designs, and I enjoy the feeling that you and I are, if only for a moment, enjoyably in accord.

2

Rhetoric as Emotion

'You do look, my son, in a moved sort, as if you were dismay'd.'
Thus Prospero to Ferdinand, at the conclusion of his tropical
island spectacular starring Iris, Ceres and Juno, with a colourful
supporting cast of nymphs and 'certain reapers, properly habited'.
It has certainly been a remarkable entertainment; but it is not the
show, not the music, not the dancing, not the girls, not the
demurely instructive script that have 'moved' Prince Ferdinand. It
is the glimpse of ferocious vindictiveness on Prospero's face as he
recollects that he has yet to deal with Caliban and the sailors. And
it is at this moment, after the prenuptial floorshow with its tinkling
rhymes and painted smiles, after we have seen the old man,
outwardly benign as a Mafia don at his daughter's wedding,
inwardly pondering the destruction of his last antagonists, that
Prospero utters words of such calm, conciliatory eloquence, that a
miraculous stillness comes over us all:

> Our revels now are ended. These our actors,
> As I foretold you, were all spirits, and
> Are melted into air, into thin air:
> And, like the baseless fabric of this vision,
> The cloud-capped towers, the gorgeous palaces,
> The solemn temples, the great globe itself,
> Yea, all which it inherit, shall dissolve,
> And, like this insubstantial pageant faded,
> Leave not a rack behind. We are such stuff
> As dreams are made on; and our little life
> Is rounded with a sleep.

These are very moving words, words spoken to us, the audience,
as much as to Prince Ferdinand. There is a sense in which they
exist outside the action of the play, as a beloved aria has a life outside the context of the opera. The audience waits expectantly for

Prospero's great aria – never mind the masquerade, never mind the conspirators, never mind Prospero's own ambivalent character; the speech gives them access to feelings virtually indissociable from the words in which the speech is framed. A paraphrase, however accomplished, would not serve the same turn. Yet all that Prospero has to say is that the solid world is a perceptual illusion, and that our lives are like dreams. Why should his particular formulation make this *koinos topos* particularly moving?

It is partly verbal technique that moves us: the skill of marshalling phrases in a frame of continually varying rhythms:

the cloud-capp'd towers	x / / / (x)
the gorgeous palaces	x / x / x x
the solemn temples	x / x / x
the great globe itself	x / / x /

The adroit rhythmic management of a sequence of phrases can operate almost automatically as a stimulus producing the required response of a shiver, a tear, a lump in the throat. But Prospero's rhetorical power involves something more than kinaesthetic skill. In this homily on the insignificance of human life, he raises the strength of our response by directing our attention to certain representations or *correlates* of human grandeur ('the cloud-capp'd towers', 'the gorgeous palaces', 'the solemn temples'); in fact – but this is by the way – he points with valedictory melancholy to the symbols of that civic life which he himself is about to resume. He relies on these correlates to work on our sympathetic imagination – 'picture these things if you will' – and they do so because they are, so to speak, superordinate abstractions: not 'the General Post Office', 'the Savoy Hotel', 'the church of St Martin in the Fields', but *towers*, *palaces*, *temples*, and the ideas which towers, palaces, temples, move in the mind.

This technique of moving by correlating is now very obvious to us thanks to our daily experience of advertisements, and of television commercials which rely on the interdependency of word, image and musical sound. British viewers are familiar with the series of bank commercials, each of which concludes, after a little masque on money, with the heartlifting image of a great black horse, galloping wild-maned, all in the unbridled gloss of his gladness, to the accompaniment of one of J. S. Bach's most serene and spiritual cantatas. The money-talk is ordinary stuff, even when the words are spoken by a highly accomplished actor, but few can fail to be moved by the free stride of the stallion, and by the effortless flow of Bach's music. Now I suspect that this is precisely the response the script-makers are seeking; for perhaps they hope that mellifluous horse and striding melody will exercise a correlative power, making us think of Lloyd's Bank as a noble enterprise, proud and strong like the stallion, civilized and humane like Bach, never dissonant, resolved like a harmony, resolute as a thoroughbred. They are certainly not the only tele-rhetoricians to explore the power of the correlate. Bach's calm glory correlates with, among other things, the enjoyment of panatella cigars; Mozart is currently helping to sell garden fertilizer; Beethoven is in the employ of the Electricity Board; Vivaldi will market anything; the image of the tiger propounds the merits of gasoline; the gull proclaims the *freedom* of packaged peas and ready-cooked snacks; high mountains, and the sun, and the incorrigibly voluble sea, are all dragooned into correlative endeavour in the interests of this one's product or that one's process. There is a claim on our feelings, but it is a claim that almost inevitably fails, because we readily perceive it, and perceiving it are amused by it, or, ceasing to be amused, come to resent it. There is a shabby incongruity between the banality of the object and the greatness of the correlate, and our perception of that makes us bridle at the attempt to manipulate our feelings.

Great images move us, it appears, but only in correlation with great themes, with matters of empathetic concern. The transience of human life is one of the great themes; patriotism is a great theme; loyalty and friendship are great themes; love in all its guises is a great theme. We are moved at a birth and at a death; we are moved by courage in the face of danger, by resolution in the face of adversity, by selfless integrity. Such things are our empathies, our great themes. Fish-fingers, cash-dispensers, condoms, cars, off-peak electricity and late-season holidays in Majorca may be peddled with the help of the most ingenious and amusing rhetoric, but they are not great themes and all the aesthetic technique in the world will not endow them with the power to touch the mind with sorrow, with peace, with wonder. The empathy is all, or, in a homelier phrase, the matter must bring its own shiver. Then the stylistic enhancement can begin.

SOME VARIATIONS ON A THEME

Times and cultures change, and yesterday's empathy may be today's abhorrence; but some themes abide, and one of them is death, or rather, the contemplation of death, the brave reduction of the monstrous to the scope of the bearable. Few things in human experience have invited more rhetoric than this. Sir Walter Ralegh on the scaffold, settling to the block, told the executioner in a last figure of rhetoric, 'So the heart be right, it is no matter which way the head lies.' This death-rhetoric is a distractive stratagem, a stubborn argument in the face of the unarguable, as, pathetically and nobly, the human mind goes on weighing its everlasting x's against its unyielding y's. Like some forms of religious ritual, it assuages fear and dismay, but raises them in order to assuage them. The classic example is surely to be found in the fifteenth chapter of St Paul's First Epistle to the Corinthians:

> Behold, I shew you a mystery; We shall not all sleep, but we shall all be changed, in a moment, in the twinkling of an eye, at the last trump: for the trumpet shall sound, and the dead shall be raised incorruptible, and we shall be changed. For this corruption must put on incorruption, and this mortal must put on immortality. So when this corruptible shall have put on incorruption, and this mortal shall have put on immortality; then shall be brought to pass the saying that is written, death is swallowed up in victory. O death, where is thy sting? O grave, where is thy victory?

Consider the rhetorical structure of this familiar passage – so familiar, perhaps, as to make the description 'rhetorical' offensive to readers convinced of its emotional and spiritual truth. But rhetorical it undoubtedly is, if by that we mean that it has clearly discernible patterns of *taxis* and *lexis*. Its procedures may be summarized thus:

1 The *Invocation* to the audience: 'Behold, I shew you a mystery'

2 The *Topic*, or *theme*, expressed in the figures of (a) *parison* and (b) *asyndeton*:

> 'We shall not all sleep, but
> we shall all be changed.' (parison)

'in a moment,
in the twinkling of an eye,
at the last trump'   (asyndeton).

3 *Argument*, continuing in parisonic figures:

'for the trumpet shall sound, and
    the dead shall be raised incorruptible, and
    we shall be changed'.

Parison then 'tightens' to *isocolon*, in conjunction with *polyptoton* (repetition of a word with the same root but a different form); the rhetorical texture grows more dense:

'for this corruptible must put on incorruption, and
    this mortal must put on immortality'.

4 *Conclusion*, with a repetition of the isocolonic construction, leading to a *sententia* (of the form 'It has often been said, 'As X says' – that is, the appeal to authority) embodying a *trope*, or metaphor:

'So when this corruptible shall have put on incorruption, and
    this mortal shall have put on immortality,

then shall be brought to pass the saying that is written,

death is swallowed up in victory .

5 *Apostrophe*, triumphantly addressed to Death, framed as yet another *isocolon*:

'O death, where is thy sting?
O grave, where is thy victory?'

This passionate utterance, the declaration of a visionary conviction, is firmly organized and controlled, in the *taxis* of its successive parts, and in the gradually intensifying figurative texture. We are led by figurative stages, from balance to balance, towards the controlling trope, the metaphor of Death as an adversary overcome in battle. This metaphor is the correlate that we visualize or in some way feel as a presence when we read the text. Then, with the triumphant assertion of victory over Death, comes the apostrophe *to* Death – almost swaggering, almost a challenge, one of the most majestic dismissals in the history of literary utterance.

This prose is majestic and moving, not because of the random workings of inspiration, but as a consequence of an inherent discipline. It is raised on a structure not so remote, after all, from the structure of argument; and without the sense of argument, with only the figurative play to appeal to us, we might not be so convincingly moved. This can even be true of poems that have the air of unconstrained emotional utterance:

> Death, be not proud, though some have called thee
> Mighty and dreadful, for thou art not so.
> For, those, whom thou think'st thou dost overthrow,
> Die not, poor death, nor yet canst thou kill me;
> From rest and sleep, which but thy pictures be,
> Much pleasure, then from thee, much more must flow,
> And soonest our best men with thee do go,
> Rest of their bones, and soul's delivery.
> Thou art slave to fate, chance, kings, and desperate men,
> And dost with poison, war, and sickness dwell,
> And poppy, or charms can make us sleep as well,
> And better than thy stroke; why swell'st thou then?
> One short sleep past, we wake eternally,
> And death shall be no more, Death thou shalt die.

Donne's sonnet, a well-known demonstration of affective rhetoric, clearly owes something – an intertextual debt – to St Paul's epistle; and like those of the Pauline rhetoric, its passions are discernibly *argued*.

The form of the argument is quite close to that of classical forensic oratory, except that the process of *confutatio* is absent. There are no objections from the other side that the poet is prepared to concede or counter, and in any case the whole poem is a confutation of Death's alleged might; *confirmatio*, the arguments of faith, and *confutatio*, the case against despair, here run together. This avoidance of the alternating or syllogistic method – 'on the one hand; on the other hand; and so . . .' – has affected the form of the sonnet. Ostensibly it follows the Petrarchan pattern, with an octave running from 'Death, be not proud' to 'soul's delivery', and a sestet from 'Thou art slave to fate' down to the ending, 'Death thou shalt die'. Its argument, however, is not constructed on the octave – sestet division. The prosodic basis of Donne's argument in this poem is the distich; he proceeds two lines at a time. The process might be paraphrased thus:

Invocation	lines 1–2	'Death, don't be proud; you're not as powerful as they say you are'
Case	lines 3–4	'Your alleged victims don't really die, and you can't even kill *me*'
Argument	lines 5–6	(a) 'Sleep, which is a mere resemblance of you, gives us pleasure; you yourself, therefore, must be even more pleasurable'
	lines 7–8	(b) 'Our greatest men are happy to go along with you, when their time comes, because you give rest to their bodies and release to their souls'
	lines 9–10	(c) 'You are *used*, like a slave, by tyrants and criminals, and you keep company with violence and corruption'
	lines 11–12	(d) 'Drugs and prescriptions send us off to sleep every bit as quickly and soundly – so why should you boast?'
Conclusion	lines 13–14	'After one short sleep, we shall all wake to live for ever. Death, *you* are the one who is going to die'

Donne moves adroitly through his supporting instances (lines 5 – 12) with the assurance, it seems, of a skilled disputant; yet there is something wrong with this argument *as* argument. The Case and the Conclusion fit together well enough:

> For, those, whom thou think'st thou dost overthrow   *Case*
> Die not, poor death, nor yet canst thou kill me;

and

> One short sleep past, we wake eternally,   *Conclusion*
> And death shall be no more, Death thou shalt die.

At the beginning and the end of the text is an assertion of faith – a presentation of the great theme of resurrection and rebirth, nullifying death. The intervening argument, however, concerns something else: the fear of death, and the psychological means of repressing or transmuting that fear. Here – as indeed throughout the poem – there is a deliberate process of hypostasis, a confusion of death (small *d*) as natural event and Death (capital *D*) as personification. Donne's theme is, essentially, the fear of death as a natural event, and he argues, in part, from the position that death (small *d*) *is* natural, like falling asleep, or easy, like taking a sleeping draught. At the same time, he raises a moral case against Death (capital *D*) as a bad character, the servant of bad masters, the associate of bad companions. The argument he urges upon us is that death (small *d*) is natural, and therefore not to be feared; and that Death (capital *D*) is a reprobate and therefore to be despised.

This is not articulated in the form of close reasoning (which the term 'argument' might suggest), but as a sequence of commonplaces (*loci communes, koinoi topoi*), the most familiar of which, no doubt, is the comparison of death with sleep. The arrangement of these *loci*, apparently casual and impulsive, is important in the organization of the poem. Two are concerned with the 'sleep' motif (lines 5–6, 11–12) and two with the motif of Death as functionary (lines 7–8, 9–10). There is thus a discernible symmetry of pattern, *sleep – functionary – functionary – sleep*, the 'sleep' instances coming at the beginning and end of the Argument. So positioned, they form links with the Case of lines 3–4 and the Conclusion of lines 13–14; they articulate a connection between two otherwise unconnected strands of meaning, the theological assertion of faith in the resurrection and the therapeutic management of the fear of dying. In this way, a text that makes an emotional (and indeed irrational) claim acquires a kind of discursive respectability. It is an outburst no less powerful for being *structured*.

The distich structure of the argument is plotted onto the conventional octave–sestet structure of the sonnet. While we follow the argument from distich to distich, however, we are not allowed wholly to lose awareness of the literary form. The shape of the poem as a rounded utterance is emphasized by the apostrophe to Death at the beginning and end; and the onset of the sestet – after the second of the four *topoi* in the Argument – is strikingly marked by a powerful asyndeton, suggesting a peak of emotional tension:

> Thou art slave to fate, chance, kings, and desperate men,
> And dost with poison, war, and sickness dwell.

The figurative management of the poem, and its lexis generally, are quite simple. The sense of elaboration, of great richness of texture, which most people have on reading this text, is partly a consequence of its play with a personifying trope (death — Death), but mostly the result of a rather complex poetic *taxis* that (a) offsets the distich procedure against the octave – sestet form, and (b) integrates two themes, concerning the doctrine of the resurrection, and our common feelings about dying. The location of pronouns in this complicated structure is worth noting. Thus, in the first distich:

> Death, be not proud, though *some* have called thee
> Mighty and dreadful, for thou art not so.

And in the second:

> For, *those* whom thou think'st thou dost overthrow
> Die not, poor death, nor yet canst thou kill *me*.

At the outset, the notion of an involvement with Death is thus set at a little distance from the reader: it concerns *some*, and *those*, and, coming only a little closer, *me*, that is the apostrophizer, the poet himself. But at the end:

> One short sleep past, *we* wake eternally,
> And death shall be no more, Death thou shalt die.

The position has shifted, *we* (the readers) are now involved, and in consequence of this involvement – which begins with the *our* of the sixth line – we are moved by an artful conduct of the great theme. We are, indeed, inevitably moved when the *rhetor* is thus able to say to us 'this touches you personally'.

TAKING IN THE AUDIENCE

The entrapment of the audience, the enforced complicity in a ritual act, is the aim and end of affective rhetoric, the secret at the centre of its often labyrinthine constructions. The purpose may sometimes be achieved by the careful location, noted above in the

Donne sonnet, of 'exclusive' and 'inclusive' personal pronouns. The pronominal manipulations may be covert, as on the whole they tend to be in Donne's text; distracted by other things (perhaps the figurative flourish at the beginning of the sestet) the reader's attention is not sharply focused on the switch from *me* to *we*. In other famous cases, however, the rhetoric demands overt, attention-focusing emphasis on the pronouns:

> Fourscore and seven years ago our fathers brought forth upon this continent a new nation, conceived in liberty, and dedicated to the proposition that all men are created equal. Now we are engaged in a great civil war, testing whether that nation, or any nation so conceived and so dedicated, can long endure. We are met on a great battlefield of that war. We have come to dedicate a portion of that field as a final resting-place of those who here gave their lives that that nation might live. It is altogether fitting and proper that we should do this. But in a larger sense we cannot dedicate, we cannot consecrate, we cannot hallow this ground. The brave men, living and dead, who have struggled here, have consecrated it far beyond our power to add or detract. The world will little note, nor long remember, what we say here, but it can never forget what they did here. It is for us, the living, rather to be dedicated here to the unfinished work they have thus far so nobly advanced. It is rather for us to be here dedicated to the great task remaining before us, that from these honoured dead we take increased devotion to that cause for which they here gave the last full measure of devotion; that we here highly resolve that the dead shall not have died in vain, that this nation, under God, shall have a new birth of freedom; and that government of the people, by the people, and for the people shall not perish from the earth.

What immediately characterizes the rhetoric of Lincoln's 'Gettysburg Address' is the pervading use of antithesis and parison – of phrases poising emphasis against emphasis. Thus:

whether *that* nation 　 or 　*any* nation
so conceived 　　　　 and *so* dedicated

　Leading to:

we *cannot* dedicate
we *cannot* consecrate
we *cannot* hallow 　　　 this ground

　And further:

The world will little note, nor long *remember*
what *we say* here
but it can never *forget*
what *they did* here

And:

| It is for *us*, the living, | rather to be dedicated here |
| It is rather for *us* | to be here dedicated |

And:

| we *take* | increased devotion |
| they here *gave* | the last full measure of devotion |

Culminating in:

government	*of* the people
	by the people
and	*for* the people

These rhythmic structures accommodate and give overt emphasis to the principal, organic counterpoise of *we* and *they*, the living
and the dead. The emphasis on personal pronouns is reinforced
and complemented by other emphases: on *this*, *that*, *those* and *these*
('this continent', 'that nation', 'that war', 'that field', 'those who
here gave their lives', 'these honoured dead'); and on the
insistently repeated *here*, with its dual sense of *here and now* ('who
here gave their lives', 'who have struggled here', 'what we say
here', 'to be here dedicated', 'for which they here gave . . .', 'that
we here highly resolve'). The distribution of these demonstrative
expressions is interesting. The 'that' type occurs preponderantly
in the first half of the speech, giving place (after the sentence 'It is
altogether fitting and proper that we should do *this*') to the 'here'
type; the text thus shifts, in its appeal, from objective distance to
subjective presence. It is elaborately orientated to its theme and its
audience, in such a way as to suggest something contemplated by
the speaker and his audience, and something immediately and
jointly felt.

The lexis of the 'Address' operates shiftily while the parisons
and pronouns do their distracting work. There are two significant
motifs. One is that of birth and death and rebirth, represented at
the beginning and end of the speech by *brought forth*, *conceived* and
a new birth. The other is a strain of religious vocabulary: *dedicate*,
consecrate, *hallow*, *devotion*. These two sets of words present the

correlates of the great theme: the image of birth and renewal, the image of consecration. A vital word is *dedicate*, which is made to slip progressively through three stages of meaning:

First   'dedicated to the proposition that all men are created equal'
             [*dedicate* = 'committed by belief or argument']

Same   'any nation so conceived and so dedicated'

Second   'we have come to dedicate a portion of that field'
             [*dedicate* = 'set aside for special reverence']

Same   'we cannot dedicate this ground' [in conjunction with *consecrate* and *hallow*]

Third   'It is for us . . . to be dedicated here . . .'
             [*dedicated* = 'devoted (by public affirmation) to a cause']

Same   'It is rather for us to be here dedicated . . .'

Evidently the 'meanings' occur in pairs, the relevant meaning in each instance being supported by other lexical items in context. Thus, the first meaning ('committed by belief or argument') draws support from *conceived*, which is in fact a pun: 'conceive' as in 'conceive a child', and 'conceive' as in 'conceive an idea'. It is the latter that supports the first interpretation of *dedicate*. The second meaning ('set aside for special reverence') occurs in self-explanatory context with *consecrate* and *hallow*. The third meaning ('devoted to a cause') is introduced in sentences which actually contain the word *devotion*. Thus Lincoln, with a rhetorical skill no less great for being, quite possibly, intuitive, involves one word in several applications: to the life of the intellect, to religious feeling, to the public quickening of political resolve. By these involvements and involutions – for it can be said that the language of the 'Gettysburg Address' is involuted, like that of Donne's verse and St Paul's prose – we are moved.

STANCE AND STRATAGEM

Rhetoric that does not involve the reader through a direct appeal ('You! hypocrite lecteur! – mon semblable – mon frere!') sets itself a harder task, if its intention is to move the feelings. The addressee, released from the conspiracy of inclusive pronouns, is free to question the sincerity of the addressor. The *ethos* of the act, the posture, tone and demeanour of the actor, become crucially important. If I wish you to weep for the death of my neighbour's little boy's gerbil, or mourn the passing of the one-legged newsagent who always gave short change, I shall have my work cut out on two counts. First, I must convince you that I am wholly serious, not laughing up my sleeve at poor Tommy or old Sniveller, not putting on a grandiose pretence of being a nobly sensitive fellow, acutely receptive to all the sufferings of a wide and wicked world. Second, I must discover, by cunning or intuition, some simple device to spring your feelings; not necessarily an elaborate thing, but – harder than elaboration – a precise thing, a momentary force that will work on you predictably, and that you cannot resist. The first problem, which we may call the problem of stance, is efficiently solved by Catullus in the famous poem on the death of Lesbia's sparrow. He opens with lugubrious humour, in a parody of the conventional invocation to the gods:

> Lugete, O Veneres Cupidinesque
> et quantum est hominum venustiorum
> passer mortuus est meae puellae
> passer, deliciae meae puellae.

('O love-goddesses, cupids, and all men of parts – weep; my girl's sparrow is dead, her sparrow, my girl's sweet pet.') The wry, joky manner begs acceptance for what at first glance is an absurd variation on the great theme. In just such a style might one begin an elegy on Tommy's gerbil:

> Ye heavens weep, and earth, be sad,
> And likewise many a Mum and Dad;
> For Gerby's dead, so dear to Tom,
> Gerby, his pride, his loyal chum.

Catullus, however, turns the trick against his smiling auditors with a grave reflection on the destiny of the poor sparrow:

> qui nunc it per iter tenebricosum
> illuc, unde negant redire quenquam.

('Who now takes the dark way to a place from which, they say, no one returns.') It is once more a pronoun *quenquam*, 'anybody' – that reminds the reader how he, too, is involved in this, and how the event is invested with the pathos of all mortality.

There is a little poem by Emily Dickinson which illustrates admirably a solution to the second of the two rhetorical problems mentioned above, that of discovering an appropriate device with which to discharge the desired emotion. Dickinson does not give the poem a title; one of her editors, however, has called it 'A Country Burial':

> Ample make this bed.
> Make this bed with awe;
> In it wait till judgement break
> Excellent and fair.
>
> Be its mattress straight,
> Be its pillow round;
> Let no sunrise' yellow noise
> Interrupt this ground.

This commemorates the nameless. Who lies in this grave? Anybody. Yet we, as readers are at least fictively involved in the act of burial, if we choose to regard the poem's directives (*make, let*) as addressed to us.[1] That supposition is in one way absurd; we are clearly not at hand with pick and shovel. Yet it becomes acceptable as a rhetorical fiction, structured in a by now not unfamiliar way:

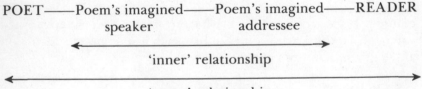

POET——Poem's imagined——Poem's imagined——READER
    speaker   addressee

'inner' relationship

'outer' relationship

The poet reaches the reader through the imagined situation, thus involving our sympathies in the death of nobody, anybody, everybody. ('Any man's death diminishes me', says Donne, 'because I am involved in mankind.')

The 'situation' in this poem – if we like, the designation from which we make our inferences – is created in two ways. First, the text depends on a *topos*, the old familiar position that as death is a kind of sleep, so the grave is a kind of bed. So completely is the wording of the poem adjusted to this theme, that if it were not for the occurrence of the word *ground* at the end of the piece, we might be misled, or be obliged to read the text as a kind of riddle:

'A Country Event'

Ample make this bed.
Make this bed with care;
In it wait till morning break
Excellent and fair.

Be its mattress straight,
Be its pillow deep;
Let no children's yelling noise
Interrupt this sleep.

Such a version *could* be a poem about death and burial, but it might just as well be a metrical Do Not Disturb notice, a cheerful intimation of a long lie-in. Certain clues that steered the reading of the original have been removed and replaced with items that collocate more banally; yet even if those words had been kept, it would still be possible to read this rewritten version ambiguously. The one indispensable word in Dickinson's poem, the word that must not be replaced if the elegiac meaning of the text if to be perceived, is *ground*. The editor mentioned above has tried to anticipate this clue in the wording of his title. In the titles of poems, as in the slogans of advertisements, there is often some item of vocabulary directly linked with some corresponding item prominently located in the text. Here, the prominent location is the very last word of the poem; it is the word *ground* that finally obliges us to admit that death is not a comfortable matter of tucking up for a nice long sleep, but that the Unknown Human of Dickinson's elegy is about to go *per iter tenebricosum unde negant redire quenquam*. It is this moment of shock at the end of the poem that enforces its emotional claim upon us.

This is one way in which the poet springs her affective trap. To make the manipulation of the *topos* work, however, she has to exploit a companion stratagem, that of the poem's design. Its verbal structures are symmetrical, reassuringly orderly, 'straight' or 'round' like mattress and pillow. There is a demure grammatical housekeeping in the figurative constructions:

Ample make this bed.
    Make this bed with awe;

The figure is called *anadiplosis*. The second stanza begins with an *isocolon*:

Be its mattress straight,
Be its pillow round;

Each stanza thus begins with a figure of parallelism. But the stanzas themselves are patterned in parallel. The first begins with the figure of the two counterpoised clauses, one clause to a line; then, after the semi-colon, follows a directive sentence ('In it wait till judgment break / Excellent and fair') occupying two run-on lines. The second stanza is constructed in like fashion; the first two lines accommodate the two parallel clauses, then, again, after the semi-colon, comes the directive sentence occupying the last two run-on lines. The syntactic tidiness expresses the ordinary emotion of the implied commonplace, 'they are only sleeping'. At last, however, a trope of extraordinary intensity ruffles the composed surface: 'Let no sunrise' yellow noise / Interrupt this ground'. The grammar goes neatly on, but the lexicon is subverted. Can the sunrise make a noise? Can the noise be coloured? Noise can interrupt sleep, but can it interrupt *ground*? Our poet guides us through the composure of her *taxis* to the ultimate discomposure of her *lexis*, to that last disturbing moment, that last unsettling word.

OVERBLOWING AND UNDERPLAYING

If Emily Dickinson's poem succeeds in moving us on behalf of a nameless stranger in another country and another age, it is because we can accept as sincere her rhetorical credentials; her stance is believable. A rather more dubious case is pesented by a frequently anthologized modern poem, Dylan Thomas's 'A Refusal to Mourn the Death, by Fire, of a Child in London'. The very title raises doubts. If you are not going to mourn, not shed so much as one furtive tear, why this fussy announcement, to the world at large, of your lofty resolve? Something is amiss; the poet appears to be bent on a bravura declaration of his unwillingness to cry over spilt milk. But here is the text:

> Never until the mankind making
> Bird beast and flower
> Fathering and all humbling darkness
> Tells with silence the last light breaking
> And the still hour
> Is come of the sea tumbling in harness
>
> And I must enter again the round
> Zion of the water bead
> And the synagogue of the ear of corn

Shall I let pray the shadow of a sound
Or sow my salt seed
In the least valley of sackcloth to mourn

The majesty and burning of the child's death.
I shall not murder
The mankind of her going with a grave truth
Nor blaspheme down the stations of the breath
With any further
Elegy of innocence and youth.

Deep with the first dead lies London's daughter,
Robed in the long friends,
The grains beyond age, the dark veins of her mother
Secret by the unmourning water
Of the riding Thames.
After the first death, there is no other.

This is highly rhetorical in the Welsh pulpit tradition of the *hwyl*, the irresistible accumulation of enthusiastic eloquence. It embodies some staggering phrases; but a good poem, a moving poem, or even a good rhetorical performance, requires something more than a catalogue of figures. It requires a *taxis*, a framework for the argument of feeling, such as St Paul and John Donne and Emily Dickinson in their various ways provide. What Thomas presents is a pseudotaxis, an apparently convincing syntactic shape contouring a sequence of propositions which, in paraphrase, would be fairly banal. ('Never until the world ends and I must die shall I mourn for this child; I will not utter prayers or elegies for her; she is deep underground with the rest of the dead, here in London by the River Thames, which does not mourn; and you only die once.') Not only banal, but absurd, for it makes no sense to declare roundly that you will not utter a syllable or shed a single tear until time ends, the heavens cease and the sea suspends its activities; you are not likely to be present on that occasion, and even if you were, your grudgingly minimal sentiments would be wholly irrelevant. *Never* is a good fist to shake at the sky, but it needs the support of rational utterance if it is not to sound petulant.

What gives the poem the semblance of important and sustained argument is a skilful marshalling of its syntax, primarily in the overlaying of sentence-units on the regular frame of four stanzas. The poem is written in four sentences, the first of which takes up thirteen lines of verse, running through the first two stanzas and into the first line of the third (from 'Never until . . .' to '. . . the child's death'). The second sentence, embodying two co-ordinated clauses, covers the remaining five lines of the third stanza (from 'I shall not murder . . .' to '. . . innocence and youth'). The third sentence (from 'Deep with the first dead . . .' to '. . . the riding Thames') is also five verse-lines in length. The last sentence coincides with the last line of the poem: 'After the first death, there is no other.' The stanzas are regularly constructed, but syntactically the poem narrows, so to speak, the sentences shortening to the curt affirmation at the close, so reminiscent of Donne ('Death, thou shalt die') or Shakespeare ('And death once dead, there's no more dying then').[2] It looks as if the poet has brought us by compulsions of thought and perception to this triumphant proposition; but all that compels us is the decreasing length of the sentences. The device, once perceived, lends itself to burlesque fantasies. See how the sentences confidently contract:

> Never until the piglet flies
> And from the chastely weeping skies
> Into my unrepentant ear
> Descend cascades of ginger beer,
> And I must eat, upon my knees,
> Plate after plate of cottage cheese
> Until the stuff runs down my legs
>
> Shall I forgo my ham and eggs.
> I shall not turn away from toast
> Or utter any idle boast,
> While stars above pursue their march,
> Of laying off the fats and starch.
>
> Down in the deep–freeze lies my beef,
> Safe from the cat, the passing thief,
> The dog prospecting for his bone.
>
> Man cannot live by verse alone.

This piece of nonsense attempts to demonstrate the principle that any truism, saw, proverb or *sententia* can be endowed with thrilling significance merely by lodging it in the nick of a narrowing form. This is all that Thomas has to do in order to endow 'After the first death, there is no other' with (it seems) sombre power.

Or perhaps not quite all; for this poem (the 'Refusal') lives by its lexis, and its lexis works within the minor syntactic forms, notably the noun phrase. The text is a procession of ornate substantives. It opens with an astonishing, almost barbarously complex nominal construction:

> the mankind making bird beast and flower fathering and all humbling darkness

The structure is less exotic if one supplies a few commas and a vulgar example: 'the chilblain-making, nose-ears-and-finger-pinching, and all-freezing winter'. The grammar is, indeed, simpler than it looks, but at first glance (as most readers of this poem may be prepared to testify) it seems difficult, because the participial modifiers ('mankind making', 'flower fathering', 'all humbling') are distractingly set in the prosodic frame. The reader does not immediately see their adjectival relationship to the headword, *darkness*, but tries to interpret the first instance, the line-end *making*, either as a noun ('mankind making' = 'the making of mankind') or as a verb ('making bird beast and flower'). The false reading of the first line induces a misreading of the whole of the first stanza. The evident strategy of the text, to begin in great syntactic complexity, both of phrase and sentence structure, and end in simplicity, is misconceived, although one can well understand how the syntax might be designedly mimetic of an emotional shift from agitation and doubt to stillness and certainty. It does not work, simply because the poem is too hard to get into, and readers begin to wonder if, after all, it is worth the effort.

The noun phrases throughout the reminder of the text fall preponderantly into patterns answering to the formula 'the N of N' (noun of noun), with variants, for example '(a)N of (a)N' ([adjective] noun of [adjective] noun]) and 'aN of Npost' (adjective noun of post modified noun). Thus:

> the still hour . . . of the sea tumbling in harness
> the round Zion of the water bead
> the synagogue of the ear of corn
> the shadow of a sound
> the least valley of sackcloth
> the majesty and burning of the child's death
> the mankind of her going
> the stations of the breath
> any further elegy of innocence and youth
> the dark veins of her mother
> the unmourning water of the riding Thames

Though other patterns (for example 'the grains beyond age') occur, it is on the whole the 'N of N' formula that rules the text; it accounts for 73 of the poem's 152 words, and in the second and third stanzas occurs in every grammatical clause and nearly every verse-line. All but one of the instances listed are figurative (the exception is marked with an asterisk), involving a metaphor or a play on words. This 'figuration' is intensive; every instance is a riddle to be solved in its own terms, not an element in the figurative progression of the immediately surrounding text. There is a vague connecting element of biblical/religious allusion (in 'the round Zion of the water bead', 'the synagogue of the ear of corn', 'the least valley of sackcloth', 'the stations of the breath'), but these intimations of Judaeo-Christian imagery are not organic to the poem in the way that the trope of 'death as sleep' is organic to Donne's sonnet and Emily Dickinson's lyric. The imagery throughout decorates the theme with somewhat diffuse correlates of feeling – the birds and beasts and the flowers, the dawn breaking, a calm sea, a cornfield, dew, valleys, majesty, church interiors, robes, motherhood. It seems that one or other of these must touch a tender spot in the reader; yet discussion of this poem with students regularly suggests that the reader is unmoved and on the whole resents the lexical elaboration of the poem as an attempt to enforce a sentiment. Thomas's bravura performance violates what appears to be a fundamental principle of affective rhetoric: always give *taxis* controlling precedence over *lexis*, even though the structural control may not be immediately apparent to reader or hearer.

SPEAKERS AND AUDIENCES

Now it is quite possible that no one reading the examples discussed in this chapter will be 'moved' by all of them, other than in the sense of recognizing that they have a claim on us, that they represent an intention to be 'moving'. Possibly they are too familiar now to beget the gooseflesh, the lump in the throat; or perhaps – a more interesting conjecture – they have absorbed and transmuted, as artefacts, the emotions they were designed both to stimulate and to allay, so that we can now consider them distantly as representations of ideas about feelings. In the same way we might look at a painting, recognizing in it a powerful affective claim, yet feeling the claim rather than the feelings originally expressed in the claim. In any case, the cited passages posit different kinds of relationship between speakers and audiences, in different contexts of emotional need. Funeral orations satisfy a need in the mourners to give significance to the lives of the departed, and so alleviate the pain of bereavement; it is this need that the 'Gettysburg Address' satisfies. Lincoln's audience, however, goes far beyond the persons gathered to hear him on that day in 1863. His audience extended, then, to the whole American nation, and has extended since to a world of idealists needing a text to which they may refer a belief that in the creation of better societies the dead have not died in vain. Lincoln's brief speech has become a powerful emblem of such a belief, and it is generally as an idealistic emblem that we respond to it. The text can thus be said to have had a real audience and an immediate need, and to have acquired an extended audience and a generalized need.

The appeal of St Paul's text may be similarly referred to an immediate and an extended audience, 'real' audiences both, whether of the churchfolk of Corinth in the 1st century, or of all the world for ever afterward. Here, however, the need is the same in either case – the universal need to be assured that death is not the end of everything. The more we feel that need, the more powerfully we are likely to be moved by St Paul's triumphal eloquence; the less we feel it, the more likely we are to read the eloquence merely as 'rhetoric'. The disposition to a belief – or in this case, the need for a belief – is an important accessory to the power of the text. John Donne and Dylan Thomas address the same disposition, rely for their affective power on the same perception of a need, but their texts do not have 'real', only 'generalized' audiences – 'readerships' rather than 'hearers'. Donne employs the fiction of addressing a personified Death, but involves his readers in the fiction, so that his poem becomes emblematic of what people in general might find to say in self-defence against death's menace. His sonnet becomes (like certain prayers) a recipe or prescription, for use in times of stress. Thomas involves none but himself, constructs no fictive addressee.

Catullus' apostrophized hearers are an odd sort of 'immediate audience' – Love-Goddesses, Cupids, *et quantum est hominum venustiorum*; but this address is a wry joke, as indeed is his domestic scolding, later in the poem, of the nasty 'shades of Orcus' which devour all good things. Whom, then, does he move – if indeed the poem is intended to move? The fact that it does, indeed, move many readers may be explained as the result of the poet's touching an extended audience, intentionally or otherwise, in the line *illuc, unde negant redire quenquam,* 'Thither, from where, they say, no one returns'. At this point the poem involves its readers and raises the universal issue of how we feel about death; pre-Christian sparrows or twentieth-century people, we are all subject to the ungainsayable power.

Emily Dickinson apostrophizes no person or power, and yet her poem implies both the fiction of immediate hearers and the intention of an audience in general. Her imperatives, fictively addressed to the gravemakers, appeal to us all, and in the appeal are transmuted into metaphors that evoke yet another need, the need for peace, the need for death itself as a release from the ordeal of consciousness. We are moved by it if we have ever found living a burden, or if, empathically, we are able to perceive how to some it may be unremittingly burdensome.

THE MAXIMS OF MOVING

We may therefore be moved by rhetorical utterance in diverse ways, responding to affective claims conditioned by the status of the utterance in relationship to the speaker, the audience and the context of its appeal; claims potentially much more sophisticated than the simple demand for a tear, a sigh, a shiver. At the same time, however, we may fairly assume that what the rhetorician would like to wring from us is in the first place just such a nervous response. 'If you have tears, prepare to shed them now', Anthony warns his Roman audience; among the common devices of affective rhetoric is that of letting your hearers know that you are bent on touching a nerve – 'Weep with me', 'Be appalled', 'I invite you to commiserate'.

Then what principles must the mover observe?; what are the *maxims of moving?* They are to be framed with reference to four discursive constituents. The first of these is *emphathetic matter.* If a speaker or writer is to move an audience, the theme must be capable of evoking feelings into which the audience can readily enter. It must be one of the 'great themes' mentioned earlier, themes which stand up either in their universal human validity (we are born, love, suffer, know defeat and triumph, die) or in the frame of a culture or an epoch. War is an example of a 'culture-framed' theme. In *Beowulf* and Malory war is treated heroically, and death in battle, or after battle, is the theme for rhetorical set pieces of great power. In modern literature the same theme commonly moves us only to dismay or revulsion, and the skills of rhetoric. if they are deployed, only serve to alienate us. If we continue to pay the tribute of heroic feeling to the dying Beowulf or the stricken Arthur, it is either because of a capacity to shed preconceptions and accept the *ethos* of another age – to 'enter into the spirit of the thing' – or because we are in some way able to translate the scene of death into emotional and moral terms that are agreeable to us. (It happens, incidentally, that as they die Beowulf and King Arthur are each attended by a single retainer, whose conduct and sentiments raise the theme of *loyalty*, which is wholly acceptable and intelligible to the modern mind.)

The second important constituent may be called *stance*. This involves both the tenor of discourse ('tone of voice') and, connectedly, the attitude of the speaker/writer to a theme and to an audience. Here are variables enough to suggest that stance is potentially a complex thing. To take one combination out of many, I may speak seriously of my theme, with apparent deference to an immediate audience, but with indications of wry humour to a wider audience. (So teachers and school visitors will sometimes communicate with bystanding parents over the heads of the children they are ostensibly 'addressing'.) Stance is deeply, sometimes bafflingly, involved in the trope of irony, the decipherment of which often requires social or institutional knowledge as much if not more than knowledge of linguistic matters.

The third and fourth elements directly involve discursive skills. There is a skill of *design*, or the patterning of a text, syntactically and figuratively, to guide the reader/hearer to a desired conclusion and to bring into focus the items that represent the play of feeling in the piece. This embraces the companion skill of *relation*, involving the devices of style, imagery and allusion: the *topoi* and *sententiae*, the tropes, the images that 'correlate' with, and thereby enhance, the emotions to be expressed or elicited. 'Design' and 'relation' have obvious affinities with the classical *taxis/dispositio* and *lexis/elocutio*, but it may sometimes be psychologically convenient, especially in describing forms of modern rhetoric, to avoid commitment to the ancient terms.

Now if an orator sets out to move his audience, he may assume, as basic principles from which he is free to depart as the occasion suggests, the following maxims:

1 *Let your matter be broadly empathetic.* Your hearer has native access to the primary feelings about life and death, and your business is to use the primary impulse in a particular application. The initial appeal is always broad, and is made narrower by your tact and skill. You may thus reduce the broad and vague theme of 'death' to 'the death of a child' or 'the death of a cat'; but you must never 'narrow' too circumstantially. A poem on 'The Death of a Cat who fell in Love with a Golf Ball' would make a very interesting and possibly witty *class exercise*, but it would raise no tears for pussy, because, though it might not lack pathos, its matter would no longer be empathetic.

2 *Let your stance be direct and uncomplicated.* In other words, let your audience be in no doubt that you mean wholeheartedly what you say. There are exceptions to this, adoptions of an oblique stance, suggesting irony or wry humour, that may succeed in being sincerely moving; but any such exception must be a calculated risk. Furthermore, a stance should be self-evident; you should not have to justify your decision to mourn (or not to mourn) for the dead, to praise courage and self-sacrifice, to celebrate loyalty and endurance.

3 *Make the design of your text compulsive.* The object of affective rhetoric is to assert, or even impose, a powerful feeling; but this is not done simply by shouting 'feel!' at an audience. There is a dialectic of the emotions, an argument of feeling, that has to be demonstrated if the audience is to be satisfied that its response to a claim is right and respectable. You must accordingly pattern your text so that the reader/hearer feels compelled, step by step, to an emotional conclusion.

4 *Let your relation focus powerfully on one or two tropes or 'correlates'.* Never pack your discourse with unrelated images and metaphors, but limit your figurative scope to a few emblems of feeling that can be so effectively placed in the design as to coincide with steps in the development of the 'compulsive' pattern mentioned above. A random and energetic scattering of images is often highly effective in humorous discourse, but will not reliably move an audience to graver feelings.

The trickiest of these rules is the maxim of stance which says, in effect, 'publish your truth'; for it is possible to be wholly sincere in terms that ring insincerely, and to be quite insincere in language that that trumpets sincerity. A speaker whose purpose is to move the deeper emotions of an audience is always a speaker at risk. If, rightly or wrongly, your audience perceives insincerity, it will no longer oblige you by being moved, however solemn and emotional your matter. It may still, however, find pleasure in what you have to say, since a questionable or ambivalent stance is the source of much that is pleasurable, as well as deplorable, in rhetoric. There is a kind of dishonesty that is the soul of charm   but this brings us to another chapter.

3

Rhetoric as Distraction

Among the many delectable passages in Chaucer's *Troilus and Criseyde*, there is an episode describing the astonishment of the hero, a man cavalierly indifferent to women, at being suddenly stricken with love. One look is enough to destroy him. Chaucer describes at some length the downfall of the cynic, but the gist of it is caught in two stanzas:

> As proude Bayard gynneth for to skippe
> Out of the weye, so pryketh hym his corn,
> Til he a lasshe have of the longe whippe;
> Than thynketh he, 'Though I praunce al byforn
> First in the trays, ful fat and newe shorn
> Yet am I but an hors, and horses lawe
> I moot endure, and with my feres drawe';

> So ferde it by this fierse and proude knyght:
> Though he a worthy kynges sone were,
> And wende nothing hadde had swich myght
> Ayeyns his wille that should his herte stere,
> Yet with a look his herte wax a-fere,
> That he that now was moost in pride above
> Wax sodeynly moost subgit unto love.

(Just like proud Bayard, swerving off the straight path because he's feeling his oats – till he gets a lash from the long whip – then he thinks, "Even though I'm the leader of the team, first in the trace, well-nourished, well-groomed, yet I'm only a horse, and I must put up with the rules for horses, and pull my weight along with my fellows": that's just how it was with this fierce, proud, knight. Even though he was the son of a noble king, and would never have expected that anything could move his heart against his will – yet with one look his heart was on fire, and he, who had been most lofty in his pride suddenly become the most humble subject of love)

Now the general sense of this is a *koinos topos*; it tells of love at first sight, and it warns that the power of love is great, so great that even the sons of kings must be obedient to it. The particular charm in Chaucer's treatment of the topic is his witty choice of an *exemplum*. An arrogant young man is like a horse feeling his oats; sooner or later the lash must bring the horse into line, and sooner or later the young man must fall in love. It was a bold stroke, to equate a Trojan prince with a *horse*, and not even a hunter or a charger, but a mere waggon puller. Certainly the the horse has a chivalric name, 'Bayard', but the editors will tell us that Bayard was a common name for a horse (much, it may be supposed, as 'Rex' is a common name for a dog). And there is something laughable, after all, about Bayard's pride. He 'praunces', he is 'first in the trays' (that is, the leader of the team), he is 'ful fat and newe shorn', and yet, as he himself admits, he is only a horse. 'Yet am I but a hors', applied to Troilus, both asserts and comically deplores his arrogance. The use of *exempla* is common in medieval narratives and sermons. Here, Chaucer uses one in a way that constitutes a minor triumph of serio-comic rhetoric. It offers an instant grasp of a situation and a character, and does so in a way that is memorable and pleasing.

The *exemplum*, or illustration, is a major resource in the rhetoric of entertainment as well as in the rhetoric of instruction. The instructor uses illustrations to free his pupil from the trance of a fixed perspective. The entertainer also induces a mental shift in the reader, but perhaps with a somewhat different intention. The purpose is not to inform, suggest the solution of a problem or justify a position, but simply to refresh the attention by distracting it. Chaucer, in the stanzas quoted, is not rehearsing an argument but inviting a comparison. The elements in his design are therefore not serially linked like the successive points of a *confirmatio*. The linkage is parallel: not 'A and furthermore B', but 'A in correlation with B', 'A reflecting or reflected by B'.

In such constructions the *exemplum* often acquires ascendancy over the thing exemplified; the correlate becomes more memorable than the primary theme. This is an effect characteristic of presentations as widely different as the TV commercial and the heroic simile. It is a common experience that the television images – of cats, dogs, beautiful women, men fishing, rainstorms, forest fires, children at play and so on – are more memorable than the names of the products of which they are purportedly emblematic.

The effect of the correlative image is often to distract the viewer rather than focus attention on the advertiser's message; the visual rhetoric disorientates with its anecdotes of mischievous puppies and tropical seas, making us forget that the real talk is of toilet rolls and chocolate bars. A comparable disorientation may be experienced in the reading of the 'classical' simile, the extended poetic comparison as practised by Milton or by Tennyson. Here is a typically rhetorical patch from one of Tennyson's *Idylls of the King*. A long central episode of the poem called 'The Last Tournament' describes how Arthur leads an expedition to put down the insurrection of a certain 'Red Knight' and his followers, who occupy a castle in a barbarous northern wilderness. When the Red Knight comes out to engage Arthur in single combat, the King merely evades the first blow and his adversary topples from his horse in a fall described thus:

> And Arthur deigned not use of word or sword,
> But let the drunkard, as he stretched from horse
> To strike him, overbalancing his bulk,
> Down from the causeway heavily to the swamp
> Fall, as the crest of some slow-arching wave,
> Heard in dead night along that table-shore,
> Drops flat, and after the great waters break
> Whitening for half a league, and thin themselves,
> Far over sands marbled with moon and cloud,
> From less and less to nothing: thus he fell
> Head-heavy;

What is this about? Strictly speaking, it is about a drunk falling into a swamp; but the televisual distraction presents a great wave resonantly breaking and dispersing along a beach lit by the moon. Between the *as* and the *thus* of the comparison there is really very little equivalence: the knight is not like a wave (except that they both have crests), his fall into the mire is not like the slap of the breaker on the beach, his ignominy is not like the dispersion of foaming water. The assertion of a correspondence, falling man/ breaking wave, is a poetic confidence trick, perhaps different in intention but hardly different in kind from the adman's play with seductive images. And Tennyson's image *is* seductive; it makes the reader momentarily lose sight of what is, at this point in the narration, a story of sordid events, and indulge in the enjoyment of words as they make their brilliant projections on the mind.

Chaucer and Tennyson are alike in having recourse to an ancient device, the *as–so* structure of an exemplary illustration.

They are unlike, as far as the present instances are concerned, in their use of the process of comparison. Chaucer's *as* is equivalently connected, point by point, with his *so*:

AS	SO
proude Bayard	this fierse and proude knyght
though I praunce al biforn	though he a worthy kynges sone were
first in the trays	and wende nothing hadde had swich myght
til he a lasshe have	his herte waxe a-fere
horses law I moot endure	wax sodeynly moost subgit unto love

The pleasure in the comparison is in tracing the ingenuity of the fit, an occupation which, far from disorientating the reader, in fact brings a theme into clear perspective. (It is the earliest hint, albeit a humorous one, of the motif of inevitable destiny which pervades this long poem.) Chaucer *equates*, whereas Tennyson's rhetoric *expands*. Tennyson's simile has no functional role in the narrative, casts no sidelight on event, character or motive, but has the curious psychological role of inducing a moment of distraction and forgetfulness – perhaps with the intention of rendering all the more vivid and urgent the 'reality' of the narrative when presently we return to it. It is comparable to the filmic 'cut' from a noisy scene of murder and mayhem, the exterior action, to the stillness of mental recollection, the distance of the interior world. This rhetoric evokes a different kind of pleasure from that of observing the wit and propriety of a pattern of equivalences. This is the pleasure of disorientation, of reverie, of illusion or delusion; the rhetoric not of the demonstrator but of the hypnotist.

In some of Milton's epic similes there is a discernible shift from 'focus' to 'distraction'; the figure begins as though an equational pattern (for example Troilus = Bayard) were to be developed, but then moves quickly into the disorientating image. This appears in a well-known passage from the first book of *Paradise Lost*, as Milton labours to impress on his readers the sheer size of Satan, sprawling in the smouldering flood:

– Thus Satan talking to his nearest mate
With head uplift above the wave, and eyes
That sparkling blazed; his other parts besides
Prone on the flood, extended long and large
Lay floating many a rood, in bulk as huge
As whom the fables name of monstrous size,
Titanian or Earth-born, that warred on Jove,

> Briareos or Typhon, whom the den
> By ancient Tarsus held, or that sea-beast
> Leviathan, which God of all his works
> Created hugest that swim the ocean stream;
> Him haply slumbering on the Norway foam,
> The pilot of some small night-foundered skiff,
> Deeming some island, oft, as seamen tell,
> With fixed anchor on his scaly rind
> Moors by his side under the lee, while night
> Invests the sea, and wished morn delays;
> So stretched out huge in length the arch-fiend lay
> Chained on the burning lake;

Most readers, uneasily tracing the syntax of this long passage through its meander of personal and relative pronouns, will be sufficiently disorientated by the mere exercise of reading. There are ellipses ('As whom the fables name of monstrous size', 'Created hugest that swim the ocean stream'). There are constructions dependent at one end on an elided antecedent and at the other on a deleted conjunction:

>   in bulk as huge
>   As whom the fables name of   monstrous size,
> Titanian or Earth-born, that warred on Jove,
> Briareos or Typhon

('Titanian or Earth-born' requires an antecedent *those*: 'huge as the limbs of those – Titanian or Earth-born – that warred on Jove'. At the same time it anticipates a *such as* or a *like*: 'Those that warred on Jove, such as the Titan called Briareos or the earth-born giant Typhon'). The sentence patterns have to be deciphered, as though one were reading Latin verse. A direct object is emphatically pre-posed, momentarily confusing the reader who expects the subject to come first and who may wonder where the verb has got to:

> Him haply slumbering on the Norway foam,
> The pilot of some small night-foundered skiff,
> Deeming some island, oft, as seamen tell,
> With fixed anchor in his scaly rind
> Moors by his side under the lee

(Read: 'The pilot of some small night-foundered skiff, deeming him – haply slumbering on the Norway foam – some island,

oft . . . moors by his side under the lee.' The sentence is introduced by a participle clause with a direct object qualified by
another participle clause.)

These syntactic displacements and convolutions induce a perhaps rather bemused acceptance of the shift from the 'focusing'
comparison to the distracting fantasy. The comparison with
Briareos and Typhon is apposite. These were, like Satan, of giant
stature, and like him they were in rebellion against the authority
of heaven. Thus far the comparison focuses on significant matters.
It is the third allusion, to Leviathan, that marks the transition to
the fantastic and distracting image. Here Milton, though intent on
his great argument, suddenly takes time off to pitch a salty yarn, a
likely tale of fetching up in the lee of a sea-monster, mistaking
him, in the dark, for an island, and dropping the hook in his hide.
That we are prepared to accept what is, after all, a grotesque idea
may be in part a consequence of our being compulsively gripped in
the coils of Milton's serpentine syntax. But the Leviathan image
also supplies a psychological need – the need for refuges from
reality, safe houses of perception from which the painful or
frightening or merely unpleasant experience is debarred. Satan as
a reality is too terrifying to bear contemplation; Satan as
Leviathan, with nightscape and fishing-boat, we may more
pleasurably consider. What Milton employs here is an exalted
form of a rather common strategy. 'Try to think of it this way', we
say to children or friends confronting some frightening or tedious
reality.

In the rhetoric of pleasure, comparison has a major place. Much
of our enjoyment of art in language, or of art generally, arises
from the designed collocation or juxtaposition, the invitation to
read B in terms of A, A in terms of B, and to enjoy the sense of illu-
mination or liberation that comes from these readings. Formulae
and conventions are developed – the small, compact formulae of
metaphor ('A is like B', 'A is B', 'the A of B', 'AB' and so on), or the
larger conventions of the extended comparison that either focuses
attention on companion images (saying 'spot the difference', like
games in the children's corner of the newspaper), or makes the
comparison a source of illusion or distraction. Thus a literary
tradition accumulates, a tradition allowing for repetition and
innovation. This poem by C. Day Lewis uses the comparison
device innovatively:

As one who wanders into old workings
Dazed by the noonday, desiring coolness,
Has found retreat barred by fall of rockface;
Gropes through galleries where granite bruises
Taut palm and panic patters close at heel;
Must move forward as tide to the moon's nod,
As mouth to breast in blindness is beckoned.
Nightmare nags at his elbow and narrows
Horizon to pinpoint, hope to hand's breadth.
Slow drip the seconds, time is stalactite,
For nothing intrudes here to tell the time,
Sun marches not, nor moon with muffled step.
He wants an opening – only to break out,
To see the dark glass cut by day's diamond,
To relax again in the lap of light.

But we seek a new world through old workings,
Whose hope lies like seed in the loins of the earth,
Whose dawn draws gold from the roots of darkness.
Not shy of light nor shrinking from shadow
Like Jesuits in jungle we journey
Deliberately bearing to brutish tribes
Christ's assurance, arts of agriculture.
As a train that travels underground track
Feels current flashed from far-off dynamos,
Our wheels whirling with impetus elsewhere
Generated we run, are ruled by rails.
Train shall spring from tunnel to terminus,
Out on to plain shall the pioneer plunge,
Earth reveal what veins fed, what hill covered.
Lovely the leap, the explosion into light.

This ingenious construction is as elaborate as Milton's and almost as bemusing in the orientations and disorientations of its syntax. The opening sentence, ending at 'beckoned', has no main, non-dependent, clause (the stem structure is 'As one who wanders into old workings . . . must move forward as tide to moon's nod'). Into this opening pseudo-statement, three 'as' constructions are set: 'as one who wanders . . .', 'as tide to the moon's nod' and 'as mouth to breast in blindness'. This is a figurative keynote. Framed in similitude, the poem is full of similes: 'whose hope lies like seed in the loins of earth', 'Like Jesuits in jungle we journey', 'As a train that travels underground track'. These comparisons are lodged in long sentences, the constituent clauses of which, particularly in the second stanza, tend to overrun the line-endings, half-suppressing the prosodic organization. Against this works a rhythmic insistence on the line as the unit of structure, a pulse marked by three alliterating staves. The alliterations commonly mark the onset of lexically important items:

*G*ropes through *g*alleries where *g*ranite bruises

But the second, unaccented element of a compound may alliterate:

*D*azed by noon*d*ay, *d*esiring coolness

Or the alliteration may fall on a conjunction, for example 'like':

Whose hope *l*ies *l*ike seed in the *l*oins of earth

Or even on an unstressed word-medial syllable:

Deli*b*erately *b*earing to *b*rutish tribes

The poet is at times forced to make shift for an alliteration. In every line, however, there are three staves – except in the last, which has one extra for good measure. (The first line may puzzle a reader unaccustomed to thinking phonetically: the alliterating words are *one, wanders, workings*.)

The distribution of the staves, line by line, is interesting. Either the arrangement is two before and one after the caesura:

Whose *d*awn *d*raws gold / from the roots of *d*arkness

Or the line follows the alternative pattern of one pre-caesural and two post caesural staves:

*T*rain shall spring / from *t*unnel to *t*erminus

Checking stave-patterns (two-one or one-two) throughout the text raises the stylistic question of whether they are deliberately controlled in relationship to a rhetorical purpose, or whether they have occurred without conscious intention, as reflexes of the changes in feeling that lead to changes of phrase-length and sentence structure. Thus if we survey the first stanza:

As *o*ne who *w*anders / into old *w*orkings	2 : 1
*D*azed by the noon*d*ay / *d*esiring coolness	2 : 1
Has *f*ound retreat barred / by *f*all of rock*f*ace	1 : 2
*G*ropes through *g*alleries / where *g*ranite bruises	2 : 1
Taut *p*alm / and *p*anic *p*atters close at heel;	1 : 2
*M*ust *m*ove forward / as tide to *m*oon's nod,	2 : 1
As mouth to *b*reast / in *b*lindness is *b*eckoned.	1 : 2
*N*ightmare *n*ags at his elbow / and *n*arrow	2 : 1

*H*orizon to pinpoint, / *h*ope to *h*and's breadth.   1 : 2
*S*low drip the *s*econds, / time is *s*talactite,   2 : 1
For nothing in*t*rudes here / to *t*ell the *T*ime,   1 : 2
Sun *m*arches not, / nor *m*oon with *m*uffled step.   1 : 2
He wants an *o*pening – / *O*nly to break *o*ut,   1 : 2
To see the *d*ark glass / cut by *d*ay's *D*iamond,   1 : 2
To re*l*ax again / in the *l*ap of *l*ight.   1 : 2

An immediately striking feature is the sequence of eight lines, from 'Has found retreat barred . . .' to '. . . time is stalactite', in which the stave-distribution regularly alternates, one – two, two – one. The lines immediately preceding that sequence, the opening lines of the poem, have the two – one pattern, and those following it, the last five lines of the stanza, are all patterned one – two. We might say that rhythmic weightings shift, over the whole stanza, from line-beginning to line-ending. The poem opens with a focus on the first half of the line, proceeds into a sequence which see-saws between pre- and post-caesural emphasis, and completes its first stanza with another sequence in which the second half of the line is weighted.

The patterning of the second stanza is less clearly suggestive of a significantly varied pulse. The last eight lines nevertheless appear to suggest an immanent design:

As a *t*rain that *t*ravels / underground *t*rack   2 : 1
*F*eels current *f*lashed / from *f*ar-off dynamos   2 : 1
Our *w*heels *wh*irling / with impetus els*ew*here   2 : 1
Generated we *r*un, / are *r*uled by *r*ails.   1 : 2
*T*rain shall spring / from *t*unnel to *t*erminus,   1 : 2
Out on to *p*lain / shall the *p*ioneer *p*lunge,   1 : 2
Earth re*v*eal what *v*eins fed, / what hill co*v*ered,   2 : 1
*L*ovely the *l*eap, / exp*l*osion into *l*ight   2 : 2

Three lines with pre-caesural weight are followed by three in which the impetus is transferred to the second half of the line. The penultimate line is one in which the alliteration is rather subdued; 'covered' is the weakest imaginable completion of the three-stave pattern. But then, as if in deliberate contrast, comes the strong alliteration of the final line, a four-stave departure from the norm, with an equipoise – two – two – around the caesura. The rhythmic sway and counter-sway ceases, the poem ends with a prosodically balanced line. Is this a willed reading, or does it correspond to something the poet intended? Our pleasure is, that we can never really know.

These, however, are stylistic details subordinate to the one major manipulation that makes 'As One Who Wanders' an original essay in the traditional simile of extended comparison. The innovative feature is simply this, that Day Lewis sets up the expectation of AS . . . SO and then frustrates it, substituting AS . . . BUT. This is why the syntax has to lapse in the opening sentence. The initial 'as' will not be followed by the expected 'so'; instead, the poet, having lured his reader into the poem, through several clauses, writes a full stop (after 'beckoned') as though a statement had been completed. There is a genuine 'as – so' comparison towards the end of the poem ('As a train- . . . [so] . . . Our wheels whirling'), but the text in its entirety is framed on a deception, or at least on a deceptive expectation. We expect comparison and are rewarded with contrast. The *we* of the second stanza contrasts with the *one* of the first; 'one' *wanders into* old workings, 'we' *seek . . . through* old workings. The most telling contrast is reserved for the final lines of the two stanzas. Each ends in *light*, a pleasing touch of formal cohesion, but we read *relax* against *leap*, and *in the lap of light* against *explosion into light*.

There is something 'ludic' about this poem, a suggestion of a game played with an alert reader, and it may be that this playful rhetoric has saved it from oblivion, or from the fate of becoming a fusty museum-piece. Written in the 1930s, it was originally the assertion of a political programme, in the 'salon communist' fashion of the time. It can no longer survive in that role, but its rhetorical ingenuity and the strength of its verbal invention guarantee for it a survival in a vaguer yet larger capacity, as the expression of any ideal, any dedication, any hope for the future. The myth it served is dead, but because it is well made it can be remythologized.

PERSONIFICATIONS

These extracts from Chaucer, Milton, Tennyson and Day Lewis illustrate a literary tradition in a rhetorical device, that of extended comparison. There are other traditional toys in the playbox of literary rhetoric, prominent among them the figure of personification:

Tired with all these, for restful death I cry, –
As, to behold Desert a beggar born,
And needy Nothing trimm'd in jollity
And purest Faith unhappily forsworn,
And gilded Honour shamefully misplaced
And maiden Virtue rudely strumpeted,
And right Perfection wrongfully disgraced,
And Strength by limping Sway disabled,
And Art made tongue-tied by Authority,
And Folly, doctor-like, controlling Skill,
And simple Truth miscall'd Simplicity,
And captive Good attending captain Ill;
   Tired with all these, from these would I be gone,
   Save that, to die, I leave my love alone.

This well-known poem presents the reader with an emotional and perceptual paradox. Its paraphrasable meaning is that the world is so hideously corrupt and unjust that were it not for fear of the ultimate injustice of abandoning his love – the one good thing in a wicked society – the poet could wish to die. This is certainly a very serious matter. But the message that the world is perverse and unfair is conveyed through personifications as vivid and interesting as the costumed personages of a pageant, or a parade of mannequins with their stylized gestures ('And now Helga, swathed in a gown of rich Italian silk'). 'Tired with all these' the poet may be; but what he conveys to his readers is a sense of lively interest. The rhetoric of personifications endows the poem with something like gaiety, as though one might, after all, have a taste for the jostle of life even when the wrong people are being jostled.

The materials of this rhetoric are quite simple. First and foremost, there is the device of the capital letter that distinguishes Nothing from nothing. This typographical credential is carried by all the personifications in the poem; so that when we read of *restful death* in the first line, we see there no invitation to regard 'death' as a personified entity. In other respects that invitation stands, for the noun in the first line is modified by an adjective possibly suggesting a human attribute, *restful*; and the use of an attributive epithet characterizes nine out of the ensuing list of sixteen personifications ('needy Nothing', 'purest Faith', 'gilded Honour', 'maiden Virtue', 'right Perfection', 'limping Sway', 'simple Truth', 'captive Good', 'captain Ill'). These duly exhibit the conventional syntactic and lexical form of the characterizing personal epithet plus the abstract noun; yet what really marks them out as personifications is a typographical device, the capital letter. Rhetoric is sometimes a matter of how it looks in writing. Read Shakespeare's sonnet aloud, and to the listener *restful death* is no less a personification than *simple Truth*; confine it to the dimension of the printed page, and the reader sees that only one of these phrases represents a personality in the verse-masquerade.

The third personifying feature, after the capital letter and the attributive adjective, is a post-modifying construction, usually in the form of a participle clause – for example, 'trimm'd in jollity', 'attending captain Ill' (the one exception is the adverbial 'doctor-like', qualifying the personification of Folly). Not all the person-ages in Shakespeare's world-pageant are distinguished by a pre-modifying epithet – Desert, Strength, Art, Authority, Folly, Skill and Simplicity are exceptions; but all are involved in postures or actions designated in each case by the post-modifying clause. It is from this that a sense of theatrical liveliness proceeds. In lines 2–7 of the sonnet, the figures of Desert, Nothing, Faith, Honour and Virtue stand in isolated poses, each the bearer or victim of some mischance or arbitrary imposition. In lines 8–12, by contrast, the personages are involved with each other, in a simulacrum of the world's familiar struggles and topsy-turvy values. The poem presents tableaux of two different yet complementary types of injustice – the injustice of inert circumstance and the injustice of society in action (or the injustice of misfortune and the injustice of oppression). In his representations of social conflict, Shakespeare is occasionally obliged to reduce a personification to its minimal form; there is, for example, nothing but a capital letter to suggest that Simplicity (= 'silliness', 'imbecility') has any personified value.[1] In other cases, however, he adroitly involves his actors in the little drama of the line; thus 'Strength by limping Sway disabled' and 'captive Good attending captain Ill' are miniature plays within the play, or particular poses in the general tableau.

It is remarkable how often, once one has made the connection, the rhetoric of writing suggests equivalents in the rhetoric of the visual media. Thus 'Tired with all these' seems to exert a motley appeal comparable to that of the video-narratives that accompany today's pop-songs and TV commercials. Through such presenta-tions there runs a thread of sense, a 'story', but essentially their claim on us is that of a sequence of striking images strikingly juxtaposed. Very few viewers can be interested in the 'argument' –

meaning 'what this song suggests', or 'how our product will help'. In most cases we are amused by particular images that reconcile us to the mere message. In current TV advertisements for Volkswagen cars British viewers may see insulted Beauty casting off her mink and bankrupt Fortune smiling at the dawn – she emerging from her love-nest in the mews, he leaving the casino, each stripped to the bare material essentials of a suit of clothes and a well-conditioned Volkswagen. It is of course not very surprising if we do not take the message of the commercial (paraphrasable as 'Through all the vicissitudes of life your Volkswagen will be your help and sustenance') very seriously; but that does not prevent us from relishing the images, finding them memorable, taking pleasure in the skill with which they are presented. In the same way, though taking a somewhat more serious view of its content (paraphrasable as 'In this world of injustice and perverted values only my love is my help and sustenance'), we relish the personified images of 'Tired with all these'.

Shakespeare's sonnet is an original performance, a foundation text upon which other texts have been based. Here, for instance, is Wordsworth in the third book of *The Prelude*, describing his freshman impressions of Cambridge as it was in the year 1787:

> And here was Labour, his own bond-slave; Hope
> That never set the pains against the prize;
> Idleness halting with his weary clog,
> And poor misguided Shame, and witless Fear,
> And simple Pleasure foraging for Death;
> Honour misplaced, and Dignity astray,
> Feuds, factions, flatteries, enmity, and guile;
> Murmuring submission and bald government,
> (The idol weak as the idolator),
> And Decency and Custom starving Truth,
> And blind Authority beating with his staff
> The child that might have led him; Emptiness
> Followed as of good omen, and meek Worth
> Left to herself unheard of and unknown.

The resemblance to Shakespeare's text can hardly be missed; indeed in one instance Wordsworth directly echoes Shakespeare's wording (*Shakespeare*: 'Honour shamefully misplaced'; *Wordsworth*: 'Honour misplaced'). The context of the rhetoric, too, appears to be similar; Wordsworth, like Shakespeare denounces the mores of a world that conspires to promote the triumph of the undeserving. Yet the texts differ quite considerably at a deeper level, because the rhetoric, the process of personifications, serves dissimilar meanings. What Shakespeare has to say is that his love is the single reason for living in a corrupt world; more than that, his relationship with his lover is equal and wholesome, unlike the indecent partnerships of the dominant and subservient, exemplified by Strength and Sway, Art and Authority, Folly and Skill, Good and Ill. If he chooses to escape from an unjust world by dying, he not only leaves his partner in vulnerable isolation, but also breaks a vital, humane, defensive bond, against which the painted semblances of wrong and misfortune otherwise have no power.

Wordsworth's rhetoric is orientated to a more obviously political purpose. His recollections of his Cambridge days present the university and academic life as a microcosm of society at large. The passage quoted above is preceded by these lines:

> 'tis enough to note
> That here in dwarf proportions were expressed
> The limbs of the great world; its eager strifes
> Collaterally portrayed, as in mock fight,
> A tournament of blows, some hardly dealt
> Though short of mortal combat; and whate'er
> Might in this pageant be supposed to hit
> An artless rustic's notice, this way less,
> More that way, was not wasted on me –
> And yet the spectacle may well demand
> A more substantial name, no mimic show,
> Itself a living part of a live whole,
> A creek in the vast sea; for all degrees
> And shapes of spurious fame and short-lived praise
> Here sate in state, and fed with daily alms
> Retainers won away from solid good;

This might be loosely paraphrased: the undergraduate quickly discovers that in back-stabbing, bitchiness, conspiracy and self-aggrandisement the university can offer models that will instruct him for the future. Academic life is a 'pageant', a 'spectacle' of things 'collaterally portrayed'. And yet it seems to Wordsworth, on reflection, that these terms are not wholly accurate, since they appear to suggest that the university and its people have no reality except as abstract signifiers of a greater theme. This, the poet concludes, is misleading, for what he evokes is also a reality, 'no mimic show, Itself a living part of a live whole'. In other words, his descriptions of Cambridge, interpretable as observations on the politics of the world at large, are still quite specifically comments on the real state of the academy.

Consequently, the reader is predisposed to relate the figures in the Wordsworthian pageant to the typical features and themes of academic life – the hard-working student and the idler; the authoritarian with no intellectual authority; the spurious, flashy reputation; the loneliness of solid, scrupulous work; the abhorrent tendency, observable in sundry times and colleges, for social and institutional convention to suppress inconvenient truthfulness. For any university teacher, indeed, Wordsworth's lines make uncomfortable reading, because one or other of these abstract instances will bring forcibly home the consciousness of something in recent experience. The description of the University of Cambridge as it appeared in 1787 might be the description of that same university, or of Harvard, or Uppsala, or any educational institution anywhere in our own day and age. But the description is also a description of contemporary Britain, and Europe, and America, and all human societies. This is the remarkable power of poetic rhetoric. It appeals to general experience even while it insists on nothing more than the particular and local fact.

Wordsworth evokes the image of a particular community figurative of a larger, general community. The invitation to find the particular in the universal, or to project the universal from the particular, is less apparent in these lines from W. H. Auden's 'Birthday Poem', addressed to his friend Christopher Isherwood. Auden deplores the apparently comfortable resolve of his countrymen to ignore the signs and omens of a dangerous decade, the 1930s:

> The close-set eyes of mother's boy
> Saw nothing to be done; we look again:
> See Scandal praying with her sharp knees up,
> And Virtue stood at Weeping Cross,
> The green thumb to the ledger knuckled down,
> And Courage to his leaking ship appointed,
> Slim Truth dismissed without a character,
> And gaga Falsehood highly recommended.
>
> Greed showing shamelessly her naked money,
> And all Love's wondering eloquence debased
> To a collector's slang, Smartness in furs,

And Beauty scratching miserably for food,
Honour self-sacrificed for Calculation,
And Reason stoned by Mediocrity,
Freedom by Power shockingly maltreated,
And Justice exiled till Saint Geoffrey's Day.

The stylistic debt to Shakespeare's sonnet, no longer very obvious in verbal echoes, is none the less apparent. We can take it for a certainty that Auden knew the Shakespeare poem – a classic text, after all – and it is a not unreasonable assumption that he had read Wordsworth's lines. Yet once again it appears that the tradition is treated with a difference. The contrast is partly stylistic, and involves Auden's handling of the personifying technique. With two exceptions ('slim Truth' and 'gaga Falsehood') his capitalized abstractions are presented without an attributive epithet. Throughout the two stanzas it is the post-modifying structures – mainly participle clauses – that bear the figurative weight, and in more than one instance this is wittily done, with intimations of some underlying word-play. Perhaps the most obvious example is 'Greed showing shamelessly her naked money', which implies the image of money as pornographic display. Less obvious is the ambivalence of 'Slim Truth dismissed without a character', where Auden puns on 'character' in the sense of a testimonial, a letter of recommendation given to a servent, and 'character' in the primary meaning of a personality, a set of moral and intellectual attributes. Truth is dismissed as having no meaningful 'character', and Falsehood, which is 'gaga' (= 'senile', 'witless', 'inarticulate') is preferred. 'Slim' and 'gaga' are vitally contrasting elements, firstly as connoting 'youth' versus 'age' and secondly in the more elusive connotation of 'fit' versus 'unfit', or 'functional' versus 'malfunctioning'. The disintegration of Falsehood is more acceptable than the integrity of Truth.

Auden's purpose is not to make a declaration of love *in extremis*, as Shakespeare does; not yet to demonstrate, with Wordsworth, the relationship of microcosm to macrocosm in human affairs; but rather to denounce and warn against the symptomatic phenomena of what in another poem he calls 'a low dishonest decade'.[2] His rhetoric is political in a quite precise and localized sense. He is not speaking retrospectively, like Wordsworth, of a little world prefiguring a larger. He is speaking in the present, about the life of the present, the 'present' being the 1930s. At the same time, his imagery is curiously surreal. The representations of disaster crowd in like allegories, and the topographical or temporal signpostings of the dream world are either unexplained ('at Weeping Cross') or patently inexplicable ('till Saint Geoffrey's Day'). What Auden makes out of the personifying device is not a pageant, a procession, a masque, or even a video script; it is a landscape of grotesques. His lines are in one sense, the sense of the job they do, quite *unlike* those of Wordsworth and Shakespeare; on the other hand, the intertextual relationship, the remarkable continuity of a verbal device, is there for all to see. There are three different acts, but the conventions of staging are the same.

STAGES AND SCRIPTS

Now much of the pleasurable distraction of rhetoric is to be sought in the observation of quasi-theatrical performances. To watch the leaders of our political parties at their annual jamborees, for example, is an entertainment spiced by our ability to predict and respond to their verbal routines. The street-market is another natural arena for the performing rhetorician. Here is a typical 'pitch', of a trader in china goods and tableware (recorded as the vendor was speaking from his stall in the open market of a town in the English Midlands):

Here you are –
Here you are –
Madam – yes – look – you won't see a better bargain than this –
This lovely dinner service –
Lovely service, genuine Wedgwood, that.
Twenty-four pieces, new out of the factory, never been touched –
No, it did *not* fall off of a lorry, I can assure you –
This is the goods, this is new out of the factory –
But I'm not asking factory prices –
No, I'm *not asking* factory prices –
I'm not asking *shop* prices –
I know what you would pay in the shops –
You know what you would pay in the shops –
But I'm not asking that.
What am I asking?
What am I asking for this lovely twenty-four piece dinner service?
Am I asking fifty pounds?
                    I am not.
Am I asking thirty pounds?

I am not.
Am I asking twenty-five pounds?
I am not.
Fifteen pounds, three fivers, *that's* what I'm asking for this lovely dinner service, straight out of Wedgwood's factory, and don't ask me how I can do it.
Fifteen pounds and a box to go with it.
Now can I say fairer?
Can I say fairer than that?
Well come on, then, who's going to take advantage of me?

The scripting of this recital imposes on it a form not necessarily implied in the original delivery; it is a case of speech being organized into something resembling literature. The transcript, however, duly records and preserves the central feature of the sales pitch, that of recursion. Certain phrases and constructions are repeated, in rhythmical sequences embodying the pattern phrase plus one or two recurrences ('Am I asking fifty pounds?' – 'Am I asking thirty pounds? – 'Am I asking twenty-five pounds?'). This recursion is an attention-fixer, partly because of the near-hypnotic power of the rhythmic insistence, and partly because it invites the audience to join predictively in the performance. In the crowd round the stall there are those who comment, respond, try to disrupt the recital or put the pitchman off his rhythm by anticipating his moves. The thing becomes a game of wits, in which even the trader must sometimes forget his stock of flawed china (the 'lovely dinner services' were seconds, factory rejects) and commit himself wholly to victory in the verbal struggle.

The hecklers round the market stall, like political hecklers, are able to take part in the game because they recognize the pattern of a performance. The study of rhetoric involves the identification of such patterns, but the task is quite a complex one because new conventions of performance for particular purposes are being generated all the time. Are you seeking a companion, with a possible view to marriage? Then perhaps you will submit to the 'Personal' columns of your local newspaper an entry like this, from the *Weekly*, a Seattle week end supplement:

GOOD LOOKING SWM, 36, creative, trustworthy, professional, successful, considerate, honest, sensitive, and is a perfect gentleman. Personal and spiritual growth are important to me. Looking for a creative and unique SWF I can feel open and compatible with.

Maturity, stability, and how you feel about youself are more important than your age or what you do. I'm open to commitment as long as it's built on the foundation of friendship. And I'm open to friendship as long as it's built on a commitment to honesty.

Or perhaps this:

COMPASSIONATE DWM, 39, Ph.D., likes bikes, hikes, tykes, prefers light jogs, friendly dogs, casual togs; seeks free thinking, reasonably fit, non-materialistic partner.

Or this:

BEAUTIFUL, BOUNTIFUL, buxom blonde, bashful yet bawdy, desires masterful, masculine, magnetic male for friendship, frolic and future. Forward photo and facts.

Or, for an extreme case, this:

CAN IT BE POSSIBLE . . .

That a 5′5″, in shape, blondish, bearded, semi-off the wall, serious about living, up energy, spiritual (Eastern type), secure, outgoing, somewhat aware, up front, career businessman, 42, having intensity, emotions, an arts educational background, loves the outdoors, can't resist the sun and would like to meet a lady friend/lover/companion/soulmate but is not sticky needy? Yes! She would be non-smoking, honest, growth-oriented, balanced, not aggressive, understands where she is going, has integrity, humor, a fit body, prefers equivalence, is assertive, loves city life but a piece of her heart is in the country and perhaps knows the feel of silk as well as denim. I wonder if she wonders what I wonder enough to write to Ad #4393, *The Weekly*.

These extracts, chosen more or less randomly from the *Weekly*'s crowded personal pages, are fair samples of performances in twentieth-century folk rhetoric. Each presents, in greater or lesser measure, a verbal elaboration in excess of the simple message 'I am looking for a partner'. In each case, moreover, the performer is clearly aware of, and perhaps amused by, the act or performing; the compassionate Ph.D. has fun with rhymes, the buxom blonde rejoices in alliteration, the perfect gentleman shows a turn for the combined figures of isocolon (parallel clauses) and antimetabole (reverse sequencing of lexical items):

I'm open to *commitment*   built on   *friendship*
And I'm open to *friendship*   built on a *commitment* (to honesty)

Each example bears some mark of individual composition; but the performance feature that characterizes all of them is asyndeton, the listing of words or phrases without linking conjunctions. These lists are either 'theme centred', related to a developing strain of meaning, or 'theme scattered', jumping from topic to topic with little or no attempt to demonstrate connections. Thus the perfect gentleman characterizes himself as '*considerate, honest, sensitive*' (theme centred), while the blondish, bearded, career businessman is presented as '*having intensity, emotions, an arts educational background, loves the outdoors*' and so on (theme scattered). Virtually all of the personal ads in the *Weekly* use asyndeton, but there is some not insignificant variation in the occurrence of theme centring and theme scattering. The more sober entries, like that of the perfect gentleman, seem to prefer theme-centred lists, while the more exuberant, like the appeal of the career businessman, tend towards theme scattering. But centring and scattering may be combined, as in this announcement from a part-time Mom:

> 34 YEAR OLD, part-time Mom, desires special male friend for fun and companionship. Should be nonsmoking, downhill ski enthusiast, and tolerant to mild infrequent herpes. I enjoy good conversation, bicycling, camping, exploring the North West. Extra points for beards and rollerskaters.

Mom's quaintly asserted needs are actually formulated with some artistic skill. The piece has a pattern:

Requirement	34 year old, part-time Mom, desires special male friend for fun and companionship.
Theme scatter	Should be nonsmoking, downhill ski enthusiasiast, and tolerant to mild infrequent herpes. (No semantic relation between listed items.)
Theme centre	I enjoy good conversation, bicycling, camping, exploring the North West. (Listed items all connected by the notion of 'pastime', 'pursuit'.)
Theme scatter	Extra points for beards and rollerskaters.

The theme scattering articulates her general requirements of the proposed partner, and the theme centring indicates her own particular characteristics; the final sentence suggests a humorous awareness of the rhetorical game she is playing. For these ads are indeed a game, and are playfully treated by those who devise and publish them; there is an 'ad of the week' in each issue, and the entries themselves often betray a consciousness of a competitive drive that has very little to do with the business of dating and mating – unless, of course, we choose to interpret these verbal extravagances as a form of courtship display. The primary impulse seems to be to enjoy performing, emulatively and competitively, in the typical styles of the 'person-to-person' column. Sometimes the entries border on parody, and might be interpreted as such, if it were not for our readiness to grant the sincerity of their intentions.

THE THEATRE OF DISTRACTIONS AND DELIVERIES

About these examples, as about all the examples in this chapter, there is an air of the theatrical, a staginess essential to rhetoric, for good or ill. It appears partly as a matter of costuming, creating masquerades designed to illuminate and distract. We are to understand the character of a Trojan prince, when suddenly a horse prances onto the scene; the theme of worldly corruption and injustice brings on a merry-go-round of masks; a simple appeal for companionship begets a frenzy of posturing and word-play. It is also in part a question of performance and delivery – the virtue of the old *genus demonstrativum*, the stuff of the good pep-talk, the good after-dinner speech, the good eulogy. The politician and the shop steward have this theatrical gift, but so do the street-trader and the fairground-barker. We pause to listen to a pitch for the Elixir of Life or the Python Woman, even though we intend to pass on presently, unparted from our money; a good spieler is always worth five appreciative minutes.

There are many ways in which rhetoric is pleasurable for its own sake. It distracts, it teases, it flirts with language, it is an unabashed show-off, strutting its stuff like a vaudeville dancer. Yet this ebullient energy is, paradoxically, a source of ill repute. The cautious critic is troubled by the power of rhetoric to disorientate, to shift the attention from *is* to *as if*, from *here* to *yonder*, from themes to variations. It is allusive and oblique in method, constantly generating analogies and comparisons; in expression it deceives simple expectations and deflects enquiry with tropes, hyperboles, figures of antithesis, gradation, recursion. Enjoy the show, it says; and against any demurral it reiterates, enjoy the show. But is this all? At least some of the examples in this chapter may hint that it is not quite all, and that it lies within the capacity of rhetoric to illuminate even as it distracts. Sometimes we can only learn to see by shifting our position, only to learn to understand by mocking our understanding; and thus rhetoric's pleasurable distractions become the serious stuff of argument.

4

Images of Argument

Achilles sulks in his tent, and meanwhile there is a war to be won, a war that without his notable assistance stands at a stalemate, and could even be lost. Compose a speech showing him how it would be in his own best interests, as well as those of the Greek army, to forget his grievances and get back to work.

Once upon a time this could have been a theme for a *suasoria*, one of those exercises in persuasion that were prescribed for rhetorical aspirants to careers in politics or the courts. In the twentieth century, *mutatis mutandis*, the theme might be an appeal to the leader of a striking union, or a plea to a reluctant candidate for office. Whatever the variations in its specific terms, the task is fundamentally the same: to get people to change their behaviour, ostensibly for their own good, ultimately for the good of some collective or interested party.

How *do* you get Achilles back into harness? What sort of thing do you say? 'Come on, old chap, this will never do.' 'Get off your idle backside, you Hellenic hulk.' 'Don't you want to be famous any more? 'How can you behave like this?' 'You know, there are plenty of young fellows coming up.' 'Ajax is in top form just now.' And so on, while our man picks at his palliasse and sneers. Remarks of this kind, well or ill chosen, fall into three categories. Some are exhortations ('Get up', 'Try harder', 'Come along, now'); some are framed as questions of the type we call 'rhetorical' ('Aren't you ashamed of yourself?' 'Why am I talking to you like this?'); and some are citations of exemplary cases ('Look at so-and-so, why can't you be like that?'). These are devices that recurrently inform our attempts at persuasion.

Such devices may be put to work within discursive structures that generally resemble the standard forensic/deliberative pattern of exposition described in the first chapter of this book. Here is a possible version of the speech to Achilles:

Achilles, I don't want to intrude on your privacy, and I wouldn't like you to think I was speaking out of turn, but I must say something, old boy, for your own good. I mean, I'm the last one to talk, I grant you that, but even so . . . you know . . .? [*the exordium*]

It's this hanging around in your tent all day while others are out doing their bit for Greece. You do realize, don't you, that people are beginning to talk? OK, sure, what you get up to with Patroklos is your own business entirely, we all have our special friends, and that mix-up with the slave-girl – what's-her-name – Briseis – well, that was a bit unfortunate, but having said that, Achilles, having said that, aren't you *over-reacting* just a little bit? I mean, this is *Troy*, man, this is the big one, we need you, you're our star performer. Lying round and sulking isn't the way to win a war. Ask Ajax. He's up at the walls every day giving it one hundred and ten per cent. He's really *dedicated*. He's the most *improved* warrior we've seen this year. And here you are in your tent. [*the case, with supporting examples*]

Of course, you may think you're indispensable, you may think you can wait till Agamemnon and the rest of them come crawling on their bended knees to beg you back, but frankly, Achilles old man, I think you might find yourself waiting a long time. It may not look like it now, but believe you me, there's always a new star, a new face. Before you know it, some kid will be leading the charge, and then where are you? Who needs you? You want to know what *I* think? Every day and in every way your dispensability gets bigger and bigger and bigger. That's what I think. [*refutation of anticipated objections*]

But look, you're not finished, it hasn't come to that, who said it had? It's all in your own hands, don't you see? You can be champ again, you can be the best, you *are* the best, if only you'll come out and show us some of that old style. We can get round our difficulties, we can come to an accommodation, just give us a chance to talk it through. There's no problem that good will won't solve. Think it over, and if I've said anything I shouldn't, I know you'll forgive me for old times' sake. Well, there it is, I've spoken my piece. I leave it with you. [*concluding appeal*]

It is not entirely the familiar colloquial language, the *stilus vulgaris,* that makes this a rather lame essay in persuasion. Even were it translated into cadences of Miltonic dignity it would probably leave Achilles snoring. The real problem is that the formal progression is wholly predictable, and that the imagined speaker grinds on through his 'piece' with no apparent sensitivity to the covertly dialogic nature of persuasive rhetoric. The skill of persuasion lies in listening to the unspoken rejoinder, observing the unarticulated reaction; and then, if need be, in changing the line of attack, the particular emphasis, the order of discourse. The tactics of persuasion do not always coincide with the standard strategy of laying out a case.

SHAKESPEARE AND THE ACHILLES PROBLEM

Among those who have attempted the Achilles problem is William Shakespeare. His demonstration, however, is something more complex than a straighforward sample of a scholastic *suasoria*. His exercise on a well-known Greek theme occurs in *Troilus and Cressida*, where he has a great deal to say about matters of politics and social philosophy which concern Elizabethan England every bit as much as they concern ancient Greece. Shakespeare's Ulysses, the self-elected spokesman of the Greek higher command, displays the tactical cunning of a Renaissance politico. He knows that a stubborn subject is not won over by a single speech. The victim has to be softened up; and to be softened up, he must be *set up*. This is the situational equivalent of the *captatio benevolentiae*; you put your victim into a position he dislikes, in order to make him receptive to your redemptory argument.

Ulysses sets up Achilles by instructing his colleagues to stroll past the great man's tent and respond to any greetings negligently, with snubs and cold-shoulderings. He himself, he tells them, will then come along to chasten the recalcitrant with a few well-chosen words. Thus the scene is set, and Ulysses in due course makes his appearance with what must be one of the oldest tricks in the repertoire of come-ons – pretending to be absorbed in a book ('Oh, hi there! You know, there's something here that would interest you . . .'). Achilles, studiously snubbed by his colleagues, takes the bait with almost pitiful readiness:

Achilles: What are you reading?
Ulysses: A strange fellow here
        Writes me, 'That man – how dearly ever parted,
        How much in having, or without or within –

Cannot make boast to have that which he hath,
Nor feels not what he owes but by reflection;
As when his virtues shining upon others
Heat them and they retort that heat again
To the first giver.'

We may conjecture that the book is a dummy and that Ulysses is
making up his *topos* as he goes along. His words may be paraphrased thus: 'Here's a queer chap – he says that however gifted you
are, however great your talents and powers of personality, you
can't be said to *possess* any quality until you see it reflected in the
reactions and responses of others.' Ulysses is careful not to claim
these sentiments as his own, but to attribute them to an authority,
the 'strange fellow'; and equally careful, at this stage, not to let
Achilles suspect that the proposition is aimed directly at him. As
Achilles himself will presently point out, it is not a particularly
unusual idea. The language in which it is dressed, however, is a little opaque, and embodies a central stylistic principle of *Troilus and
Cressida*, namely that the Greeks all speak Latin; or rather, that
the Greek commanders (particularly in the great council scene,
Act I, Scene iii) use many words borrowed from Latin, learned
words, 'ink horn terms', some of them quite recent entrants into
Elizabethan English, some, indeed, invented by Shakespeare
himself.[1] In his opening remarks to Achilles, Ulysses significantly
uses two such 'aureate' words: *reflection*, in the sense of 'throwing
back heat and light', and *retort*, with the same sense. These are
appropriately bookish words for a man purportedly quoting from
a book.

Presented with a familiar notion couched in language just
difficult enough to flatter an unphilosophical fellow's powers of
decipherment, Achilles is encouraged to help Ulysses out of his
perplexity. It's quite easy, he implies, I'm surprised you find it
difficult, and you such a clever chap, look, let me explain:

This is not strange, Ulysses.
The beauty that is borne here in the face
The bearer knows not, but commends itself
To others' eyes: nor does the eye itself
That most pure spirit of sense, behold itself,
Not going from itself; but eye to eye opposed
Salutes each other with each other's form:
For speculation turns not to itself,
Till it hath travell'd, and is mirror'd there
Where it may see itself. This is not strange at all.

This is no more than a lumbering paraphrase (he has particular trouble with 'itself' and 'each other') of what Ulysses has already said, though Achilles is keen to show that he is no laggard when it comes to a scientific vocabulary. If Ulysses is going to talk about *reflection*, he will talk about *speculation*. All done by mirrors; not in the least strange.

Ulysses politely replies that he is not concerned with the 'position' (*topos*, *locus*), which is 'familiar' (*koinos*, *communis*), so much as with the 'circumstance' (*narratio* and *confirmatio*) elaborating the argument:

> I do not strain at the position –
> It is familiar – but at the author's drift;
> Who, in his circumstance, expressly proves
> That no man is the lord of any thing,
> Though in and of him there be much consisting,
> Till he communicate his parts to others;
> Nor doth he of himself know them for aught
> Till he behold them formed in th' applause
> Where they're extended; who, like an arch, reverb'rates
> The voice again; or, like a gate of steel
> Fronting the sun, receives and renders back
> His figure and his heat.

All that Ulysses does here is to resummarize the argument, or 'position', that Achilles has already summarized after Ulysses' first statement of it. They appear to be like faculty wiseacres, each telling the other in other words what the other has told him in his own words. It is the *words*, however, that are important; the real aim of Ulysses' speechifying is to establish a semantic base in words like *reflection*, *retort* and now *reverberate*. The latter is particularly to his purpose, because what is reverberated (by those tokens of military honour, the arch and the gate of steel) is the *voice*. There is a connection between 'voice' and 'reputation', a connection which Achilles has already been made to recognize. Suddenly no one is speaking *to* Achilles, or *about* Achilles. Even Ulysses, who has stopped by for a friendly talk, appears to have been talking about someone else. 'When you caught me reading this book', he says 'do you know, I was thinking about *Ajax*?' Ajax is an exemplary instance to goad and disgruntle Achilles:

> I was much rapt in this
> And apprehended here immediately
> The unknown Ajax.

Heavens, what a man is there! a very horse
That has he knows not what. Nature, what things there are
Most abject in regard, and dear in use!
What things again most dear in the esteem,
And poor in worth! Now we shall see to-morrow –
An act that very chance doth throw upon him –
Ajax renown'd. O heavens, what some men do,
While some men leave to do!
How some men creep in skittish Fortune's hall,
Whiles others play the idiots in her eyes!
How one man eats into another's pride,
While pride is fasting in his wantonness!
To see these Grecian lords! – why, even already
They clap the lubber Ajax on the shoulder,
As if his foot were on brave Hector's breast,
And great Troy shrieking.

Ajax – the unknown Ajax, Ajax the horse, the lubber Ajax – is instanced in reproof of Achilles, though the name of Achilles is not mentioned; he is a mere pronoun in a sidelong play of 'some' and 'others', occurring in a sequence of antithetical figures:

What some men do / While some men leave to do
  (='What Ajax does while you are idle')

How some men creep . . . / Whiles others play the idiots
  (='How you go unnoticed, while Ajax is fortune's favourite'; or possibly 'How Ajax prospers while you fool around'; but *idiot* has the sense of 'licensed fool', and Ajax, like the professional entertainer in a great house, enjoys a special position denied to Achilles, who goes unnoticed, on sufferance, like a scullion or mendicant)

How one man eats into another's pride . . .
  (='How Ajax is feeding on the glory meant for you')

While pride is fasting in his wantonness
  (='While you wilfully starve yourself of fame')

'Ajax, who is too stupid to know his own luck, is revelling in it, the favourite of the moment, while you, an intelligent man, stubbornly insist on depriving yourself of the status that is rightfully yours.' This is the tenor of Ulysses' message, but it is conveyed indirectly, through the indefinite pronouns ('some', 'others', 'one') and through a strain of imagery which contrasts feeding and starving, status and neglect. Ulysses will presently return to this theme,

after Achilles has spoken words that tell how the setting-up and
the softening-up have succeeded:

> I do believe it; for they pass'd by me
> As misers do by beggars, – neither gave to me
> Good words nor look: what, are my deeds forgot?

This is Ulysses' cue for a speech that now has the familiarity of a
set piece, an anthology passage; the lines beginning 'Time hath,
my lord, a wallet at his back', *Troilus and Cressida*, Act III, Scene
iii, 145–90. One might suppose that this would be the point at
which to produce the rehearsed argument, the scripted appeal,
but the speech is not like that. It is much more of an impromptu,
reflecting Ulysses' current responses to Achilles' reactions and to
his own words. Thus he begins with a *koinos topos* – time devours
everything – expressed in a trope which picks up the themes of
eating, fasting, patronage and beggary touched on in the preceding dialogue:

> Time hath, my lord, a wallet at his back,
> Wherein he puts alms for oblivion,
> A great-siz'd monster of ingratitudes:
> Those scraps are good deeds past; which are devour'd
> As fast as they are made, forgot as soon
> As done:

An attempt at paraphrase might produce something along these
lines: 'Time is [like a] man who carries on his back a little bag in
which he keeps charitable offerings for a fat and scandalously
ungrateful pensioner called Oblivion. Those alms-gifts take the
form of good deeds. No sooner is one of them offered than it is
snapped up by Oblivion and promptly forgotten.' Such, it appears,
is the overall sense of the lines. Shakespeare's image – or rather,
Ulysses' image, if we agree to make him an honorary Elizabethan –
is in fact rooted in the social culture of his time, when alms-giving
was a charitable duty, and the collection and distribution of alms a
more or less institutionalized business. Oblivion here is personified in the shape of an alms-man, or beadsman ('pensioner' is a
paraphraser's rough guess), one who eked out a living on charity
and in turn prayed for the souls of the charitable. We may suppose
that an alms-man, living on slim pickings, would be rather lean, yet
would be expected to show gratitude to his benefactors. Oblivion,
on this supposition, is a very unlikely sort of alms-man: he grows

fat ('great-siz'd') on a surfeit of charities, and is monstrously ungrateful.

Many sermons and uplifting addresses begin in this fashion, with some picturesque example or minor fable which provides threads for the stranding of an argument. It might be expected that Ulysses would develop from this opening image the stuff of his 'circumstance', or elaborated appeal: 'Now, my lord, *you* in your time have done many good deeds, *you* have put a lot into the wallet, *you* have fed the ingrate . . .'. Yet he abruptly breaks the continuity of his oration at this point. Does he perhaps pause there, reading blank incomprehension in Achilles' face? Or does he sense that the terms of the personification may be a little confusing, because Time gets mixed up with Oblivion, so that we are never quite sure which of the two it is that 'forgets' the good deeds? For whatever reason, Ulysses' aborts his opening, stops talking about charities and pensioners, and attempts to establish a new position from which to unfold the circumstance of his argument:

> perseverance, dear my lord,
> Keeps honour bright: to have done, is to hang
> Quite out of fashion, like a rusty mail
> In monumental mockery.

Here is a more promising start, a stiff *sententia*, a bracing moral maxim for a military man, 'perseverance keeps honour bright'. Dramatically, too, this is appropriate. Achilles, the text informs us, 'stands i' th'entrance of his tent' – from which position, presumably, an observer might glimpse the armour hung on the tent-pole or on a spear-shaft. Your very armour, Ulysses implies, is a standing reproach to your idleness.

This military motif allows a transitional development into imagery that suggests soldierly activity; imagery of men running pell-mell in order to be the first to enter a defile. You must go for it, Ulysses says, because if you give way or swerve, they will all come past you like the sea rushing into a channel, and you will be stranded behind them:

> Take the instant way;
> For honour travels in a strait so narrow
> Where one but goes abreast; keep, then, the path;
> For emulation hath a thousand sons

> That one by one pursue: if you give way,
> Or hedge aside from the direct forthright,
> Like to an entered tide, they all rush by,
> And leave you hindmost;

New personifications have entered the argument; Time and Oblivion having been put aside for the moment, now Honour and Emulation appear. Honour is the warrior-runner, Emulation the father of warrior-runners. The theme of running for the prize, or charging for the honour of leading the vanguard, prompts a supplementary image, of the cavalry charge in which the fallen rider is trodden underfoot by those who follow:

> Or, like a gallant horse fall'n in first rank,
> Lie there for pavement to the abject rear,
> O'er-run and trampled on:

The argument is banal, and we have heard it so often: 'If you don't stay right up there, well, there are plenty of others coming along, and I'm telling you they're going to walk right over you.' But this is the sort of stuff that Achilles understands, and Ulysses knows that he understands it. What is important is not so much the argument as the method. Earlier, Ulysses has observed, in anticipation of this encounter with Achilles, that 'pride hath no other glass to show itself but pride'. It is Achilles' military pride that Ulysses aims at; and he rounds off this section of his argument with a pointedly formulated paradox:

> then what they do in present
> Though less than yours in past, must o'ertop yours.

Thus might one say to a cricketer or baseball player, a poorer bat than you will top the averages; or to a boxer, some small-town bruiser will be the new champion. You persuade your man according to his personal persuasions, those shadows and phantasms of private conviction that Francis Bacon called Idols of the Cave.[2] Achilles' particular *eidolon* is a competitive notion of honour, and Ulysses uses that notion to make Achilles an accomplice in the argument levelled against him. 'Pride hath no other glass to show itself but pride.' These observations on competitiveness and honour are the real 'circumstance', the *confirmatio*, of Ulysses' argument. He now reverts to his original topic, the representation of Time:

For Time is like a fashionable host
That slightly shakes his parting guest by th' hand
And with his arms outstretch'd as he would fly,
Grasps-in the comer: welcome ever smiles,
And farewell goes out sighing.

Here is a new mini-drama, or emblematic tableau, with new
personae: Time (the host), Welcome (the in-comer) and Farewell
(the departing guest). This trope is better organized than Ulysses'
earlier attempt to conjure with the notion of Time as an alms-
gatherer. In this second appearance, Time is not presented in a
dubiously benevolent or even a neutral light. Time here is fickle,
pretentious, a hypocrite, not a truly warm-hearted host but an
entertainer of celebrities and a scorner of has-beens. Ulysses is still
telling Achilles that people have short memories, but he has now
put Oblivion out of the picture, in order to make Time the
complete and only villain:

O, let not virtue seek
Remuneration for the thing it was;
For beauty, wit,
High birth, vigour of bone, desert in service,
Love, friendship, charity, are subjects all
To envious and calumniating time.

'Beauty', 'wit' and so on may possibly recall the 'scraps' or 'alms' of
the earlier image, but now the theme of alms-giving has yielded to
some talk of commercial business, of payment, or *remuneration*, for
services rendered. Not only is this word *remuneration* prosodically
focused, as the first pulse in a line of verse; it is also something of a
neologism, one of those 'aureate' or 'ink-horn' words mentioned
earlier. (Shakespeare uses the word in only two of his plays: in
Love's Labour's Lost, where he openly laughs at it, and here, where
he uses it seriously – or is he quietly smiling at the oracular
pomposity of Ulysses, who knows everything, including the posh
word for 'wages'?) His message is that you do not go on being paid
just for being Achilles; that you cannot deposit your good qualities
in some ideological bank and go on drawing against them; or as
Margaret Thatcher has put it, in her own briskly rhetorical style,
'there's no such thing as a free lunch'. Time is not, after all, an
alms-giver; Time is not a trustee paymaster; Time is not a source
of unending hospitality; Time is, in the last resort, a tyrant who

envies and calumniates (another aureate word) all who come into his power. In the space of thirty verse-lines the persuasive tenor of Ulysses' oratory is allowed to shift a little. At the outset, the accent is on *oblivion*: your deeds are soon forgotten. But at the end of the extract thus far examined, the stress is on *calumny*, Your qualities are misrepresented; not only does Time refuse to reward you for your good deeds, he actually tells lies about them, out of envy. In thus gradually changing the psychological thrust of his argument, Ulysses is undoubtedly gauging the responses of Achilles, who in fact says, somewhat later in the scene:

> I see my reputation is at stake;
> My fame is shrewdly gored.

This suggests that it may be the immediate calumny (being 'shrewdly gored') as much as the distant prospect of oblivion that produces a reaction from Achilles; and that Ulysses, indeed, has been quite 'shrewd' in slightly adjusting his line of appeal. In the game of persuasion, such procedural mutations are allowed, even under the pretence of conducting a consistent, well-formed argument. In logical demonstration they are not; and this is one of the recurrent quarrels between logic and rhetoric.

Such, indeed, has been the drift of Ulysses' address that when he comes to his summing up, his tone is consolatory rather than one of exhortation. 'So you've been passed over', he says 'but never mind, that's just the way of the world, and you're not entirely a has-been, you can make a come-back if you move smartly':

> One touch of nature makes the whole world kin –
> That all, with one consent, praise new-born gawds,
> Though they are made and moulded of things past,
> And give to dust, that is a little gilt,
> More laud than gilt o'er-dusted.
> The present eye praises the present object:
> Then marvel not, thou great and complete man,
> That all the Greeks begin to worship Ajax;
> Since things in motion sooner catch the eye
> Than what not stirs. The cry went once on thee,
> If thou wouldst not entomb thyself alive,
> And case thy reputation in thy tent;
> Whose glorious deeds, but in these fields of late,
> Made emulous missions 'mongst the gods themselves,
> And drave great Mars to faction.

No one would suppose from this that the Greeks desperately need to get Achilles into the field again. Ulysses' tone is that of a counsellor talking the disconsolate star through a career crisis; his implication is that Achilles needs his public far more than his public needs him. Ulysses' rhetoric is now suddenly busy with *sententiae* and saws, maxims and morals: 'the present eye praises the present object', 'things in motion sooner catch the eye than what not stirs'. Proverbial formulae of this kind often supply the 'moral' that closes the didactic fable. Here also they are symptoms of closure. A perhaps less obvious sign is Ulysses' reversion to the theme of reputation as the reverberated voice:

> The cry went once on thee,
> And still it might, and yet it may again.

'And yet it may *again*'; the plaudits may yet reverberate. But Achilles, a 'great and complete *man*', must earn the 'praise', the 'laud', the 'worship' now given to Ajax as though he were a *god*. Ulysses' apparently casual use of religious language is extremely shrewd; emollient though his closing remarks may seem to be, he continues to goad Achilles to the very end with the prospect of being less than the first and the highest.

What emerges very clearly from this scene is Shakespeare's dramatic grasp of the dynamism of rhetoric in face-to-face encounters. The participants do not speak from a script or a brief; they manoeuvre, or change their discursive ground in response to transient stimuli. Ulysses in particular appears to play the game by god and by guesswork, the 'god' being the general principles of rhetorical address, the 'guesswork' being the moves dictated by assessment of the situation as it unfolds. Much of that situation we as readers of course do not see; it is up to the producer and the actors to realize it for us – and particularly for the actor playing Achilles to demonstrate, through mute expressions of incomprehension, protest or vulnerability, the developing sense of the interaction. There is a plan to what Ulysses does, but it is a plan he is ready to adjust to the needs of the moment.

In these positional shifts he has constant recourse to little illustrations, analogies, conceits, images, tropes, *topoi* – local maps of ever-changing territories. These points of discursive reference include:

1 The representation of Time as an authority collecting and distributing alms.

2   The revised representation of Time as a host, bidding goodbye
     to the old guest and welcoming the new.
3   A picture of men running all out to be first through some gap,
     defile or narrow passage.
4   A picture of a cavalry charge in which the front runner falls
     and is trampled on.
5   An allusion to armour, which is customarily burnished but
     which is allowed to rust when it falls into disuse.
6   Allusion to phenomena in optics and acoustics.

Between them, Ulysses and Achilles cover a great deal of
imaginative and iconographic ground. What is most striking about
Ulysses' tactics, however, is that he repeatedly and deliberately
breaks away from or circumvents the literal facts of the situation in
order to evoke fictive circumstances. He does not use logic or
inference or connected demonstration to persuade Achilles; he
works on him with miniature fables and just-supposes, from which
he then 'infers' certain consequences. His method, indeed, is more
than iconographic; it is *mythographic*. Here is Shakespeare's
inspired understanding of the Achilles problem: if you go to
persuade, take your myth with you.

A DIGRESSION: ON MYTH AND RELATED MATTERS

Since much of our ordinary communication is through assumptions based on convenient fictions, it is not surprising that myth –
or fable-making – or parables – or analogies – should be a
prominent element in the rhetoric of persuasion. We use myths all
the time; we are imaginatively and institutionally committed to
them; and no politician could survive six months in office without
them. But what is a myth? First, it is a kind of narrative, but not a
narrative plain and simple. It is a story that betokens something; it
has an interpretative and explanatory significance, supplying a
way of understanding the otherwise elusive – the sunrise, the
thunder, the changing of the seasons, the vagaries of fortune, the
pattern of nature. Myths represent a pre-logical, concrete phase of
thought, and as such may be regarded as primitive; but they are
also highly sophisticated in giving access to otherwise fugitive
ideas, and in promoting the necessary illusion of the world and the
mind as theatres of meaningful activity.

    For this reason, teachers and preachers have always made use of myth, and every age tends to generate its own favoured scenarios and mythic types. Medieval theologians regarded nature itself as no more than a physical token of a spiritual purpose, a mere shadowing of the mind and purposes of Almighty God; the human and animal realm, the very stocks and stones of the common earth, could be interpreted as myth. Medieval zoology, for example, was bizarrely unscientific, but that was because the authors of the so-called 'bestiaries' were more concerned with spiritual significance than with what we should now insist on as scientific accuracy. They thought, among other things, that the elephant had no knee-joints and was obliged to sleep standing up. No one appears to have gone to the trouble of testing this curious notion by actually observing the beast – or perhaps elephants were hard to come by. At all events, the belief remained in scholarly circulation for a long time; we find it uncritically recorded in the *History of Four-Footed Beasts* by the Elizabethan naturalist Edward Topsell, and it was one of the popular fallacies that Sir Thomas Browne found it necessary to demolish in his *Pseudodoxia Epidemica* (1646). What medieval writers like Theobaldus (of Monte Cassino) or the Anglo-Norman poet Philippe de Thaün made of it was, in effect, a lesson in religion.

It went like this. The elephant, having no joints in his knees, has to lean against a tree when he wishes to rest. The cunning hunter waits until the elephant is asleep, digs a pit on the reverse side of the tree, then chops the tree down so that the elephant topples into the pit. To get the elephant on to his feet again, the services of a younger, stronger elephant are required; the young animal gets his trunk under the body of the fallen beast, and by main strength raises him. All this was taken to be the literal truth – or rather, the literal *fact*, for the truth embodied in the fact was a matter of much greater concern. The elephant with his unbending legs (so the commentary went) represents unredeemed humanity in all the stubbornness of its pride. The hunter is of course the devil, who, knowing our nature, plots to bring about our fall; and the young elephant is our Saviour who, as one of us, abases Himself to raise us up again.

As one of Chaucer's characters says, 'glosynge is a glorious thynge, certeyne'; but indeed no medieval orator would have thought it worth while to tell a story that did not invite some 'glosynge', or interpretation. It is apparent that we can put a gloss on the elephant story in one or more of four ways. First, we can take it quite straightforwardly as an account of what elephants are like and how hunters go about catching them. Second, we can assume that this account, of tangible events, is a pattern of the invisible and intangible. Third, and consequently, we can take it that each element in the outward pattern (the old elephant, the hunter, the young elephant) has a symbolic correspondence with some value or notion in the inner scheme. And finally, we may think that the whole story points to a doctrine, a moral, an evaluative summary, for example 'Pride goeth before a fall'. There are, in short, four possible and interrelated levels of interpretation – the *literal*, the *allegorical*, the *tropological* and the *anagogical*.

In myths and parables – in all fictions that set out in some way to instruct, enlighten or persuade – the literal, or what we are asked to take literally, is accompanied by one or more of the other interpretative possibilities. Sometimes it is possible to demonstrate convergent allegorical, tropological and anagogical interpretations of a story or an emblem; sometimes one possibility is more prominent than others. Fables like those of Aesop (and the European literary genre that has sprung from them) are powerful anagogically: they are constructed to emphasize a doctrine or to recommend a mode of conduct. The realistic narratives used by Jesus to teach his disciples also have a clear anagogical intent, as guides to behaviour and attitude; but the stories, however realistic, are also allegories with a complex tropological structure. In the parable of the sower (*St Luke*, chapter 8) Christ tells how a man goes out to sow, and how some of the broadcast seed falls by the roadside, some on a rock, some among thorns and some on good grounds. The seed that falls by the wayside is picked up by birds or trodden underfoot; the seed that falls on a rock simply withers; but the seed that falls on good ground springs up and flourishes. 'He that hath ears to hear, let him hear', says Jesus, and goes on to make his own tropological exposition of the tale:

> Now the parable is this: The seed is the word of God.
>
> Those by the way side are they that hear; then cometh the devil and taketh away the word out of their hearts, lest they should believe and be saved.
>
> They on the rock are they, which, when they hear, receive the word with joy; and these have no root, which for a while believe, and in time of temptation fall away.
>
> And that which fell among thorns are they which, when they have heard, go forth, and are choked with cares and riches and pleasures of this life, and bring no fruit to perfection.

But that on the good ground are they, which in an honest and
good heart, having heard the word, keep it, and bring forth fruit
with patience.

Thus Christ makes it clear that his story – about something within
the literal experience of his hearers, something of common
occurrence – is an allegory of how God's word is received among
men; and then proceeds to explain the tropes or metaphors that
make up the allegory indicating that the birds stand for the devil,
the thorns for 'the riches and pleasures of this life' and so on. The
literal, the allegorical, the tropological and the anagogical (the
moral of the tale – 'if you want to live, listen') converge in this
narrative.

A typical passage from St Paul invites comparison with Christ's
parabolic method. St Paul does not tell stories, but he likes
symbols, analogies and allegorical pictures. Among the best
known of his inventions is this, from the sixth chapter of his Epistle
to the Ephesians:

Put on the whole armour of God, that ye may be able to stand
against the wiles of the devil.
For we wrestle not against flesh and blood, but against principali-
ties, against powers, against the rulers of the darkness of this world,
against spiritual wickedness in high places.
Wherefore take unto you the whole armour of God, that ye may
be able to withstand in the evil day, and having done all, to stand.
Stand therefore, having your loins girt about with truth, and
having on the breastplate of righteousness;
And your feet shod with the preparation of the gospel of peace;
Above all, taking the shield of faith, wherewith ye shall be able to
quench all the fiery darts of the wicked.
And take the helmet of salvation, and the sword of the Spirit,
which is the word of God.

Rather than allegory, in the sense of consistently patterned
symbolic narrative, it is tropology that takes prominence here.
There is a discernible allegorical sense – that spiritual life is a
battle against the devil – but it is inferred from the metaphors Paul
constructs after his first invention, 'the armour of God', metaphors with a common linguistic form represented in English by *the
A of B*: 'the breastplate of righteousness', 'the shield of faith', 'the
helmet of salvation', 'the sword of the Spirit'. One figure, it
appears, provides the impulse to another.

This tropological style may imply allegory, may suggest parable, may invoke myth, but does not spell out these larger, explicatory forms in terms of a narrative pattern. It resorts to tropes that carry some hint of narrative, as convenient adjuncts to persuasion: the tropes of transient make-believe. Although the texts and intentions are worlds and eras apart, what St Paul does in the 'armour of God' passage is not wholly unlike what Shakespeare represents Ulysses as doing in his persuasive confrontation with Achilles. Ulysses also has recourse to tropes that suggest, however vaguely, the possibility of full-blown myth. He never completely develops, however, the narrative/mythic argument implicit in any of his tropes. That is not his purpose. His particular act of persuasion requires the invention of little fables that will fill the context of a moment before giving place to new inventions. His mythography is casual and fragmented, unlike that of Christ in his parables. Each story that Jesus tells is an entity complete in itself, a fully re-solved *mythogram* supplying the pattern for a moral or ideational construction. Ulysses' strategy, on the other hand – if we may amuse ourselves by inventing yet another term – is that of the *tropodrome*, a set of figures from which an underlying pattern may be inferred by the obliging reader/hearer.[3]

CHESTERTON AND THE CAUSALITY PUZZLE: 'THE WIND AND THE TREES'

Now here is another problem for the persuasive: *A sceptic is convinced that material effects are to be traced only to material causes: that unemployment causes drunkenness, that poor housing leads to the break-up of marriages, that financial inequality promotes crime and so on. Try to convince him that material effects are, after all, consequent upon spiritual causes.*

This is the problem to which G. K. Chesterton addresses himself in a fine essay called 'The Wind and the Trees'. He begins his argument like this:

> I am sitting under tall trees, with a great wind boiling like surf about the tops of them, so that their living load of leaves rocks and roars in something that is at once exultation and agony. I feel, in fact, as if I were actually sitting at the bottom of the sea among mere anchors and ropes, while over my head and over the green twilight of water sounded the everlasting rush of waves and the toil and crash of

shipwreck of tremendous ships. The wind tugs at the trees as if it might pluck them root and all out of the earth like tufts of grass. Or, to try yet another desperate figure of speech for this unspeakable energy, the trees are straining and tearing and lashing as if they were dragons each tied by the tail.

As a piece of description, this certainly merits the adjective 'rhetorical'; but let us enumerate some of the significant facts of its rhetoric. First, it posits something manifestly false, a deception that in fact would deceive none but a simpleton. No one supposes that Chesterton actually wrote these words while he was sitting out of doors, in a gale; and certainly no one is so innocent as to believe that the present tense means what it says – that even as the reader starts to read, he is addressed by someone experiencing the situation described. What the writer proposes is a stratagem of reference, a scheme which the reader accepts, thereby becoming an accomplice to falsehood, if falsehood is the right word. But it is not really falsehood. It is the proposed ground of a persuasive argument, the poetic setting for a philosophical play. It is, in short, a mythogram. When we say 'let's pretend', we are not lying.

What is ostensibly a declarative clause describing an actual state of affairs, 'I am sitting under tall trees', is to be understood as a directive to the reader: 'Imagine that I am (and therefore that *you are*) sitting under tall trees', 'Let it be posited that we are at this moment sitting under tall trees.' The reader is asked to accept the implications of *as if*, a conjunction that occurs three times in four sentences. *As if* is the proposed 'fact', the literal ground; 'as-ifness' is adroitly confounded with factuality: 'I feel, in fact, as if I were actually sitting at the bottom of the sea.' But Chesterton knows that he is not *actually* sitting at the bottom of the sea; he knows that he is not actually sitting under any trees; so that whatever it is he feels, he cannot be actually feeling it in a factual situation; yet he writes, 'I feel, in fact.' His assertion can only be rescued from the charge of blatant mendacity by supplying what any sensible reader will instinctively offer, the interpretation of 'I feel, in fact', as 'In such a situation one might very well feel.' To supply such an interpretation is, of course, an act of complicity. 'One' has only reached the second sentence of the essay, and 'one' is already persuaded; 'one' has assented to the terms of the mythogram. By the end of the paragraph the assent is so complete that Chesterton can unabashedly refer to his own rhetorical procedures, in the phrase 'a desperate figure of speech'.

'Desperate' here is a double-sided word. Ostensibly it implies that he despairs of finding expressions adequate to describe the fury of the wind in the trees – a descriptive purpose to which the minor rhetoric of the passage is palpably devoted, for example in the alliterations of 'their *l*iving *l*oad of *l*eaves *r*ocks and *r*oars' and in the end-chime of 'strai*ning* and tea*ring* and lash*ing*'. But the word suggests something else: a determination at all costs to establish a position from which all subsequent discussion can be controlled. That position may be roughly paraphrased thus: that invisible causes produce sensational effects, and worldly events are steered by spiritual powers. It is stated quite explicitly later in the essay, but its statement and acceptance at that later point, as a 'dialectic' proposition depends vitally on its initial appeal in mythographic guise. The rhetorician is 'desperate' to make an audience accept his scenario; that done, he can more or less quietly unfold the plot of his argument.

After this spectacular opening, the next stage in Chesterton's argumentative business is the execution of a well-tried rhetorical move: the appeal to external witness, whether in the form of an acknowledged authority, a friend, an unbiased observer or any convenient face in the audience. In this case the necessary outsider is a small boy:

> He did not like the wind at all; it blew in his face too much; it made him shut his eyes; and it blew off his hat, of which he was very proud. He was, as far as I remember, about four. After complaining repeatedly of the atmospheric unrest, he said at last to his mother: 'Well, why don't you take away the trees, and then it wouldn't wind?'

This charming utterance represents a point of view that Chesterton is about to rebut; a point of view which, indeed, he despises. The whole point of his essay is to reject the notion that worldly things can affect the motions of the spirit. But he does not begin by propounding his intention in terms such as: 'There are modern philosophers so utterly wrong-headed as to be capable of supposing that the trees make the wind blow.' He will get to the modern philosophers in due course. At the outset, he guilefully attributes the erroneous idea to a mere child of four, a nice, amusing little boy, and comments amiably: 'Nothing could be more intelligent or natural than this mistake.' Within two pages he will abandon the tolerant concession of 'intelligent' and 'natural', and will write:

'The man who represents all thought as an accident of environment' (in mythic terms, the man who supposes that the trees govern the wind) 'is simply smashing and discrediting all his own thoughts – even that one.' The rhetorical value of that little boy, handily playing in the mythographic park, lies in his *childishness*, which is a proper ornament to a child but a reproach to the adult. Chesterton writes: 'My small friend was, in fact, very like the principal modern thinkers; only much nicer.' We notice once more a smuggled *in fact*, which invites the reader to accept an underlying proposition or maxim: 'It is a fact that the principal modern thinkers have the mentality of four-year-old boys.'

And now, having charmed, tricked or otherwise tamed his reader, Chesterton proceeds to his thesis with propositions analogous to the demonstrator's *Let x equal* . . . :

> the trees stand for all visible things and the wind for the invisible. The wind is the spirit which bloweth where it listeth; the trees are the material things of the world which are blown where the spirit lists. The wind is philosophy, religion, revolution; the trees are cities, and civilizations.

Here is the explicit foundation upon which the various propositions might be constructed: for example, 'Our philosophers determine the kind of cities we live in', or 'Religion changes the material character of civilization.' Chesterton goes on to suggest one such construct:

> You cannot see a wind; you can only see that there is a wind. So, also, you cannot see a revolution; you can only see that there is a revolution. And there never has been in the history of the world a real revolution, brutally active and decisive, which was not preceded by unrest and dogma in the region of invisible things. All revolutions began by being abstract. Most revolutions began by being quite pedantically abstract.

The style, we see, is subtly changing, from the descriptive to the propositional. More and more sentences have the form of some generalizing assertion: 'All revolutions began by being abstract.' Such assertions have a thrillingly adventitious air, as though conceived in intellectual vacancy; but we know of this one, at least, that it depends on the fable of the wind in the trees. Indeed, Chesterton keeps reminding his readers of the rhetorical origin of his argument, only to develop the argument into further stages of dialectic:

> The great human dogma, then, is that the wind moves the trees.
> The great human heresy is that the trees move the wind. When
> people begin to say that the material circumstances have alone
> created the moral circumstances, then they have prevented all
> possibility of serious change. For if my circumstances have made me
> wholly stupid, how can I be certain even that I am right in altering
> those circumstances?

The grammatical forms of the sentences now begin to suggest
processes of reasoning rather than myth-making, though the
argument continues to be rooted in the mythogram; we begin
from *the a is b*, and proceed through *when . . . then* to *for if . . . how?*
Certain qualifying expressions, furthermore, are carefully placed
as links in the chain of assertions: 'material circumstances have
alone created . . . then they have prevented *all* possibility'; 'if my
circumstances have made me *wholly* stupid, how can I be certain
even that I am right in altering those circumstances?'
  This shift into dialectic assertion is even more marked in the
paragraph following the one cited above:

> The man who represents all thought as an accident of environment
> is simply smashing and discrediting all his own thoughts – including
> that one. To treat the human mind as having an ultimate authority
> is necessary to any kind of thinking, even free thinking. And
> nothing will ever be reformed in this age or country unless we
> realize that the moral fact comes first.

Here are three sentences, two of which have the outline of general
propositions ('Each/all/every x is/are y'; 'x is required by y'),
while the third proposes conditionally 'not x unless y'. The essay
has at this point taken on the linguistic habit, so to speak, of logic;
furthermore, any one of these three sentences might in itself be
the point of departure for extended dialectic.
  By this time, however, Chesterton has effectively concluded his
demonstration. Although he devotes a further page to the
rebuttal of false positions in specific social or political cases, his
assertion that 'the moral fact comes first' is the logical terminus of
the short discursive journey beginning from the rhetorical position that the trees do not make the wind. The rest is commentary
on possible counter-argument – *refutatio*, according to the
precepts of the classical rhetoricians – but Chesterton cannot
resist one final dig at his 'modern thinkers':

I get up from under the trees, for the wind and the slight rain have ceased. The trees stand up like golden pillars in a clear sunlight. The tossing of the trees and the blowing of the wind have ceased simultaneously. So I suppose there are still modern philosophers who will maintain that the trees make the wind.

Thus he returns to his rhetorical base, to the mythogram. The pragmatic four-year-old has disappeared from the scene, having played his part in emphasizing the folly of his philosophical elders. 'I get up from under the trees', says Chesterton, meaning 'I am through with my argument', and 'the trees stand up like golden pillars in a clear sunlight' – which sounds a little as though he were congratulating himself on his own lucidity and sturdy independence of mind; or at least as though he were saying *quod erat demonstrandum*.

Anyone who reads this essay by Chesterton will immediately feel its persuasive force. Its logic seems, if not irresistible, at least difficult to subvert. A second reading, however, may bring demurral. Can it never be the case that a physical fact may have a moral consequence? Is it logically indefensible to allege, for example, that insanitary housing will eventually subvert moral values? Or that drug-taking leads to despair and the collapse of the moral being? But Chesterton debars any such attempt at a defence, because he has framed the discourse with his fable of the wind in the trees – *framed* both in the conventional sense of enclosing within a limiting reference, and also in the old underworld slang sense of providing evidence which must produce a conviction. (The modern British criminal says *fitted up*.) The reader is taken in, perhaps willingly, by Chesterton's 'evidence'. Of course it would be absurd to allege that the trees make the wind. There is a powerful compulsion upon us to reject that absurdity; we must accept the order of the universe. But we are by no means compelled to accept whatever follows from an author's analogies of 'wind' and 'spirit', or 'trees' and 'pillars'. Such tropes, however striking, do not preclude us from arguing that architecture can affect habits of thought, or that slum conditions can cause civic unrest. The analogous inference, however, is crucial to Chesterton's persuasive strategy. It is just at the point of accepting it ('the wind is the spirit . . . the trees are the material things of the world . . . the wind is philosophy, religion, revolution . . . the trees are cities and civilizations') that the reader surrenders all his rights in the debate and becomes the essayist's voluntary dupe. What makes the acceptance difficult to withhold is that it is required after a page of the most beguiling mythopoiea – the turmoil in the air – the little boy who is in danger of losing his hat and his temper, and who says such a charming thing – most of all, that opening paragraph of strenuously emotive language, in which the author is *desperate* to find a figure of speech. We now understand why he is desperate. It is in the first paragraph of the essay that the argument is won or lost, because it is there that rhetoric must establish the conditions in which dialectic may be effectively conducted. The mythogram is the foundation of the argument; it is also a *captatio benevolentiae*.

'The Wind and the Trees' is an essay of great charm, but it appears on sober analysis merely to support Plato's general view that rhetoric is a way of lying, or at any rate of bamboozling your audience into a partisan position. Rhetoric may certainly exercise great power over the mind. It is possible, nevertheless, to overstate that power. In some respects, rhetoric is of no consequence at all and will deceive no one. No rhetoric in the world will support or subvert a manifest, absolute, unconditional truth, the truth of what philosophers call brute facts. I cannot rhetorically establish that grass is green, nor may I discolour it with rhetoric. No rhetoric in the world can break a logical chain or fracture a mathematical consequence. I cannot rhetorically unsettle the proposition that $(a + b)(a + b) = a^2 + 2ab + b^2$. Rhetoric only begins to come into its own when the 'truths' it invokes are complex and conditional and require interpretation: in short, when there is a case to be made. If I want to argue, for example, that state welfare undermines individual morale, I shall be advocating a thesis to which some will immediately assent, murmuring 'true!'; which others will as spontaneously reject, crying 'lies!'; and of which others still will observe judiciously, 'it all depends'. I shall find myself in a refracted realm which is not truth, and perhaps not even belief, but the country of what I want to believe to be true. As it happens, I do not believe it; but I might begin to make the case on the basis of the possibility of believing it. Now this is the domain of most political, social, moral and aesthetic questions: the domain of making plausible cases. To make my case I have to elaborate a postulate into a scenario which will then supply the principal bearings of the case: I may devise a mythogram, which is what Chesterton does in 'The Wind and the

'Trees', or I may rely on a casual tropology, as Ulysses does in *Troilus and Cressida*. In any event I shall be subordinating to a rhetorical purpose, to the advocacy of a predetermined principle, those elements of observation and reason which many would suppose to be superordinate in the unconditional search for truth. This is what affronted Plato, whose objections to rhetoric were not stylistic, but moral.

TO PERSUADE, DISTRACT

A strict moralist might certainly object that persuasive rhetoric often operates by coaxing people into looking at things as they are not, rather than as they are; in effect, by luring them into the theatre of distractions discussed in the last chapter. Ulysses disorientates Achilles with clever little fictions, Chesterton takes us in with an animated picture, even the grave St Paul allows himself a touch of fantasy, offering his beleaguered Ephesians a vision of themselves in military costume. (Thus making them the first beneficiaries of a trope that has sustained forlorn congregations down the ages and begotten staunch hymns and fiery sermons.)

Persuasion includes distraction. To persuade, distract; make your audience see matters in a different posture, a new light, an amusingly original costume. But distraction is not the whole of persuasion, nor can we stand the recommendation on its head and say, to distract, persuade. This, for instance, is intended to distract us:

> There were nearly two dozen of them in the cages. They were weak and scrawny and didn't even have the strength to stand. Most squatted on the filthy floor, the rest leant against the wire mesh. And there were to be so many noises and so many bumps on the journey that even the mercy of sleep was to be denied them.

What is it? It is the opening of an article in the *Observer*, 7 August 1988, an article headed '17.45: When the Strain is in Taking the Train'. And what can it be about? – for the terms of this introductory paragraph suggest that this is going to be another piece about the scandalous maltreatment of animals in transit. We are distracted, we are tempted to read on; and the next paragraph brings enlightenment:

But bleak and distressing as the scene was, it's unlikely to outrage,
or even surprise anyone. For they were not dumb animals in those
cages, but a lesser, far more expendable species: commuters on the
17.45 from Waterloo to Winchester.

The piece is accompanied by a photograph showing city-suited
passengers standing uncomfortably in a wire-meshed guard's van.
We have been fooled just for a moment, by a distractive exercise in
ambiguity, depending on our reading of 'cages' and 'mesh' and
our response to some items of vocabulary – 'weak and scrawny',
'the filthy floor', 'the mercy of sleep' – that would ordinarily be associated with the style of a piece on cruelty to animals rather than
a commentary on the inadequacy of British Rail's commuter
services. The writer creates a jocular image which certainly
distracts but which has no further persuasive intention. It might
be made to work mythographically, but in this case it does not. It is
only there to shock for a moment, or provoke a smile, and then it is
forgotten. It has, furthermore, a marked characteristic of images
and examples in distractive rhetoric, in that we cherish and linger
over the example itself, rather than anything it may be supposed
to imply. The correlate takes attention away from the primary
motif. We see a funny, or a clever, or a shocking, or a silly way of
putting something; we do not look for a wider, abstractable
significance in the way it is put. In persuasive rhetoric, on the other
hand, the image-correlate, or *exemplum*, or trope, is valued less for
itself than for its expository power, its capacity to make certain implications available, or indeed to enforce certain inferences.

The play of rhetoric can be a very entertaining thing, but it
always has designs on the entertained. It legitimates the logic of
persuasion; it beguiles us with endearing notions from which, if we
will only accept them, the rest follows quite reasonably. Persuaders attach importance to reasonableness and seek respectability in logical or common-sense exposition. Distractors care less
about providing a foundation for inference; they fabulate for the
fun of it, or the surprise of it, or to wrench your attention away
from some piece of plotting, or perhaps to beguile you while old
dungareed ideas shuffle on to shift the scene. (A little scene-
shifting is going on at this very moment.) And in general our
response to distraction differs from our reactions to being
persuaded. We are inclined to forgive distractors, whereas it is
very common to feel that persuaders take unfair advantage – they
are 'glib', they can 'make you believe anything', they will 'tell you

black's white'. To react thus, however, is to make oneself a victim, and we are rarely victims, we are – let it be said again – accomplices. Achilles is persuaded of what he is already inclined to believe; Chesterton's readers if they go along with him, go along because here at last, they think, is someone articulating what they have always felt. Persuasion, like hypnosis, only works on willing subjects. And if we dislike what it does to us, we have the remedy discovered in a moment of frantic inspiration by Alice, who, when the absurd images of Wonderland began to drive *her* to distraction, shouted 'Who cares for *you*? You're nothing but a pack of cards!' And woke up. She was a sensible girl, and had a mind of her own.

5

Figures of Speech, Facts of Language

Everybody knows, because Suetonius mentions it (note this intimidating rhetorical trick), that Julius Caesar described his Pontic campaign in the boastful assertion *veni, vidi, vici*. Everybody knows the saying and everybody finds it easy to remember, as figures of speech usually are, being compact in form and marked by recurrent or counterpoising features of sound and syntax. The mnemonic features of Caesar's boast are these:

1   It is alliterative; the three words of which it is composed all begin with the same consonant, /v/.
2   It has a kind of rhyme – an 'end chime', known in Greek as *homoioteleuton*; each word ends with the same vowel, /i/.
3   It is rhythmical; each word consists of two syllables, and in each the accent is on the first syllable (or the first syllable is quantitatively longer than the second): / x, / x, / x.
4   The three constituent elements (the three words) follow in sequence with no intervening conjunctions or connectives: not *veni, tum vidi et mox vici* (a + b + c), but *veni, vidi, vici* (a,b,c). The learned name of this pattern is *asyndeton*.
5   The three constituent words all have the same tense form, the perfect tense, which in this instance we translate into English as the simple past. Caesar did not say 'After I had arrived, I surveyed the situation and since then I have overcome the enemy', or 'Upon arrival I saw how things stood and proceeded to destroy the opposition'; he said 'I came, I saw, I conquered.'

What we must notice about this simple word-pattern is how deeply it draws upon the ordinary resources and possibilities of the Latin language. It makes use of phonological features of sound and rhythm, syntactic possibilities of word-sequencing, the rules of word-formation, the usage of tense. An interesting little exercise is to compare this dense convergence of linguistic features with what happens in the English translation. Of the English version we may note:

1 That it does not alliterate.
2 That there is no end-chime.
3 That it *has* a rhythm, but not the recursive, disyllabic rhythm of the original. The Latin has / x, / x, / x (strong syllable leads); in English we have x /, x /, x / x (weak syllable leads, with an additional weak syllable at the end). This has to do with the morphology of English, in which the category of 'person' is expressed in a pronoun (for example *I*) and not in an affix (the Latin *-i* ending); and in which some verbs are 'strong', forming their past tenses with a change of vowel (*come – came, see – saw*) and others are 'weak', forming the past with a suffix of the type *-d, -ed* (*conquer – conquer/ed*).
4 That it *does* make use of asyndeton (a, b, c); this is in fact the major resemblance of the translation to the original.
5 That it uses the simple past rather than the perfect (thus not 'I have come, I have seen, I have conquered'); and that the emphasis of the regular pattern is somewhat affected by the fact, noted above, that one of the verbs falls into a different morphological category from the other two.

In only one feature, the asyndetic pattern, does the English come anywhere near to reproducing the rhetorical impact of the Latin. Does this mean, then, that English must be an inferior medium of expression with fewer resources to draw upon? Not at all. A rhetorician can find in English all the material he needs to make figures as powerfully devised as Caesar's boast: we have alliteration, we have homoioteleuton and rhyme, we have diverse rhythms of word and phrase, we have syntactic patterns that include asyndeton, we have in grammar the common, recurrent features that can be transformed into the substance of an appealing phrase.

Take as an example the copywriter's invention cited in the first chapter of this book: the slogan FASTER. SMARTER. SPOILER?, used to advertise Peugeot cars. This is in one very obvious way like *veni, vidi, vici*: it is another instance of asyndeton. A further similarity is the regular rhythmical pattern based on the recurring syllabic structure of the three constituent words. There is no alliteration, but there is a marked, obviously intentional *homoioteleuton* in the *-er* endings. Where the figure becomes localized as an English product is in the derivation of those endings. In English the same ending commonly forms the comparative of adjectives (for example *cooler, slower, brighter*) and the *nomen agentis*, 'name-of-the-doer' substantives (for example *singer, driver, teacher*). This incidental fact of English word-formation is the derivative ground for a piece of word play that might be difficult to translate with undiminished effect into another language, even into a language with similar rules and morphological resources. On the other hand, we can readily produce imitations in English – for example, a caption for a noisy concert: LOUDER. HARSHER. SINGER?; or a description of a suspect sausage: BIGGER. FATTER. FILLER?; or a government health warning: HOARSER. SICKER. SMOKER?; or a political criticism: SADDER. MADDER. LEADER?

Veni, vidi, vici and FASTER. SMARTER. SPOILER? are figures of speech, products of a rhetorical impulse to put something across – a point, a boast, a conviction. In their general design they somewhat resemble each other. They are unlike each other in the way they subsume features made available through the structure of the languages they represent. Those languages, like all other languages, work to a pattern, constructing their ordinary messages by making regular and combinative selections from the limited sets of elements that constitute their code. Those same elements become available for a less 'ordinary' kind of message: for the emphatic expression of emotion, humour, persuasiveness, for the devising of supernumerary patterns that convey, or at least focus attention upon, 'affective' meanings. Every language can make such patterns; every language has resources which facilitate the production of certain rhetorical effects; every language can produce specific instances which are not readily matched in another language, even though the other language offers access to comparable resources.

THE RHETORICAL PROVISIONS OF LANGUAGE

This preamble has a point to make about the so-called 'figures of speech'. One of the reasons why ordinary sensible people are terrified by a *hysteron proteron* and would be desperately shy of a *zeugma* is that the names of these Greek museum monsters are intimidatingly remote from the workshops and playgrounds of common usage in which we fool around with words, make puns, balance phrases, try turning sentences this way or that, give voice to our feelings, give order to our thoughts and generally get our ducks in a row. (A demotic trope which incidentally expresses rather well the purpose of a figure of speech.) If the classical names are frighteners, they are frauds; because they make us haplessly aware of our unlearnedness and unhappily unaware that we are producing the most intricate and ingenious figures all the time, that it is hardly possible for us to write a sentence without giving prominence to some feature that rhetoric might seize upon. The figures of speech are not costly foreign ornaments with which we give our humble native discourse a touch of class: 'if madam would try a *syllepsis* she would find the effect quite striking'. The figures of Greek and Latin were implicit in the way Greeks and Romans used their language; the figures in English lurk all the time in our common practice. Language, we may say, makes provision for rhetoric; and understanding these provisions is more important than trying to memorize a bemusing catalogue of Greek names.

Rhetorical figures are not children of irregular inspiration; they are bred out of the morphology and syntax of a parent language. To present even a sketch of the syntax of English would make too long a digression, but it may be of interest to consider some of the things we require of our syntax, the better to understand the things we require of our figurative rhetoric. It is almost a proverbial saying in linguistics that 'language is linear' (note the alliteration, a sure sign of progress towards folk-wisdom), meaning that the verbal signals we put out cannot be made simultaneously but must follow in sequence. The words we put on the page run in line from left to right, in spatial sequence; the sounds we utter fall on other people's ears in a temporal sequence; language is linear. The order of events is arbitrary, in the sense that there is no god-given command dictating what sort of thing should come where in the sequence. Where English asserts 'We have just eaten dinner', German states 'We have just the dinner eaten', or possibly 'Just have we the dinner eaten'. Such sequences nevertheless become syntactically normative in their respective language communities, so that in the case of the English example the word-order is fixed. Or apparently fixed; there is still a possibility, as we shall see, of breaking away from this particular norm.

The problem that arises here is the problem besetting all things standing in line. Linearity breaks partnerships, disguises connections, thwarts emphasis, not infrequently mismanages the distribution of information. It is the linearity of language that underlies many ambiguities, failures to make the right kind of relation, inabilities to place emphasis where it should lie. We read that 'Many conservative parents are accusing their local Directors of Education of failing to provide for their children a choice of schools meeting standards they have a right to demand', and immediately we are shuffling in a characteristically English queue, tolerably certain of the message that comes down the line but still not wholly clear as to what goes with what: 'Many conservative parents are accusing their local Directors of Education of failing to provide for their [the parents'? the Directors'?] children a choice of schools meeting standards they [the parents? the Directors? the children?] have a right to demand.' Or we hear something like this: 'I've always enjoyed Jim and Mary's company, but Dick can't stand her.' The trouble now is that unless *and* and *her* are adequately emphasized, the personal pronoun tends to loiter somewhat disconnectedly at the end of the sentence. And if we rephrase, 'I've always enjoyed Mary's company as well as Jim's, but Dick can't stand her', then another problem of linear emphasis arises, and we are obliged to put a focusing stress on *stand*, These are typical instances of problems attending the sequencing of quite ordinary and acceptable constructions.

There are interrelated problems of *sequence* (word-order), *connection* (or linkage), *focus* (or emphasis) and *contrast* (or balance, or co-occurrence). Isolated sentences, such as text-book examples, rarely highlight these problems, which are essentially the products of continuous discourse in certain situations. It is nearly always the case, however, that we can adjust a sequence in order to focus on particular words, bring out balances and contrasts, or suggest different kinds of connection. Here are some simple examples of word-order in English:

Bears like honey

Beer is good

The cat sat on the mat

They called him Ishmael

I think I know whose woods these are

These examples represent severally the 'normal' English word order for sentences constructed on the patterns SVO, SVC$_s$, SVA, SVOC$_o$ (Subject – Verb – Object, Subject – Verb – Complement, Subject – Verb – Adverbial, Subject – Verb – Object – Object Complement); and for a three-clause structure consisting of a 'reporting' clause (*I think*) followed by a 'reported' clause (*I know*, and so on) with an embedded subordinate clause (*whose woods these are*). (Other examples of this last structure would be 'She said she remembered where she left the scissors' and 'They claimed he'd forgotten to turn off the dishwasher.')

All these instances can be taken as the normal, or as some linguists say, *unmarked* word order. Their normality is such that at first glance anyone unaccustomed to playing grammatical games might suppose it to be inescapable. But we can certainly escape from it, and in one or two of these instances the escape might be recognized as a fairly common possibility. It is in fact possible to 'front' or 'pre-pose' an Object, a Complement, an Adverbial, an embedded subordinate clause; to put at the beginning of the sentence some element that would not 'normally' go there:

Honey, bears like

Good, beer is

On the mat the cat sat (Or: On the mat sat the cat)

Ishmael, they called him

Whose woods these are I think I know

These are so-called *marked* forms. The first and the last example may look a little strange, but they are both discursively possible in English. (The last is actually a line of verse from a well-known poem by Robert Frost, and the first recalls the celebrated Pooh, who would perhaps have preferred what is sometimes called a Topic – Comment construction, 'Honey – that's what bears like', but who *could* have said 'Honey, bears like' without disgracing himself).[1] What the marked forms do is change the perspective of the sentence, making *honey*, for example, not *bears*, the principal topic in hand, or *correctively* focusing attention on the fronted item: 'Bears don't like cabbage! Bears don't like cockles! Honey, bears like!' When the marked forms are contextualized in this way it seems that one of their functions is to plot moments of discursive intensity, suggesting, perhaps, some prominence of feeling appropriate to a situation, real or fictional. The word-order of 'We've just eaten dinner' is to all intents and purposes fixed, and yet a marked form is available to express the marked situation and the marked attitude: 'They served breakfast at 11.30; we got our lunch at half-past five; dinner we've just eaten – and it's after midnight. What sort of hotel is this?' The verbal pattern in such cases is not far from figurative rhetoric, which elaborates the principle of marking.

Connections between words, phrases or clauses also create the conditions of rhetorical choice. The referee tells the grimacing pugilist, 'Go to your corner and come out fighting and may the best man win.' Those co-ordinating conjunctions, those *ands*, are symptomatic of the mode of construction rhetoric calls *polysyndeton*. Contrast the bruisers with the poor, pallid Lady of Shallott. For her (as for Julius Caesar and the Peugeot copywriter) *asyndeton* rules. Tennyson tells us, 'She left the web, she left the loom, she made three paces through the room' – with never a particle to connect one doom-laden clause to the next. Sports commentators provide numerous examples of polysyndetic leisure and asyndetic haste. From the commentary box the resident pundit describes the cricket match, for the benefit of his TV audience: 'And Smith bowls round the wicket this time, and the ball turns in a little and Jones plays him off the back foot down to mid-on but there's no one there and they take a quick single.' Polysyndeton. Then from the sweating ringside, some half-price, high-revving Homer hoarsely proclaims that 'Thumper scores with a left, a right, a left again, he's putting these combinations together with ruthless efficiency, Wobbler tries to stave him off, he can't, his legs are going, how long can he keep this up, you have to give him credit, he's brave – THERE! – he's gone, he's gone, that's it, that's a knock-out punch, it's all over.' Asyndeton – to the point of incoherence. Of course the cricket commentator may muse asyndetically if he pleases, and the boxing expert may grow polysyndetically excited, and either of them may mingle asyndeton and polysyndeton. The object of our illustration is only to remind every speaker of English of something that every speaker of English intuitively knows: that these alternatives exist in the language, in its common provision, and that where there is such an alternative there is the possibility of a rhetorical application.

Consider some other ways of linking sequent events in sentences. There is, for example, the linkage of a sequence of constructions, asyndetically or polysyndetically, to a common Subject: 'The janitor swept the floor, stacked the tables, locked the main door and took a look round the yard.' In that sentence, the Subject (*The janitor*) of the first clause is the implied Subject of each clause that follows. Or everything in the constructional line may depend on a common verb: 'The men came and painted the woodwork, the brickwork, the stonework, the whole domestic framework.' Here *painted* takes as its Object not only *the woodwork* but also every subsequent phrase in the sentential line. These subject-dependent and verb-dependent patterns represent another kind of choice in which possibilities of rhetorical playfulness may lurk. Or rhetorical pomp – of the kind we often meet in eighteenth century verse:

> On what foundations stand the warrior's pride,
> How just his hopes, let Swedish Charles decide.

Johnson's couplet illustrates the dependency of parallel constructions (the clauses 'On what foundations . . .' and 'How just his hopes') on a main verb ('decide'), though here the rhetoric is intensified by the pre-posing of the dependent constructions. It looks like, and is, an artifice, and yet it is not 'artificial' in the sense of using spurious material; Johnson has a licence for what he does in common English practice.

In complex sentences the relationship of a string of clauses is sometimes 'recursive', each clause having as its antecedent the main verb of the first clause, and sometimes 'serial', the antecedent for each clause being the last word of its predecessor. Thus, recursive structure: 'Their parents taught them how to hunt, how to find water, what creatures to avoid, where to look for food.' (*How . . .how . . .what . . .where . . .* are recursively connected with *taught*.) But serial structure: 'This is the dog that chased the cat that killed that rat that ate the corn that stood in the house that Jack built.' (The points of antecedence are the last words of each clause – *dog, cat, rat, corn, house*.) 'The House that Jack Built' is serialism gone crazy, a rigmarole for children joyfully discovering what funny things their language will do; but adults will quite often resort to serial constructions in humorous or satirical narrative. One might, for example, complain of the tortuous ways of the British National Health Service: 'You go to your optician, who refers you to your doctor, who writes out a chit for you to go to a clinic, where you are given an appointment to see a specialist, who tells his nurse to tell you to see the receptionist, who gives you the word to come back in three months.' The recursive style may also produce humorous essays: 'His wife instructs him how to hold his knife and fork, how to speak, where to buy his clothes, what to say at funerals, when to stop at traffic lights, what books to read, which seat to sit in, whose bed to sleep in, and how to make instant love.' This may be recursiveness run mad, but English readily allows it. It is in fact one of the bases, in English, of *parisonic* rhetoric, parison being (as we may be reminded by instances quoted in an earlier chapter) the parallel matching of constructions.

In figurative rhetoric, the creation of parallels is an important operation; its corollary is the devising of couplings and contrasts, the play of thesis and antithesis that informs the essays of Francis Bacon, the verse of Alexander Pope, or the Sunday lunchtime colloquy round at the local pub ('That's not cricket, it's crap', 'And then again . . .', 'But having said that . . .', 'There's them'll rubbish her, but I reckon she's right'). Once more, linguistic provision supports rhetorical invention. The encoding devices of 'ordinary' language include bracketing constructions like *Both . . . and, Not only . . . but also, Neither . . . nor, On the one hand . . . on the other*. These, together with contrastive conjunctions and conjuncts such as *but, yet, although, whereas, while, however, nevertheless*, provide material for figures of equipoise and counterpoise. Other useful operators are *therefore* and *not* ('I think, therefore I am', said Descartes; 'I'm thirsty, not dirty', said the tramp when the housewife offered him a glass of water). See how in a passage of classic eloquence, the simple antithesis of *but* provides the frame that contains an elaboration of asyndeton and parison:'

> When I was a child, I spake as a child, I understood as a child, I thought as a child; but when I became a man I put away childish things.
> For now we see through a glass, darkly; but then face to face: now I know in part; but then shall I know even as I am known.

HOW THE FIGURES TAKE SHAPE

The figures represent our attempts to give point and controlling shape to our thoughts and observations. Common speech reflects this attempt so often that we might consider everyday usage to be naturally figurative, or at least figurative by preference. The lady who was overheard to say 'Now and then of a lunchtime I'll take a glass – two glasses and I'll take to my bed' was producing a verbal design very close to the cross-over pattern rhetoricians call *chiasmus* or *antimetabole*; to say nothing of her witty essay in the trope called *antanaclasis*, requiring two meanings of 'take'. Almost certainly she could not have put learned names to her sport with language, nor, probably, would she have cared. But if we are to talk about rhetorical patterns in language, we must have recourse to some sort of terminology, and the Graeco-Roman words, marmoreal marvels though they be, at least have the claim of long standing.

It is an old difficulty, this unease with an alien nomenclature, made for dead tongues, so remote from the bartering and badinage we know. The Elizabethan rhetorician George Puttenham (author of *The Arte of English Poesie*, 1589) was so perceptive of the problem as to try to replace or at least gloss the classical terms with English names expressing the nature and characteristic operation of the figure. Some of the names read like personifications; *hyperbaton* is called 'the trespasser', *litotes* 'the moderator', *hyperbole* 'the loud liar, otherwise called the overreacher'. Many are imaginative – for instance the rendering of *epizeuxis* as 'the Cuckowspell' (cuckoo-call); some are almost as opaque as the Greek they translate, for example the glossing of *micterismus* as 'the fleering frumpe'. In all instances, however, Puttenham's concern is to give his readers access to the psychology of the figures and to show how in using them writers monitor and evaluate their own creative processes. He also presented his own classification of different kinds of figure, distinguishing between 'figures pertaining to clauses', 'figures which . . . alter and affect the minde by alteration of sense . . . in single words' and 'figures appertaining to whole speeches'.[2] This was a useful and sensible attempt to relate the methodology of rhetoric to the language and literature of his own time; and while his plan is occasionally puzzling, his precept at least invites imitation. Let us therefore propose a simple taxonomy of general terms. The word *figure*, we shall say, is the superordinate term, applicable to any rhetorical device. *Scheme* will refer to figures of word-order and syntactic patterning; *trope* will refer to figures that play on the sense of words. We shall further distinguish between tropes that confine their play to a single word or phrase, and those that pervade longer stretches of discourse; these last we shall call *modes*. There are thus figures of syntax and figures of semantics, the latter being roughly divisible into word-semantics and discourse semantics. The proposed hierarchy of terms is represented in the following sketch:

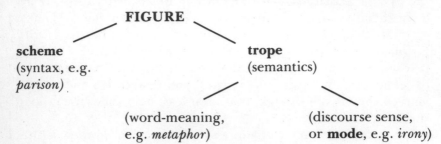

FIGURE

scheme
(syntax, e.g.
parison)

trope
(semantics)

(word-meaning,
e.g. *metaphor*)

(discourse sense,
or **mode**, e.g. *irony*)

This is a way of looking at stylistic resources in rhetorical terms. To 'English' the names of the figures, after Puttenham's example, might be to court trouble; but it is feasible at least to try to understand the schemes quasi-diagrammatically, as basic patterns outlined by words.

First, two kinds of linear figure: progressions and parallels. Progressive figures mark the steps from one construction to the next in line, making particular words function like links in a chain. *Anaphora, epistrophe, anadiplosis* and *symploce* are characteristic figures of progression, and here are some examples:

anaphora

The first word of a phrase or clause is repeated in each sequent construction: 'Children are a comfort, children are amusing, and children are sometimes a nuisance'; 'These are good laws, these are wise provisions, these are sensible responses to social need'.

epistrophe

The last word of a phrase or clause is repeated in each sequent construction: 'You may not like rules, you may spend your time devising ways to break the rules, but in the end you must admit that we have to have rules'; 'Old money, sound money; new money, funny money'.

anadiplosis and climax

In anadiplosis, the last word of a phrase or clause becomes the first word of the next: 'there he met a friend, a friend who was to stand by him throughout his life'. In the similar figure of climax, the last-and-first progression delineates a kind of stairway, with mounting or descending steps of declamation: 'You pay twenty-five pounds for a ticket, the ticket admits you to a seat in the upper circle, the upper circle is up four flights, four flights is your ticket for a heart-attack.'

symploce

A combination of *anaphora* and *epistrophe*; the first and last words of sequent constructions are repeated: 'Our demagogues are in love with freedom; our demagogues, it seems, would give their right arms, if not their money, to secure their freedom; our demagogues are only a little uncertain about other people's freedom.'

The constructions serially linked in these examples also suggest, in some cases, a linkage in parallel. Such linkage is more explicit, more evidently a major element in the design of the figure, in schemes like *parison*, *isocolon* and *chiasmus*. Examples:

parison

One of the commonest and most powerful figures of rhetoric, a key element, above all, in the prose style of the Elizabethan masters. It means (but we have already mentioned it several times in the course of this book) the fairly exact matching, or 'comparison' of constructions usually occurring in pairs or threes. In Shaw's *Pygmalion*, the dustman Doolittle tells Professor Higgins, 'I'm willing to tell you, I'm wanting to tell you, I'm waiting to tell you.' This is an example of parison. It also exemplifies *isocolon* (see below). Other instances of parisonic figures: 'The government proposes to reduce some taxes, the electorate would prefer to abolish all of them'; 'Nothing, they say, succeeds like success, and everything, it appears, collapses in failure.' Parison is quite often combined with figures like anaphora, epistrophe or anadiplosis so that the effect is simultaneously one of sequence and comparison: 'The public might like to arm the police, but the police would not want to accept this measure'; 'Mr Brown drinks in moderation, his wife thinks in moderation, and their son washes in moderation.'

isocolon

This is an exact parison of *cola*, or clauses, matching word for word. (The etymological elements of the name are *iso-*, 'equal', and *colon* 'clause'.) Thus Doolittle's remark, quoted above, is an instance of isocolon. The figure is easily managed if the *cola* are fairly short ('Jim drank the beer, Jack ate the sandwiches, I read *The Times*') but not so naturally or easily produced on the model of a longer clause ('Jim inconsiderately drank the generous supply of beer, Jack incontinently ate the liberal provision of sandwiches, I disconsolately read a tattered copy of *The Times*'.)

chiasmus

Another name for this figure, which has been mentioned earlier, is *antimetabole*, A standard example is Moliere's *Il faut manger pour vivre, et non pas vivre pour manger*, 'One should eat to live, not live to eat.' Another is the remark made by an eighteenth-century wit about the author (Gay) and the producer (Rich) of *The Beggar's Opera*: that this notable success at the Augustan box-office 'made Gay rich, and Rich Gay'. The name is ultimately based on the Greek word for the letter X, and describes a two-clause figure in which the second clause is an inverted parallel of the first. 'You should take care of your wife's money, then your wife's money will take care of you'; 'All professors are clever men, but clever men aren't all professors; 'Good mothers make children happy, happy children make mothers good.' The latter is a very strict example, in which the word order in the second clause exactly mirrors that of the first.

These shapes of parison, isocolon and chiasmus all underlie a parent or superordinate figure of *antithesis*, which is a general name for any pattern of parallel or counterpoising propositions. In literary composition, excessive resort to antithesis results in a stylistic dandyism that is often tedious. A good deal of eighteenth-century verse is blemished by antithesis, and ornate prose like that of John Lyly (see p. **136**) is almost stultified by it. It is nevertheless a useful general figure, virtually indispensable in argument and exposition.

Other figures are of a type that might be called (somewhat in imitation of Puttenham's proceeding) *couplers*. These figures link words or phrases which are in some instances semantically similar, in others semantically disparate. The suggested distinction between scheme and trope here begins to blur; in figures such as *hendiadys, oxymoron* and *zeugma* a play on meaning underlies the word-order pattern. Instances:

hendiadys

This figure conjoins two nouns or adjectives of similar or contingent meaning: 'It was an occasion of much *merriment and hilarity*'; '*a noble and uplifting* melody began'. In our medieval and Renaissance authors, it is often associated with the phenomenon of *diglossia*, the co-existence in our language of familar Germanic words (for example 'earthly') and less homely words of classical origin (for example 'terrestrial'). Hendiadys could be used to introduce and explain the less familiar word by coupling it with a native counterpart. This dictionary function could in its turn be raised to an aesthetic principle: thus Shakespeare, 'the dark backward and abysm of time'; 'in the wind and tempest of her frown'. Coupled nouns sometimes express the sense of adjective + noun, for example 'It is laid down by *rule and statute* [=statutory rule]'; 'The situation calls for *kindness and humanity* [= human kindness]'.

oxymoron

This figure surprisingly juxtaposes words expressing contrasted or opposed meanings. It is most commonly a phrasal figure, and the collocations which carry it are usually adverb + adjective, or adjective + noun, or adjective + adjective, or noun + noun: 'It was a *brilliantly boring* lecture'; 'His students performed feats of *inspired plagiarism*'; 'The cat lay on the sofa, looking all *drowsy and vivacious*'; 'Filling in a tax return calls for absolute *honesty and cunning*'. The examples may suggest that the figure is most often used to frame witticisms, often of a mordant kind. Sentences are sometimes connected semantically by what is in effect oxymoron: 'John was a polite, kind, clean-living boy, who always told the truth. No one could stand him.'

zeugma

Zeugma is a clause pattern, designed to bring out an ambivalent relationship between the verb and the dependent elements which it yokes together. (The word in fact means 'a yoking'.) The forms it commonly takes are: (a)Two nouns or noun- phrases are the conjoint Subjects of a verb semantically appropriate only to one of them: 'Her beauty and bank-account faded.' (b)Two nouns or noun-phrases are the conjoint and semantically disparate Objects of one verb: 'He lost his bet and his temper.' (c) Two semantically disparate adverbial phrases are governed by one verb: 'The chairman left in high good humour and a Rolls Royce.'

Zeugma is sometimes called *syllepsis*, though a distinction may be drawn which is not always very clearly apparent in English. In zeugma, the verb is in grammatical concord with the constructions it yokes, but is in semantic concord only by virtue of some ambiguity (for example by reading *fade* in the dual sense of 'wither' and 'dwindle'). In a syllepsis, the verb accords grammatically with only one of the yoked elements, though it may well be semantically appropriate to all. Thus the not uncommon form of singular verb and plural Subject: 'Here comes my son, my neighbour, and a whole packet of trouble.'

In addition to figures of progression and coupling – lines and linkages – it may be important to cite one or two schemes of *repetition*. Reiteration is a front-line weapon in rhetoric. Shakespeare's Antony, it may be remembered, uses it very effectively in his ironic onslaught on the Brutus gang after they have assassinated Caesar: 'For Brutus is an honourable man; So are they all, all honourable men.' Some reiterative figures are *epizeuxis*, *epanorthesis*, *antanaclasis* and *polyptoton* Examples:

epizeuxis

The repetition of a word with emphasis: 'Take, O take those lips away'; 'Corrupt, I call it, utterly corrupt'; 'When, when, when will you learn?'

epanorthesis

The recalling of a word in order to suggest a more precise or appropriate expression: 'This ill-advised, nay, this wantonly irresponsible act'; 'In winter the climate is humid, or downright damp'; 'Tax inspector did I say? – robber baron, I mean'; 'Her manner was brisk and cool, not to say boreal.'

epanalepsis

Authorities explain this figure in at least two ways. In one version, a construction (clause, sentence, verse, distich) begins and ends with the same word. Thus Puttenham gives the example 'Much must he be beloved, that loveth much.' The Graeco-Roman Demetrius, however, defines epanalepsis as the repetition of the same particle in the course of a lengthy sentence.[3] His illustration involves the use of the word 'indeed' (Greek μὲν) to signal the resumption of a sentence after some digression. In English, *then* is sometimes used in that way: 'Then, after we have achieved our aims, after we have regained a little of our lost pride and showed the world what we can do – then we can talk of taking a rest.'

antanaclasis (ploce)

Antanaclasis requires the repetition of a word in an altered sense: 'If I take two glasses I'll take to my bed'; 'He saw sense when he saw her father's shotgun'; 'The dumb may not be as dumb as you think'; 'He's a handsome fellow, and he's paid a handsome salary'; 'We've paid rates for many years, and at this rate we'll never stop paying them'. It will be evident from these examples that antanaclasis is a form of punning. This figure is sometimes called *ploce*, which, however, is strictly a device of repetition without alteration of sense. The Roman rhetoricians called it *traductio*, and Puttenham describes it as 'the *doubler* . . . a speedie iteration of one word, but with some little intermission by inserting one or two words between'.[4] The sayings 'Boys will be boys' and 'Handsome is as handsome does' are examples of ploce.

polyptoton

The repetition of a word in a different inflectional form: 'I don't much care for *singing*, and I personally dislike the *singer*'; 'The *flower show* was more *showy* than *flowery*'. This kind of repetition may be clumsily unintentional; when it is deliberate it is often (as the second example must suggest) a form of word-play. Strictly speaking, this figure is proper to richly inflected languages like Greek and Latin, with their variety of word-endings denoting case, tense, mood and so on. The English examples are approximations, and might be described as pseudopolyptoton.

TROPES AND MODES

The other kind of rhetorical device, the trope, is a conceptual sport, a game about meaning. There are, however, two senses in which the game can be played, and the senses are well illustrated by the terms *metaphor* and *irony*, both of which may be called tropes. The major principle of metaphor is one of substitution or transference. If I remark that 'My car tends to *grumble* at gradients steeper than one in twenty', I am speaking metaphorically, and one way of explaining my metaphor would be to say that I have selected a verb implying the associations 'human being' and 'speech', and placed it in a context properly requiring the attributes 'inanimate' (or 'machine') and 'noise'. The metaphor thus created is localized in the linguistic framework of the clause, and even if I augment this notion of grumbling with concordant metaphors in subsequent constructions – 'My car *grumbles* at steep gradients, but otherwise seldom *protests*, and most of the time *mutters happily* to itself' – these extending metaphors are none the less localized in the sense that they reside in the linguistic patterns of phrase or clause, where there is always a locus, a particular verbal item that realizes the trope.

Now here is an example of irony, from Jonathan Swift's 'An Argument to prove that the Abolishing of Christianity in England, may as Things now stand, be attended with some Inconveniences, and perhaps not produce those many good Effects proposed thereby'. The title is in itself heavily ironic; the text, of which the following is a short extract, is continuous irony:

> If Christianity were once abolished, how would the Free Thinkers, the Strong Reasoners, and the Men of profound Learning, be able to find another Subject so calculated in all Points whereon to display their Abilities. What wonderful Productions of Wit should we be deprived of, from those whose Genius by continual Practice hath been wholly turned upon Raillery and Invectives against Religion, and would therefore never be able to shine or distinguish themselves upon any other Subject. We are daily complaining of the great decline of Wit among us, and would we take away the greatest, perhaps the only Topick we have left?

Not even the most naive reader could take this at its face value. From the title onwards, Swift makes it profusely clear that his proceedings are a pose, a stance, that his assertions are solemn mendacities, wry masks of a hidden sincerity. This is irony; irony says what it does not mean and means what it does not say. And yet, in the passages quoted above, there is no clear locus of the ironic, no key word, no linguistic focus that announces the trope of irony. We might argue that *some Inconveniences* (= 'wholesale disasters') or *wonderful productions* (= 'talentless rubbish') are fairly specific signals of ironic intent, but if we interpret them ironically (as indeed we do) it is not in response to the working of a verbal mechanism, like that of metaphor. Our interpretation is based on our assumptions about Swift's assumptions about every-body's assumptions about life and society. Swift assumes that his readers are sensible people who cannot believe that atheistic tracts could truly be *wonderful* productions. He assumes that Christianity is self-evidently a matter of overwhelming importance, so neces-sary to our well-being that the timid qualifications of '*some* Inconveniences' and '*perhaps* not produce' will be perceived immediately as serio-comic posturing, a stance which he will adopt and maintain throughout his whole discourse. From this example it may appear that irony, if it is to be called a trope, is a different kind of trope from metaphor. The *tropos*, or 'turning', in metaphor is a switcharound of linguistic elements, of particular words and their references. The 'turning' in irony is a rotation of attitude towards a topic in discourse. Stylistic manipulations of language are of course involved in both instances, but perhaps it will now be clear what we mean if we call both metaphor and irony tropes, yet reserve for irony and other discursive tropes the particular designation of *mode*.

SOME RECURRENT TROPES

Among the commonest tropes are *simile, metaphor, metonymy, synecdoche, paronomasia* and *personification* (*prosopopoeia*). Simile and metaphor are closely related as processes involving a transfer of meaning or a substitution of one meaning for another; they are 'replacement' tropes. Metonymy and synecdoche are related as processes denoting that one meaning is a part of, or contingent upon, another; they are 'contact' tropes. Paronomasia ('punning') and personification have affinities both with tropes of the 'replace-ment' type and those of the 'contact' type.

simile

This is the weakest, or least compressed, kind of replacement trope. Metaphor in some way displaces, or entirely suppresses, one of the elements in the transfer process; simile presents both. In other words, simile always announces that *A is like B* ('my desk is like a paper pigsty'), whereas metaphor can say, for example, *BA* ('my paper pigsty desk'), or *B of A* ('my paper pigsty of a desk'); or simply *B* ('the paper pigsty where I fatten up my pieces' – but here is a second metaphor, another *B* with a buried *A*, in 'fatten up'). In his *Rhetoric*, Aristotle uses the term *eikon*, which he defines as a metaphor with a particle of comparison. Quintilian, in the *Institutio*, formulates the distinction that continues to govern any discussion of metaphor and simile: *metaphora est brevior similitudo, eoque distat, quod illa comparatur rei, quam volumus exprimere, haec pro ipsa re dicitur* ('metaphor is briefer than simile, and also differs thus, that whereas the latter presents a comparison with the thing we wish to express, this propounds the thing itself').[5]

There is some variation, particularly in poetry, in the way the *A*'s and *B*'s of similitude are presented and linked, and in the kinds of resemblance that are suggested. Similarities are sometimes suggested via adjectives (in which case *as* is the linking conjunction) and sometimes through verbs (when *like* is the linker). The conventional order is *A – link – B* (for example *A* 'Her face' – *link* 'was white as' – *B* 'a sheet') but poetic constructions allow *B – link –A, link – A – B, A – B – link, link – B – A, B – A – link*. The functions in verse of such formulaic similes are mainly of three kinds: they compare the abstract and the concrete, or make sensory comparisons; they suggest intensifications of feeling by comparing greater entities with lesser, and vice versa; and they are mechanisms of personification.

The simile, as described above, was a favourite device, indeed a mannerism, among poets of the 1930s. W. H. Auden, as a stylistic leader, may have set the fashion. Here are some instances picked out at random from Auden's work:

The lilac bush like a conspirator
Shams dead upon the lawn

. . . those whose brains are empty as a school in August

The fortress like a motionless eagle eyeing the valley

And the cry of the gulls at dawn is sad like work

          for the long lost good
Desire like a police dog is unfastened

You alone, O imaginary song
Are unable to say an existence is wrong,
And pour out your forgiveness like a wine

Here are some of possible variants in the ordering of the figure (for example *A* 'fortress, – *B* 'eagle' – *link* 'eyeing the valley'; *link* 'pour out' – *A* 'forgiveness' – *B* 'wine'). Here too, some characteristic functions (for example personification – the lilac bush becomes a 'conspirator'; abstract – concrete transfer – 'forgiveness/wine'; or concrete – abstract switch – 'cry of gulls'/'work'; intensifying by comic reduction, 'brains'/'school in August'; a combination of several functions – intensifying, abstract – concrete switch, and personification, or inanimate-animate transfer – in 'desire'/'police dog').

The *A* and *B* of this kind of simile are proportionately related; *B* does not outbalance *A* in the figure, and in theory at least *B* can be said to resemble *A* as *A* can be said to resemble *B*. (Though the case is not always easy to argue.) In what is variously known as the 'Homeric' or 'epic' or 'Miltonic' or 'long-tailed' simile, the *as...so* pattern discussed in Chapter 2, *B* is not proportionate to *A*, and the figure is a one-way street – often a long way, and sometimes a blind alley.

metaphor

It is difficult to say a brief word about metaphor, and impossible to say the last word; there is very considerable body of academic writing on the subject. Its substitutive character is mentioned above. Its linguistic forms are protean, and can involve constructions with a semantic locus in any of the major form-word categories of noun, verb, adjective and adverb ('That fox of an accountant has cheated me of a thousand pounds'; 'I've been foxed out of a thousand pounds by that accountant'; 'My foxy accountant has stolen a thousand pounds'; 'My accountant has foxily pinched a thousand pounds'). Metaphor is often discursively extended in running tropes: 'That fox of an accountant has gone to earth, but I'll hound him out, never you fear.' When the speaker/writer is insensitive to the need for figurative consistency, we have so-called 'mixed' metaphor: 'That foxy accountant has submerged, but I've got my ear to the bush telegraph.'

In rhetorical and poetic discourse, complexes of metaphor are very carefully organized. Metaphors interlace one with another, and there is frequently a commingling of metaphor with the looser patterning of simile. Thus Auden:

Ridges of rich apartments rise tonight
Where isolated windows glow like farms

This is from a poem called 'Brussels in Winter'. The first thing to take the eye is perhaps the simile: isolated windows glow like farms

– the windows glow like isolated farms – the lighted windows stand
out in the urban darkness as lighted farmhouses would stand out
in rural darkness. But this is all extravagant and unmotivated
without the background metaphor located in the word *ridges*.
That word supplies the key to the figurative riddle. As ridges are
to the landscape, so apartment blocks are to the townscape; then as
farms appear among the ridges, so lighted windows appear among
the apartment blocks.

metonymy and synecdoche

These related – and not always clearly distinguishable – tropes
exploit the relationship of larger entities with lesser. Synecdoche
substitutes the part for the whole, and its terms of reference are
concrete. Thus:

for *worker*   read *hand*
for *person*   read *head*
for *house*   read *door*

These commonplace instances occur in usages such as 'They're
taking on hands down at the steelworks', 'We had to pay ten
pounds a head just to get in', 'Mr Jones lives four doors down the
way'. Synecdoche is not uncommon in colloquial usage and slang;
skirt used to signify *woman* ('I saw him out with a skirt') and
recently I have noticed, in film-criminal language, *face* for
(*unidentified*) *person* ('There's a face outside asking for Lou').

Metonymy, a subtler and much more productive trope, substitutes the token for the type; substitutes, that is, a particular
instance, property, characteristic or association, for the general
principle or function.[6] Its terms of reference very often bridge the
abstract and the concrete. Thus:

for *government*   read *the crown*
for *law*   read *the bench*
for *command*   read *flag*
for *war*   read *the sword*
for *authorship*   read *the pen*
for *democracy*   read *the ballot box*
for *terrorism*   read *the bullet*

These are the metonymic cliches that we find in 'The powers of
the crown', 'the dignity and authority of the bench', 'forces under

the flag of General Popgun', 'the pen is mightier than the sword', 'they prefer the bullet to the ballot-box'.So far the distinction between synecdoche and metonymy seems quite clear. But there are overlaps and near-misses. In some instances a turn of phrase might be regarded as a synecdoche in one perspective, a metonymy in another. When we read, for example, that 'Cetewayo had ten thousand spears at his command', or, more prosaically, that 'Lord Roughbore was out on the moors with a party of guns', we may suppose *spear* and *gun* to be synecdochic (part for whole) references to 'warrior', 'sportsman', and equally we might take them as metonymies (token for type) signifying 'warlike power' and 'game shooting'.

A rather more troublesome difficulty arises with instances of usage that do not quite answer to the part-for-whole requirement of synecdoche, or exactly meet the token-for-type definition of metonymy, but which none the less bear a resemblance to these tropes. There is a whole stylistic genus of quasi-metonymies. Suppose, for instance, that I conceive two narrative sentences: 'They were told to expect the Minister at twelve next day. Punctually at noon the car drew up in front of the house.' I would expect *car* to be read as an expression tantamount to *Minister*, or as the *token* of a *type*. Yet this is not a textbook metonymy, a free-standing example; it is conditional upon the larger structure of discourse. Some descriptive difficulties might be avoided if we were to consider both synecdoche and metonymy as categories contained within a governing linguistic/stylistic principle of *holonymy* and *meronymy*, the naming of a whole and the naming of a part or an associated feature. This principle can be taken to apply not only to strict instances of synecdoche and metonymy, but also to any instance suggestive of semantic inclusion or contiguity. Thus it might appear, given an appropriately constructed context, that *winter* and *frost*, or *time* and *clock*, or *love* and *kiss*, have a holonymic-meronymic relationship.

Since the late 1950s, writings on stylistics and tropology have given prominence to what is sometimes presented as a productive polar contrast between metaphor and metonymy. Roman Jakobson, who writes illuminatingly on this theme, cites as a potential sequence in Russian folk poetry:

A bright falcon was flying beyond the hills.
A fierce horse was coming at a gallop to the court.
A brave fellow was going to the porch.
Vasilij was walking to the manor.[7]

Each of these lines, Jakobson argues, refers to Vasilij (a bridegroom); the last two literally and the first two tropologically. But
the trope of the first line is metaphoric – there is resemblance
between the 'brave fellow' and the 'bright falcon', while in the
second line there is an overlap of the metaphoric and the
metonymic. 'A comparison between the appearing bridegroom
and the galloping horse suggests itself', says Jakobson, 'but at the
same time the halt of the horse at the court actually anticipates the
approach of the hero to the house. Thus before introducing the
rider and the manor of his fiancée, the song evokes the conti-
guous, *metonymical* images of the horse and of the courtyard:
possession instead of possessor and outside instead of inside.'

paronomasia

This can be taken as an inclusive term for the whole family of puns
– of which there are species and sub-species. A prominent type is
the homophonic pun – playing on words of like sound but
different meaning:

> Seyton! – I am sick at heart,
> When I behold – Seyton, I say! – This push
> Will chair me ever, or dis-seat me now.

Even at this moment of mortal crisis, Macbeth can make a pun, on
'chair' and 'cheer'. The two lexemes that converge at the central
point of the punning phrase each allude to something in the
immediate context; 'chair' points forward to 'dis-seat', and 'cheer'
back to 'sick at heart'. This is no mere fooling with words;
Macbeth's rhetoric is the angry excitement, the racing wit, of a
man under great stress. So also John Donne, punning on his own
name as he asks God to forgive his sins: 'When thou hast done,
thou hast not done, for I have more.' ('When you have done
forgiving my sins, you will still not be able to receive me, Donne,
because I have yet more sins.')

Punning is akin to metaphor in that a pun necessarily turns on
two meanings, one at least of which is transferred from its proper
sphere. At the beginning of *Twelfth Night*, the courtier Curio asks
the lovesick Duke Orsino, 'Will you go hunt, my lord?' 'What,
Curio?' asks the Duke, and Curio replies, as one giving a straight
answer to a silly question, 'The hart'; to which his lordship replies,
'Why, so I do, the noblest that I have.' At this point Curio
probably rolls his eyes heavenwards ('my God, chaps, he *has* got it

bad'), because the play on *hart* and *heart* is well tried, not to say corny. In this context, however, it is metaphorically implicated with the word *hunt*. 'To hunt the heart' is a metaphor for the pursuit of love, in which Orsino is effetely if pleasurably engaged.

There is also a casual kinship, depending on the particular substance of the trope, between punning and personification. An ancient piece of musical-hall patter goes thus. *Question*: 'I say, I say, I say, is life worth living?' *Answer* (after some intervening banter and pratfalling): 'Is life worth living? Is life worth living? Well, it all depends on the liver, doesn't it?' This dates, I think, from the era of Kruschen Salts, Andrews Liver Salts and Carter's Little Liver Pills, from the days when one was not 'out of sorts' or 'under the weather', but 'liverish', from a time, in fact, when medical practice and popular hypochondria attached importance to the liver as a seat of health or disease. Hence 'it all depends on the liver'. But also, 'it all depends on the Liver', the person doing the living. An element of personality, or an implication of animate properties, commonly enters into puns on personal names ('X by name and X by nature'), or puns on occupations and functions. In his *Verrine Orations*, Cicero puns sarcastically on the name of Verres, whom he was prosecuting on charges of maladminstration. In Latin, the common noun *verres* means 'a boar', not a happy name for an extortioner, which Verres was. Fiction offers many examples of mordantly humorous play on names.[8] In Shakespeare's English, for example, the name *Jacques* (a character in *As You Like It*) was homophonous with the common noun *jakes*, meaning a privy; a rather coarse pun in tune with the taste of the time.[9] But puns that confer names, and puns about names, are common everywhere and at all times. More generally, there are puns about people's activities and offices: 'Our chairman was charming'; 'The postmaster is a past master at finding excuses'; 'They sent for a joiner and he wrecked the joint'; 'Punctuality is the courtesy of princes – earls get there early'. Puns are the common stock of wit; and popular wit most often concerns personalities.

personification

This hardly needs definition; examples of this trope in passages of verse by Shakespeare, Wordsworth and W. H. Auden have been discussed in Chapter 3. It is closely connected with traditional forms of myth, in which natural phenomena are personified as gods or supernatural beings. There is a half-way stage to mythic or literary personification in the common tendency to ascribe personality or agentive power to parts of the body, to physiological and psychological events, or, indeed, to any of the contingent facts of our lives: 'My feet are killing me', 'Her hands suddenly reached out', 'Pain was a frequent visitor', 'Unhappiness always hits you when you are unprepared'. The extent to which, in such cases, we feel that personality is attributed to the noun placed in the thematic role in the sentence ('feet', 'hands', 'pain', 'unhappiness') must depend on whether the verb, or some other part of the predicate, correlatively implies human or animate activity. If 'Unhappiness always hits you when you are unprepared' suggests personification, it is no doubt because of *hits*. The suggestion would be less powerfully conveyed by 'Unhappiness affects you most when you are unprepared'. Similarly 'Pain was a frequent visitor' personifies 'pain', whereas 'Pain was a regular occurrence' surely does not. What such examples suggest is that practically any common noun can be 'personified' because our grammar makes available constructions that promote the illusion of personal agency. The constructions within which personifications most commonly operate are those of the noun phrase – 'cruel pain', 'grim unhappiness' – and the clause – 'pain racked him', 'unhappiness haunted her'. In these constructions, the adjectives or verbs that establish the personification are by necessity metaphorical. Personification thus has affinities on the one hand with metaphor, on the other with punning. It is a kind of pun to write about *death* as *Death*, because the small orthographic change suggests a homophone with two distinct references, to the natural termination of life and to a mythical agent: 'Long before death came, Death came and talked to him.'

A passage from Dr Johnson's *The Vanity of Human Wishes* illustrates the adroit management of personifications in a figurative framework. These lines are a part of the celebrated portrait of Charles XII of Sweden:

> The march begins, in military state,
> And nations on his eye suspended wait;
> Stern Famine guards the solitary coast,
> And Winter barricades the realms of Frost;
> He comes, nor want nor cold his course delay! –
> Hide, blushing glory, hide Pultowa's day.

This short passage begins with a discreet but perceptible onomatopoeia (a sensitive reading should bring out the rhythmic rataplan or drum-roll of the first line), after which it is dominated by two figures: the *parison* of the third and fourth lines ('Famine guards . . .', 'Winter barricades . . .') and the *epizeuxis* (the reiteration of 'hide') in the final line. We should notice how subtle the passage is, rhythmically, and how the figures of parison and epizeuxis are accommodated to changes of pace and emphasis; more than that, how the changing figuration is accommodated to a heightening of feeling, culminating in the pathos of the last line. This is the figurative frame that contains four personifications, three (*winter, frost* and *famine*) in the parisonically balanced lines, and one (*glory*) in the epizeuxis of the closing line. The personifications of Winter, Frost and Famine are conventionally marked by capital letters, and their metaphorical character is expressed by an adjective ('stern Famine'), by verbs ('Famine guards', 'Winter barricades') and by an incorporating noun phrase ('the realms of Frost'). The line that follows the parisonically balanced couplet reads:

He comes, nor want nor cold his course delay!

Although the verb *delay* might possibly suggest the attribute of personality, or at least animacy, there is no suggestion here, nor can the reader feel, that *want* and *cold* are personifications. They are merely common nouns; and yet they have their place in the figurative and tropological pattern, because they are metonymically, or at least *meronymically* related to what *famine* and *winter* designate. A component of famine is want; a component of winter is cold. The two nouns are carefully placed so that we shall notice the correspondence. Johnson does not write 'nor *cold* nor *want*', but 'nor *want* nor *cold*', setting the two words that balance in the line in the same order as the two words balanced in the couplet. And then follows the last line, with a personification (of *glory*) not typographically marked, although the noun is accompanied by an adjective ('blushing') that makes the personifying intent quite clear. 'Glory', in fact, is here both personification and a common noun of general designation; it personifies Glory as a kind of deity, but it also designates Charles's military successes and the distinction of his career. It is a paronomasia, like *death/Death*. The line further illustrates the figure of *oxymoron*, in that 'blushing' and 'glory' have powerfully contrasting connotations. Altogether, six lines of complex rhetoric, figurative and tropological; but a rhetoric that grows out of sense and feeling, not a cold artifice or a mere mannerism.

TROPES OF DISCOURSE

A striking stylistic fact about Johnson's verse-portrait of Charles
XII is that of the sixteen couplets that constitute the passage in its
entirety, twelve are written in the present tense. Johnson writes as
though the events of Charles's reign were unfolding before our
eyes, as though Charles's actions were there for us to see, Charles's
words uttered for us to overhear:

> No joys to him pacific sceptres yield,
> War sounds the trump, he rushes to the field.
> Behold surrounding kings their powers combine,
> And one capitulate, and one resign;
> Peace courts his hand, but spreads her charms in vain,
> 'Think nothing gained,' he cries, 'till nought remain,
> On Moscow's walls till Gothic standards fly,
> And all be mine beneath the polar sky.'

'Behold', says Johnson, as though he were our impresario and our
guide to the History Show being enacted before us. This is a
convenient discursive stance, of mediating between his topic and
the reader; it is, in other words, a trope of discourse, or, to use our
proposed term, a *mode*.

Discursive modes convey the attitudes of an author or speaker
towards the topic of discourse, towards the process of creating a
written or spoken address, and towards the reader. *Irony*, discussed a little earlier, is a discursive mode; so is *paradox*, so are
hyperbole (overstatement) and *litotes* (understatement). There are
some fearsomely named but easily recognized tropes concerning
common elements and strategies in speech-making. *Aporia*, the
affectation of perplexity, is one of these ('I hardly know how to account for what I am about to tell you') others are *anacoenosis*, the
process of inviting the reader/listener's opinion, *comprobatio*, the
paying of compliments to one's audience ('you, as educated and
sensitive people, can readily understand...'), and *epitropis*, the
referral to the good judgement or imagination of the audience ('I
need hardly say more on this head; I leave it to you to conceive . . .').

All these modes reflect the speaker's awareness of a listener;
more than that, they reflect a writer's awareness that his work is
dead on the page unless it takes on the character of speaking and
compels a manner of reading that may be fitly compared with

listening. Among the commonest, it might be said the most primitive, of discursive devices, is that of framing a proposition in the form of a question – a device so well known, indeed, that we habitually speak of 'rhetorical questions'. A rhetorical question either requires no answer (Puttenham calls this kind of questioning *erotema*), or, in the form of *anthypophora*, it is followed by an answer as though in dialogic response. A classic passage of anthypophora is Falstaff's speech on the topic of honour in King Henry IV, Part I:

> Can honour set to a leg? no: or an arm? no: or take away the grief of a wound? no. Honour hath no skill in surgery, then? no. What is honour? a word. What is that word honour? air. A trim reckoning! – Who hath it? he that died o' Wednesday. Doth he feel it? no. Doth he hear it? no. 'Tis insensible, then? yea, to the dead. But will it not live with the living? no. Why? detraction will not suffer it. Therefore I'll none of it; honour is a mere scutcheon: – and so ends my catechism.

This is anthypophora. Does knowing that add to our enjoyment of the speech? no. For any device of narrative or appeal, for any piece of verbal cunning, any move in the discursive game, there is a learned label to be discovered somewhere in the copious writings on rhetoric. But the names, let it be said again and again, ought not to be our first concern. If they were, we should never be done naming and burrowing for a nomenclature. There is probably a name somewhere for the stylistic act in which I am at present consciously engaged, of reverting at my chapter's end to a position stated near the beginning. Never mind – or do not mind too much – the names of the figures of speech; only be aware of them as patterns latent in the language we use every day. Equally, do not mind too much, or only inasmuch as names help to trap otherwise fugitive concepts, the names of tropes in discourse. These moves in the game are part of our social and verbal competence. We command them before we even know that they are worth naming, and they are familiar to us in argument, in story-telling, in the structures of literature.

6

Patterns of Writing, Processes of Art

The traditional view grants literary status to rhetoric in two respects. It assumes that every literary work has a style which is in some way extraordinary; discernibly the language of the speaking millions, and yet different from the common tongue, idiosyncratic, even in casualness bearing the mark of design, capable of the transparency of report and yet receptive of all the colours of emotion. It further assumes that the literary work has a structure, not only in the sense of having a discernible outer form (like the conventional octave–sestet pattern of a sonnet, for example), but also in its adherence to some informing scheme of elements or episodes, so disposed as to make up the plot of a novel or the 'argument' of a long poem. Stylistic choice, and options taken in constructing the plot of the fable, are not merely ornaments to please the writer at work, but are intimately bound up with the claims the author makes upon the reader; and thus are inherently rhetorical.

This view of a two-sided rhetoric in literary art reflects the older view of a two sided rhetoric in social and political debate; the sides are essentially *taxis* and *lexis*. The literary lexicon, however, is frequently innovative, at times subversive, unpredictably obedient or resistant to notions of decorum, stylistic level and propriety of register; and the *taxis* of literary works, though often comparable to the patern of an oration or sermon, sometimes requires its own categories. Aristotle's analysis of the structural pattern of tragedy (beginning with the famous assertion that it has 'a beginning, a middle and an end') is an early attempt to demonstrate a poetic taxis.[1] Rather more recently, we have William Labov's model, also well known, of the art of oral narrative as practised by black youths in inner-city areas in the United States. Labov has demonstrated that the stories told by his informants move through certain well-defined structural phases. A fully formed narrative, he says, has firstly an *Abstract*, encapsulating the point of the story; then an *Orientation*, identifying time, place, situation and participants; then the *Complicating Action*, which develops the events of the narrative, then the *Evaluation* which answers the question 'Why am I telling this tale?', and so to the *Result* which tells how it all ends, followed, possibly, by a *Coda*, a phase of rounding-out and retrospective commentary, exemplified in fairy-tales by pronouncements of the type 'and they all lived happily ever after', or in the case of Labov's oral narrators by remarks like 'And ever since then I haven't seen the guy 'cause I quit.[2].

What Labov discovered among the fabulists of the inner city we can as easily discover in the books on our library shelves. His narrative scheme is in fact a classic *taxis*, the conventional pattern of many an anecdote, fable or mythical tale; it is also the *taxis* of some elaborate literary recitals. It is quite clearly discernible in, for example, the passage from Johnson's *The Vanity of Human Wishes* quoted in the previous chapter, the story-portrait of Charles XII of Sweden. Here is the passage in its entirety, with, on the right, a commentary on its procedure through the Labovian categories:

On what foundations stand the warrior's pride How just his hopes, let Swedish Charles decide.	*Abstract* ('Listen, do you know about Charles XII?')
A frame of adamant, a soul of fire, No dangers fright him, and no labours tire; O'er love, o'er fear, extends his wide domain Unconquered lord of pleasure and of pain; No joys to him pacific sceptress yield, War sounds the trump, he rushes to the field. Behold surrounding kings their powers combine, And one capitulate, and one resign: Peace courts his hand, but spreads her charms in vain: 'Think nothing gained,' he cries, 'till nought remain, On Moscow's walls till Gothic standards fly, And all be mine beneath the polar sky.'	*Orientation* ('Well, he's *tough*; no one can lick him; and he gets this idea he's going to invade Russia;')

The march begins, in military state,	*Complicated Action*
And nations on his eye suspended wait;	('So he gets to it,
Stern Famine guards the solitary coast,	never mind he's
And Winter barricads the realms of Frost;	cold and hungry,
He comes, nor want cold his course delay! –	but then there's a
Hide, blushing glory, hide Pultowa's day:	big battle and he's
The vanquished hero leaves his broken bands	beaten and he has
And shows his miseries in distant lands;	to run away and
Condemned a needy suppliant to wait,	beg for help and
While ladies interpose and slaves debate.	humble himself')
But did not Chance at length her error mend?	*Evaluation* ('Why
Did no subverted empire mark his end?	am I telling you
Did rival monarchs give the fatal wound?	this? You think
Or hostile millions press him to the ground?	there's a big finish
	coming?')
His fall was destined to a barren strand,	*Result* ('He died out
A petty fortress, and a dubious hand;	there in the middle
	of nothing, and
	they still don't
	know who killed
	him')
He left the name at which the world grew pale,	*Coda* ('So that's Mr
To point a moral, or adorn a tale.	Big for you, just a
	name in the story
	books')

This little game with a classic text, a kind of rhetorical commentary on rhetoric, is designed to make the point that Dr Johnson's narrative, for all its literary dignity and noble elevation of style, in fact conforms to the very principles of structure that any knockabout raconteur might instinctively observe. In Johnson's case the structure is, as we have seen, supported by intricately organized figures of rhetoric; but Labov's street-narrators also narrate rhetorically, adapting the patterns of their syntax to the changing purposes of narration. These twentieth-century Americans in the city of New York have something in common – an artistic principle – with the eighteenth-century Englishman in the city of London; the principle that stories and sermons and sonnets and such rise in their *lexis* but stand on their *taxis*.

THE PHANTOM TEXT

The traditional view puts the text first, and last, and there an end of it; but that assumes something about the text that modern critics will not always allow. It presupposes that here we have an object, an artefact, a 'work', like a piece of sculpture or a Grecian urn, immutable, self-sufficient, requiring for its everlasting existence no dependence on any context, any person whose perceptions or preferences or needs may furnish it provisionally with a 'meaning'. Poets, by and large, like to think of their poems as independent entities, liberated from time, place and the rash intrusions of personality. Writers of fiction are deeply concerned with the business of 'crafting' their narratives – the very term, the implicit metaphor of the workshop, suggests a way of looking at what is done; not as a bargain with the times or a contract with any reader, but as a solid piece of work that is going to be looked at and enjoyed.

But God also made critics, and critics have an interest in interpretation, which literary artists are to a greater or lesser degree inclined to dismiss as irrelevant, or humbug, or even as a form of parasitism. In response to this, the ultimate plea and accusation of the interpreters is that if they are parasites upon poets, poets are equally parasites upon them: that poems and fictions are not self-sufficiently informed with their own vital principles, but depend for their continued life on critics who re-create them and re-endow them with meaning. This position has two corollary implications. One is that creative writers are no more the complete masters of what they do than are any other writers ; specifically, they delude themselves into thinking they know what their own *intentions* are, and consequently into thinking they can perceive when and how they have failed to realize those intentions. They meet the apparent failure by making another attempt: a new poem, a new story. But, say our critics, that is not wholly the point, and not the critical point. The real point is that they are frequently blind to their own intentions, and to the nature of what they are doing; the truth of their undertakings is revealed to the careful reader in the language and tropes of their poems and stories, close appraisal of which may even show that the latent tendency of the writing is actually the reverse of what is overtly claimed. This may seem preposterously arrogant – in the earlier sense of *preposterous*, 'getting things the wrong way round', and the historical significance of *arrogant*, 'taking too much upon oneself' – but we can present a reasonable case for critical presumption, with reference – yet again! – to Johnson's portrait-narrative of Charles XII.

The case relies on a subjective perception that many readers may share: the perception of a curious tension or ambivalence in Johnson's lines, the sense that here is a message with an attitude inside it trying to get out. Ostensibly this sketch of Charles's career is a cautionary tale; the teller, superior to vanities he portrays, sadly shakes his head over the folly and emptiness of military ambition. But it is difficult to read the passage without sensing that the overtly head-shaking moral is countered by a latently hand-clapping panegyric: that Johnson approves of the soldierly persona in general and of Swedish Charles in particular, and is affronted rather than saddened or philosophically satisfied by the soldier-king's loss of face and authority. The discrepancy of attitudes might be regarded as a deliberate exercise in irony, as indeed it is in the Tenth Satire of Juvenal, on which Johnson's poem is based; but Johnson manifestly speaks in grave earnest, without one flickering moment of ironic banter. His admiration for Charles and for soldiership can incidentally be documented from Boswell (10 April 1778): 'Every man thinks meanly of himself for not having been a soldier ... were Socrates and Charles the Twelfth of Sweden both present in any company, and Socrates to say, "Follow me, and hear a lecture on philosophy"; and Charles, laying his hand on his sword, to say, "Follow me, and dethrone the Czar;" a man would be ashamed to follow Socrates.' This is what we perceive in the passage from *The Vanity of Human Wishes*, but we do not need Boswell to confirm the perception. The ambivalence lurks in the language of the poem, though to demonstrate it would require much detailed and patient work, a ransacking of the lexicon. We would have to *deconstruct* the apparent ideology of Johnson's text, by showing how word and trope reflect attitudes he is patently trying to resist or ignore, or to which, indeed, he may be for the moment blind.

The critical claim that texts have provisional meanings that can be dismantled and re-created thus implies the dependence of the writer on those who will continue to give meaning to his work; and it implies as a further corollary the legitimate creative activity of the reader. So it comes about that the text which seems so solid, self-evident, monumentally possessed of a meaning that can be methodically elucidated and established once and for all, is haunted by a phantom text, a ghost that the gifted reader sees; more than that, the substantial presence itself becomes a phantom, one reflection among many of that subjective, eidetic image we call the poem or story. These are interesting notions, but if we accept them we must be prepared to accept some extension of what 'rhetoric' means, and what the rhetorician's activity involves. Classical rhetoric takes for granted the view of the text as objective artefact, so that when we talk of the rhetoric of a speech by Cicero, we mean its structure, its figures, its tropes, discrete features to which we attribute discernible significance. In this the reader/listener has no part to play; the craft of the work is the work itself. Rhetoric in this traditional definition is a *thing*, or at least a property of a thing. In recent critical usage, however, 'rhetoric' means something much more like an *activity*, not of production but of perception and reception, not of an author but of a partnership between author and reader, not of discrete significance but of provisional and dependent value. This second sense of rhetoric does not cancel out the first; rather, we are obliged to accommodate two notions of rhetoric as it is programmed into literary texts. We are obliged to think of *rhetorics* diversely perceptible in the verbal texture, the tropes, the content and the overt or latent ideology of the work.

FIGURES IN THE FOREGROUND: SOME RENAISSANCE EXAMPLES

Figures of speech, such as those discussed in the preceding chapter, turn up surprisingly in all kinds of writing. The dullest, most prosaic, least fanciful page may well yield one or two. There are cases, however, in which figures of speech are very much figures in the foreground; in which figuration is a creative principle of the text. Such cases are not very common in modern literature but the prose and poetry of the Tudor–Jacobean era will yield examples enough. Here is an extract from John Lyly's *Euphues: The Anatomy of Wit*, a book famous in its own day but now, like its companion work, *Euphues and his England*, more often mentioned than read. Its soporific unreadability results from its author's unremitting production of rhetorical figures spiked with alliteration and laced with similes drawn from allegedly natural history. In this typical passage, a woman called Lucilla uneasily questions the morality of forsaking her lover Philautus and transferring her affections to his friend Euphues, who has bewitched her with his courtly manners and silver tongue:

> 'Ah, fond wretch, dost thou think Euphues will deem thee constant to him, when thou hast been unconstant to his friend? Weenest thou that he will have no mistrust of thy faithfulness, when he hath had trial of thy fickleness? Will he have no doubt of thine honour, when thou thyself callest thine honesty in question? Yes, yes, Lucilla, well doth he know that the glass once crazed will with the least clap be cracked, that the cloth which staineth with milk will soon lose his colour with vinegar, that the eagle's wing will waste the feather as well of the phoenix as of the pheasant, that she that hath been faithless to one will never be faithful to any.
>
> 'But can Euphues convince me of fleeting, seeing for his sake I break my fidelity? Can he condemn me of disloyalty, when he is the only cause of my disliking? May he justly condemn me of treachery, who hath his testimony as trial of my good will? Doth he not remember that the broken bone once set together is stronger than ever it was? That the greatest blot is taken off with the pumice? That though the spider poison the fly, she cannot infect the bee? That although I have been light to Philautus, yet I may be lovely to Euphues? It is not my desire but his deserts that moveth my mind to this choice, neither the want of the like good will in Philatus but the lack of the like good qualities that removeth my fancy from one to the other.'

Attempting a rhetorical analysis of this would be rather like boning fish, an exercise calling for a good deal of patience, justified only by the prospect of pleasure. Perhaps some comment on the sentences constituting the first paragraph will suffice. The figures generally are parisonic, and their parallels and counterpoises are in various ways contoured by alliteration or assonance:

sentence 1: parisonic antithesis

does thou think   Euphues will deem thee   *constant   to him*
                  when thou has been   *unconstant to his friend*

sentence 2: parison + alliteration + homoioteleuton

Weenest thou   that he will have   *no mistrust of thy faithfulness*
               when he hath had   *trial of thy fickleness*

sentence 3: polyptoton

Will he		have no doubt of thine	*honour*
when thou thyself		callest thine	*honesty* in question

(Note: In this context 'honour' and 'honesty' have the same meaning; the variation in the form of the word constitutes the rhetorical figure. The sentence also suggests the counterpoise of 'have...doubt of' and 'call . . . in question', but the balancing of these expressions is not figuratively defined.)

sentence 4a: epizeuxis + antithesis + alliteration + assonance

Yes, yes, Lucilla,
Well doth he know   that   *the **gl**ass once **cr**azed*
                                          will   *with the least **cl**ap be **cr**acked*

(Note: The phonetic figuration is rich, and requires some elucidation. Of course /g/ does not alliterate with /k/, but there is a quasi-alliterative link of the clusters /gl/, /kl/ (*gl – cl*), in '*gl*ass' and '*cl*ap'. The alliterative pattern that spans the figure is a pattern of clusters in alternating sequence, /gl/ – /kr/ – /kl/ – /kr/, '*gl*ass – *cr*azed – *cl*ap – *cr*acked'. This is accompanied by an assonance-pairing of 'glass' and 'clap' – in Lyly's time these words had the same short vowel; and the more open assonance of 'crazed' and 'cracked'.)

sentence 4b: parison + alliteration

that	*the **cl**oth that staineth*		*with milk*
will soon		*lose his **c**olour*	*with vinegar*

sentence 4c: parison + alliteration + assonance

that	*the eagle's **w**ing will*	*waste*	*the **fea**ther*
	as	*well*	*of the **phoe**nix*
	as		*of the **phea**sant*

(Note: The two alliterating series are /w/ – /w/ – /w/, in '*w*ing – *w*aste – *w*ell', and /f/ – /f/ – /f/, in '*f*eather – *ph*oenix – *ph*easant'. They overlap in the pattern w–w–f–w–f–f.

The point of the allusion is that the eagle's plumage was

believed to retain, after the bird's death, the destructive power of the living creature.)

sentence 5: parisonic antithesis

that   *she that hath been faithless to one*
will   *never be faithful to any*

(Note: This is a close parison, virtually an isocolon. It is noteworthy that the paragraph ends as it begins, with an antithetical counterpoise: of 'constant' and 'unconstant' in the first sentence, 'faithless' and 'faithful' in the last.)

Analysis of the second paragraph would reveal very little more about Lyly's style than an examination of the first has produced. The reader learns to predict what will happen from sentence to sentence: that in most sentences the characteristic antitheses and parallels are worked out in subordinate clauses after an introductory conjunction – a 'for', a 'but', a 'yet', an 'as', a 'though' – and are often presented in the syntactic bracket of a 'neither . . . nor', or a 'not (only) . . . but (also)'; that speakers will apostrophize themselves with exclamations and questions; that there will be quite a dense texture of alliteration and assonance, features that often encrust the prose most thickly when the meaning is at its thinnest; and that the similes of homely life and nature-myth will crowd thick and fast, if not always very informatively.[3]

It is unendingly ingenious, but finally the question remains: what is the point of it? On the strength of this one extract, we might argue that the obsession with certain figures and figurative variations, and with the nagging repetitions of sound, projects a state of mind; that Lucilla, for instance, is distraught and that Lyly accordingly supplies her with the rhetoric of distraction. Alas, this wil not do. Lyly writes like this on page after page after page, furnishing one character after another, in this state of mind or that, with a plethora of parisonic pattering. The Euphuistic style was unrelated, by and large, to the content and psychology of the text. It was an extravagance, the tendency of which was, if anything, to discredit the serious literary pretensions of figurative rhetoric.

Those pretensions are better represented by a piece of writing from an author whose work generally appears to repudiate any claim to rhetorical elaboration of the kind practised by Lyly. The opening of Francis Bacon's essay 'Of Studies' is well known:

Studies serve for delight, for ornament, and for ability. Their chief use for delight is in privateness and retiring*; for ornament, is in discourse; and for ability, is in the judgement and disposition of business. For expert men* can execute and perhaps judge of particulars, one by one, but the general counsels and the plots and marshalling of affairs come best from those that are learned. To spend too much time in studies is sloth; to use them too much for ornament, is affectation; to make judgement wholly by their rules is the humour of a scholar* They perfect nature and are perfected by experience, for natural abilities are like natural plants, that need proyning* by study; and studies themselves do give forth directions too much at large, except they are bounded in by experience.* Crafty men contemn studies;* simple men admire them*; and wise men use them, for they teach not their own use, but that is a wisdom without them and above them,* won by observation. Read not to contradict and confute, nor to believe and take for granted, nor to find talk and discourse, but to weigh and consider. Some books are to be tasted, others to be swallowed, and some few to be chewed and digested; that is, some books are to be read only in parts; others to be read, but not curiously*; and some few to be read wholly and with diligence and attention. Some books may also be read by deputy, and extracts made of them by others, but that would be only the less important arguments and the meaner sort* of books: else distilled books are like common distilled waters, flashy things.* Reading maketh a full man, conference* a ready man, and writing an exact man. And therefore, if a man write little, he had need have a great memory; if he confer little, he had need have a present wit; and if he read little, he had need have much cunning, to seem to know that he doth not.*

(Note: The asterisks mark some words and phrases that may need to be translated. 'Privateness and retiring' = privacy and retirement, a *hendiadys*; 'expert men' = men of experience, not learning; 'the humour of a scholar' = a typical characteristic of the scholar; 'proyning' = pruning; 'do give forth directions too much at large ... experience' = studies in themselves provide general principles that only experience can apply to particular cases; 'crafty men contemn studies' = clever people despise studies; 'simple men admire them' = plain folk marvel at them; 'without them and above them' = over and above them; 'curiously' = carefully; 'meaner sort' = more ordinary sort; 'flashy' = insipid, flavourless; 'conference' = conversation; 'to seem to know that he doth not' − to seem to know what, in fact, he does not know.)

Figuratively, this is almost as complex as the extract from Lyly, and indeed exploits comparable stylistic features: the repeated use of parallel structures and the resort to metaphors and similes drawn from common experience (the pruning of plants, food and drink). One difference is the almost complete absence from Bacon's style of the phonaesthetic bravura, the alliterative efflorescence that pervades Lyly's writing. But there is a much deeper difference. Lyly's manner has no more than a tenuous relationship with his matter; Bacon's figurative schemes are essential to his discursive strategy. Any page of Lyly is stylistically similar to any other page, but no two essays by Bacon are wholly alike in style. This one, perhaps more than most, is modelled on the principle of parallel constructions.

The constructions notably occur in threes. Thus the essay begins, 'Studies serve for delight, for ornament, and for ability.' This triadic form provides the pattern for the next sentence, the three *cola* of which expand successively the three propositions of the first sentence: 'Their chief use for delight is in privacy and retiring; for ornament is in discourse; and for ability, is in the judgement and disposition of business.' The third sentence follows as a kind of general commentary and excursus, with no markedly figurative pattern: 'For expert men can execute and perhaps judge of particulars, one by one, but the general counsels and the plots and marshalling of affairs come best from those that are learned.' The pattern established at the outset if that of the figured proposition and the unfigured commentary. The figured sentences generally follow the rule of three, though there is one instance of a fourfold pattern. The essay opens, then, with the figure–expansion–comment sequence cited above and goes on to repeat the procedure:

figured construction

To spend too much time in studies is sloth;
to use them too much for ornament is affectation;
to make judgement wholly by their rules is the humour of a scholar

comment

They perfect nature and are perfected by experience, for natural abilities are like natural plants, that need proyning by study; and studies themselves do give forth directions too much at large, except they be bounded by experience.

figured construction

Crafty men contemn studies;
simple men admire them;
and wise men use them . . .

comment

. . . for they teach not their own use, but that is a wisdom without them and above them, won by observation.

figured construction (fourfold pattern)

Read not to contradict and confute,
nor to believe and take for granted,
nor to find talk and discourse,
but to weigh and consider.

figured construction

Some books are to be tasted,
others to be swallowed,
and some few to be chewed and digested;

expansion

that is, some books are to be read only in parts;
others to be read, but not curiously;
and some few to be read wholly, with diligence and attention.

comment

Some books also may be read by deputy, and extracts made of them by others, but that would be only in the less important arguments and the meaner sort of books; else distilled books are like common distilled waters, flashy things.

figured construction

Reading maketh a full man,
conference a ready man,
and writing an exact man.

expansion

And therefore,
if a man write little, he had need have a great memory;

if he confer little, he had need have a present wit;
and if he read little, he had need have much cunning, to seem to
know that he doth not.

The figured constructions are with one exception triadic; the
exception being a fourfold pattern which occurs centrally in our
extract. Using the notations F, for 'figured construction', E, for
'figured expansion', and C, for 'comment', we may tabulate as
follows the rhetorical procedures of the essay, from the beginning
down to the words 'to seem to know that he doth not':

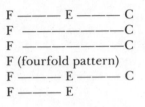

The figures occur regularly, echoically, but not as merely decorative repetitions of a pattern. They are part of a technique of
exposition, and they alternate with other elements, which either
reassert the figurative design in a somewhat more open form,
elucidating the epigrammatic utterance of the tighter scheme, or
supply a non-figurative amplification. The triadic patterns have
mnemonic power (we remember 'reading maketh a full man,
conference a ready man, and writing an exact man', much as we
remember *veni, vidi, vici*), and also a predictive function. We grasp
Bacon's strategy almost from the beginning and quickly learn to
anticipate that each triadic figure will be followed by an expansion
or a comment, or both. By allowing himself room to expand his
style, he secures the laconically striking effect of his figurative
utterances, the lexicon of which would in places be puzzling
without an explanatory note. Knowing what is meant by a *full*
man', 'a *ready* man' and 'an *exact* man' depends to a very great
extent on the explanatory sentence which follows – and which,
incidentally, is constructed on a chiastic (*chiasmus* – the 'X' figure)
scheme, for it reverses the order of key words, 'reading', 'conference' and 'writing', and presents them in the sequence 'write',
'confer', 'read'. [4]
There are other figurative touches in this extract, for example

an inclination towards the coupling figure called *hendiadys*:
'privateness and retiring', 'judgement and disposition', 'plots and
marshalling', 'contradict and confute', 'believe and take for
granted', 'talk and discourse', 'weigh and consider', 'diligence and
attention'. His similes are reiteratively framed: 'natural abilities
are like natural plants', 'distilled books are like common distilled
waters'. There is a *polyptoton* in 'they perfect nature and are
perfected by experience'. There are a few scattered occurrences
of alliteration, most obviously in 'Crafty men contemn studies'.
The discursive trope of *paradox* appears in 'to spend too much
time in studies is sloth', but the general intention of the passage is
not paradoxical. Indeed, all of the rhetorical features just mentioned are incidental colours. The major stylistic framework is a
design of parisonic figures and expanded commentary. This is the
significant rhetoric of the piece, a rhetoric intelligently conceived
and controlled, a rhetoric that both expresses and generates an
argument.

Bacon's rhetoric is cool; his schemes reflect a regulative power
of mind. Now here is Donne, as ever hot-hearted, as ever
appearing to speak on impulse:

> At the round earth's imagined corners, blow
> Your trumpets, angels, and arise, arise
> From death, you numberless infinities
> Of souls, and to your scattered bodies go,
> All whom the flood did, and fire shall o'erthrow
> All whom war, dearth, age, agues, tyrannies,
> Despair, law, chance. hath slain, and you whose eyes
> Shall behold God, and never taste death's woe.
> But let them sleep, Lord, and me mourn a space,
> For, if above all these, my sins abound,
> 'Tis late to ask abundance of thy grace,
> When we are there; here, on this lowly ground,
> Teach me how to repent; for that's as good
> As if thou hadst sealed my pardon, with thy blood.

Any account of the figurative rhetoric of this sonnet would be
meaningless without the statement of a crucial distinction between
octave and sestet, a distinction between roles adopted by the poet-
speaker. In the octave, the poet addresses the multitudes of the
dead, bidding them rise from their graves. More than that, he
commands the trumpeter angels to sound the call that will begin
the Resurrection; in fact, he assumes, in fiction, the role of an

immortal or a divine being. In the sestet, this role is abandoned and reversed; the speaker is now the miserable sinner, confessing to God his need for repentance and atonement. The octave– sestet contrast is thus something more than the sonneteer's conventional change of tone – though such a change is indeed clearly perceptible; it is a change of tone symptomatic of a change of authorial role, of stance. The power-posture of the octave yields to the stance of humility in the sestet.

That change of stance is reflected in the distribution throughout the whole poem of figurative schemes. The octave is crowded with figures, the sestet much less so. Only the first and last lines of the sestet have a structure that suggests a schematic counterpoise:

But let		*them*	*sleep*	
and		*me*	*mourn*	

and				
As if thou hadst sealed	*my*	*pardon*		
	with	*thy*		*blood*

The intervening lines are free from any figurative heightening. By contrast, nearly every line of the octave is rhetorically busy. The poem opens with a form of *oxymoron* ('round earth's imagined corners') in a trope derived from the Book of Revelation (Chapter 7). It apostrophizes the angels, and the dead; the *apostrophe* carries the additional force of *epizeuxis (in 'arise, arise');* the next figure is the antithesis of *flood* and *fire, did* and *shall*, expressing the first and the last of our human world; then follows, in a great oratorical flourish, a list of nouns and noun phrases: 'war, dearth, age, agues, tyrannies, despair, law, chance . . .'. This is the figure of *asyndeton*, and it brings us to the last clauses of the octave, which are an allusion to St Paul's assurance in his First Letter to the Corinthians (Chapter 52) that 'we shall not all sleep'.

The resultant impression of the octave is one of hectic, high-voiced excitement, an exhilaration at once virile and morbid, a pathological state of tension. The sestet supplants this with a healthier sense of reality, 'here on this lowly ground'; the bluster of 'arise, arise . . . and to your scattered bodies go' gives way to 'teach me how to repent'; the poem changes from performance to prayer. The sonnet is an illustration (there are many, many others)

of how the so-called 'figures of speech' can have organic significance in works of literature. When they are put effectively to
work, we may not always be able to find names for them, or
disentangle them from their involvement with the surrounding
text, but we feel the effect none the less; because they are markers
some creative concept. Donne's figuration is imaginatively conceived, as the embodiment and symptom of a changing psychological state. Bacon's is intellectually conceived, as the programme of
an argument. Lyly's, by contrast, is conceived only as decoration,
and his rhetorical method in general confirms Bacon's warning
about studies: 'to use them too much for ornament is affectation.'[5]

TROPES IN TEXTS

Metaphor and other tropes may similarly be 'markers of some
creative concept' in a poem, an essay, a story. To assign to any
trope a merely decorative value is greatly to undervalue the
linguistic and literary power of these devices. In so-called 'ordinary language' they are often illuminating, giving access to otherwise evasive ideas and perceptions. In the language of literature
they are frequently keys to the understanding of a part or even the
whole of a text. Literary tropes influence the reading of texts in
ways that vary from the fuzzy or half-realized, to the overt and
fully worked-out. There is, for example, a fuzzy tropology in this
well known piece by Wordsworth, the sonnet 'Composed upon
Westminster Bridge, September 3, 1802':

> Earth has not anything to show more fair:
> Dull would he be of soul who could pass by
> A sight so touching in its majesty;
> This City now doth, like a garment, wear
> The beauty of the morning; silent, bare,
> Ships, towers, domes, theatres, and temples lie
> Open unto the fields, and to the sky;
> All bright and glittering in the smokeless air.
> Never did sun more beautifully steep
> In his first splendour, valley, rock, or hill;
> Ne'er saw I, never felt, a calm so deep!
> The river glideth at his own sweet will:
> Dear God! the very houses seem asleep;
> And all that mighty heart is lying still!

The poem is not in the least difficult, and its meaning is generally accessible to paraphrase. Wordsworth is struck by the prospect of a great city at a time when it is least like a city; when it is not busy, not noisy, not smoky, but invested in a stillness that magically transforms it, creating something as mysteriously affecting as natural landscape. The text offers this meaning without asking for much effort on the reader's part. It also offers, however, metaphors that never become wholly distinct and cogent yet still influence the way in which the poem is understood.

One of these tropes is the characterization of the city, which 'now doth, like a garment, wear / The beauty of the morning'. The metaphor of dress implies the metaphor of the city as a personage, and perhaps (in view of the 'majesty' mentioned in the third line) a royal personage: the city, personified, puts on a dress, a new and beautiful dress, a strange dress, and – why not? – a regal dress. The word 'bare' in the fifth line does not cancel this reading – we are allowed to suppose that the bare body of the city (its buildings, ships and so on) is swathed in the wonderfully brilliant morning light. It is at the beginning of the sestet that this 'dress' trope, tentatively yet perceptibly realized in the octave, is put aside in favour of a new metaphor, that of 'steeping' or immersing something in a fluid. The city looks as though it were dipped in light and stillness. It is immobilized by this; there is no movement, no activity, though the river continues to flow unimpeded. And at this point the text reverts, it seems, to the image of the city as a person. To talk of a 'sleeping city' is a metonymic cliche, meaning only that the people in the city are asleep. But Wordsworth appears to intend metaphor rather than metonymy. He writes 'the very houses seem asleep', and he is talking of the buildings, not their occupants. Consequently 'that mighty heart' must also suggest something more than the cliche phrase 'the heart of the city', meaning 'the centre of the city'. This 'heart' is surely a metaphorical heart, a heart whose beat is suspended while the majestic body of the city is brilliantly shrouded, beautifully immersed in a lucid, hypnotic stillness. This reading, however, is possibly more controversial than the summary of the poem offered earlier, because the metaphors on which it depends are fuzzed; they are not unmistakably realized in a clear, coherent pattern, but they can be retrieved from the text and they do make available an interpretation along the lines sketched out above.

In such cases, the metaphoric language is an option which the reader can take up or ignore. Contrast that with a poem which at first reading appears to leave nothing to chance, Browning's 'Memorabilia':

Ah, did you once see Shelley plain,
    And did he stop and speak to you
And did you speak to him again?
    How strange it seems and new!

But you were living before that,
    And also you are living after;
And the memory I started at –
    My starting moves your laughter.

I crossed a moor, with a name of its own
    And a certain use in the world no doubt,
Yet a hand's breadth of it shines alone
    'Mid the blank miles round about:

For there I picked up on the heather
    And there I put inside my breast
A moulted feather, an eagle-feather!
    Well, I forget the rest.

A generation accustomed to thinking of *memorabilia* as German war-helmets, cut-glass door handles or cigarette-card pictures of the flags of all nations may need to be reminded that the word means 'memorable events or things'. This is the definition supplied by the *New Collins Concise Dictionary*, and it comes appositely into context, since both events and things are remembered in the Browning poem. It is evidently a kind of dialogue, although one of the participants is not heard; merely 'overheard' in the responses of the poem's speaker. This hidden interlocutor, it seems, recalls meeting and exchanging a few words with the poet Shelley – an event so remarkable to the speaker that it startles him into a recollection of his own, that of walking across a moor, the name of which he has forgotten, and finding an eagle feather.

This eagle feather is the tropological key to a text which is apparently related off-handedly, inconsequentially – 'Well, I forget the rest.' It takes no effort of imagination to see that there is a correspondence between the eagle feather and the desultory conversational exchange with a great man; and thus between the brief period of time occupied by the conversational exchange and the small patch of ground on which the feather lies. This is the manifest pattern of the poem:

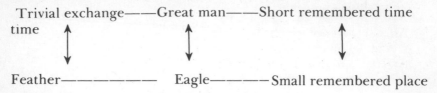

Trivial exchange——Great man——Short remembered time
time

Feather——————   Eagle————Small remembered place

The before and after of time are forgotten; the larger details of place are forgotten; it is the particular moment and the particular spot that are memorable because of their casual, trivial records of greatness. Shelley's ordinary politenesses are, as it were, metonymic of Shelley the poet. A single feather of the eagle is metonymic of the noble, soaring bird. Note, however, that the eagle, written into the poem's equation as set out above, is actually not present in the text. The great man, Shelley, is there ('did you once see Shelley plain'), along with his words, but we do not see the eagle plain; only its feather. There is, after all, a slight fuzziness in the poem's tropology, an option that eludes the four-square enclosure of the piece. The option is to read the encounter with Shelley as a merely finite event; 'strange' and 'new' perhaps, but none the less limiting, and somehow reductive of Shelley's poetic persona to a banal physical presence. The discovery of the eagle feather, on the other hand, opens access to a world of the imagination; the eagle is not seen, but its power and beauty dwell and grow in the mind of the man who carries in his breast pocket (or next to his heart) the palpable token of a huge impalpable life. This interpretation is by no means enjoined upon us, but it exists residually, almost subversively, in the overtly symmetrical, clearly organized tropology of the text.

However we choose to read 'Memorabilia', the fact remains that the reception of the text as something meaningful (it is of course open to the unreceptive reader to say 'so what') depends on the understanding of the eagle feather as a metonym of the eagle and arguably as a metaphor for the power of the creative imagination. It is the dominant trope. Another of Browning's lyrics, 'Two in the Campagna', contains a very elaborately developed trope which is not dominant in the sense of providing a necessary key to the interpretation of the piece, but which interestingly and beautifully

creates a correlate, both distracting and illuminating, to the
feeling expressed in the poem. The text unfolds quite slowly,
ruminatively:

> I wonder do you feel to-day
>   As I have felt since, hand in hand
> We sat down on the grass, to stray
>   In spirit better through the land,
> This morn of Rome and May?
>
> For me, I touched a thought, I know,
>   Has tantalized me many times,
> (Like turns of thread the spiders throw
>   Mocking across our path) for rhymes
> To catch at and let go.
>
> Help me to hold it! First it left
>   The yellowing fennel, run to seed
> There, branching from the brickwork's cleft,
>   Some old tomb's ruin: yonder weed
> Took up the floating weft,
>
> Where one small orange cup amassed
>   Five beetles – blind and green they grope
> Among the honey-meal: and last,
>   Everywhere on the grassy slope
> I traced it. Hold it fast!
>
> The champaign with its endless fleece
>   Of feathery grasses everywhere!
> Silence and passion, joy and peace,
>   An everlasting wash of air –
> Rome's ghost since her decease.
>
> Such life here, through such lengths of hours,
>   Such miracles performed in play,
> Such primal naked forms of flowers,
>   Such letting nature have her way
> While heaven looks from its towers!
>
> How say you? Let us, O my dove,
>   Let us be unashamed of soul,
> As earth lies bare to heaven above!
>   How is it under our control
> To love or not to love?
>
> I would that you were all to me,
>   You that are just so much, no more.

Nor yours nor mine, nor slave nor free!
　　Where does the fault lie? What the core
Of the wound, since wound must be?

I would I could adopt your will,
　　See with your eyes, and set my heart
Beating by yours, and drink my fill
　　At your soul's springs – your part my part
In life, for good or ill.

No. I yearn upward, touch you close,
　　Then stand away. I kiss your cheek,
Catch your soul's warmth – I pluck the rose
　　And love it more than tongue can speak –
Then the good minute goes.

Already how am I so far
　　Out of that minute? Must I go
Still like the thistle-ball, no bar,
　　Onward, whenever light winds blow,
Fixed by no friendly star?

Just when I seemed about to learn!
　　Where is the thread now? The old trick!
Off again! Only I discern –
　　Infinite passion, and the pain
Of finite hearts that yearn.

This is a meditation on inconstancy, the inconstancy of the perfectly and painfully sincere. The poem's speaker is a lover who wonders ruefully why he cannot rest in this sweet moment, this warm and desirable relationship; why, even as he perceives the beauty of the season, the landscape, the woman who so completely offers him her love, his feeling is already changing, his thoughts straying off towards objectives yearned-for yet undefined.

This meaning (if such be the meaning) is available to the reader without the support of some lines which are none the less poetically crucial. The second, third and fourth stanzas, elaborating the image of the spider's thread (an image originating in a parenthesis) might in fact be omitted, and with some minor adjustment to a line and a half in the final stanza the poem would still make sense, still present the puzzlement of the lover unable to say yes to his own happiness. But something would be missing, something indispensable to the completeness of the poem, and to its moral integrity; something that rescues the poem from the suspicion of being a philanderer's apology or the complaint of someone for whom enough is not as good as a feast, and conveys a genuine sense of pained perplexity. In part, the poem is concerned with the human fact that even our sincerest feelings are never wholly stable; but it is also importantly concerned with the baffling difficulty of articulating those trains of thought that marshal and objectify the drift of feeling. The observer is caught in the paradox of being involved in what he tries to observe.

The image of the spider's drifting, elusive thread catches perfectly, by its very obliqueness, this dual theme of the heart's restlessness and the mind's bafflement. It has the appeal of the distracting correlate, an appeal we have examined in earlier chapters. The third and fourth stanzas are a poem within the poem, charming us with their pictorial essay on the fennel, the crumbling brickwork, the weeds, the bright orange of the flower, the green of the little beetles foraging in the flower's cup. They might be prized for this distractive power alone, but of course their value goes beyond that. As the poetic argument progresses, we realize that each objective apparently sought out by the mocking, drifting thread, each place in which it can be observed, seemingly at rest, seemingly caught at last, correlates with each new objective of the heart, each station of the puzzled mind – though the correlation is never of the kind that might allow the naive reader to assert,' the fennel symbolizes *this*, the yellow flower stands for *that*.' The beautiful image is a working metaphor, not a set of symbols. In the last stanza of the poem the metaphor comes decisively into its own. The thread disappears from view. 'Just when I seemed about to learn!' cries the poet. 'The old trick! Off again!' When we think we have settled the heart and believe we understand the workings of the mind, the heart moves on, the mind stalls. And because the mind boggles, the lover's reflections close in ambiguity and paradox. The paradox, that limitless feelings are perceived in the limitations of feeling (infinite passion and finite yearning), is rhetorically expressed in a chiastic, antithetical, alliterating figure:

Infinite *p*assion and the *p*ain of finite hearts

The chiasmus is in the X-form of infinite – passion – pain – finite. The antithetical counterpoises are of 'infinite' and 'finite', 'passion' and 'pain'; but also of 'passion' and 'hearts'. It is an elaborately rhetorical finish to an elaborately subtle poem. But his ending is also ambiguous. 'Only I discern', says the speaker; and does he mean 'I alone discern', or 'Nevertheless I discern', or 'I can only discern'? Any of these would fit the context – the first as a counterpart to the poem's opening, 'I wonder do you feel . . . only I discern' (hence, 'you do not grasp, after all, what I am trying to say'); the second as a response to 'the old trick' of the fugitive perception (hence, 'all the same, I can understand something'); and the third as a despairing acceptance of his inability to learn anything about the world of feeling ('all I can see is this'). These ambiguities also have their correlate in those 'turns of thread' which the spiders throw, *mocking*, across the path of the lover and his companion.

The image of the spider's thread, that incidental, parenthetical detail, thus grows into something like a programme for a sympathetic reading of the poem. Its status is almost mythographic, in the sense defined in chapter 4 (p. 88). Mythograms are important in literary structures, no less than in structures of argument and persuasion. In fiction, they often occur towards the beginning of the story, sometimes in the first chapter or even in the first paragraph. Here is the opening of a story by F. Scott Fitzgerald, called 'The Cut-Glass Bowl':

> There was a rough stone age and a smooth stone age and a bronze age, and many years afterward a cut-glass age. In the cut-glass age, when young ladies had persuaded young men with long, curly moustaches to marry them, they sat down several months afterward and wrote thank-you notes for all sorts of cut-glass presents – punch-bowls, finger-bowls, dinner-glasses, wine-glasses, ice-cream dishes, bonbon dishes, decanters, and cases – for, though cut glass was nothing new in the nineties, it was then especially busy reflecting the dazzling light of fashion from the Back Bay to the fastnesses of the Middle West.
>
> After the wedding the punch-bowls were arranged on the sideboard with the big bowl in the centre; the glasses were set up in the china-closet; the candlesticks were put at both ends of things – and then the struggle for existence began. The bonbon dish lost its little handle and became a pin-tray upstairs; a promenading cat knocked the little bowl off the sideboard, and the hired girl chipped the middle-sized one with the sugar-dish, then the wine-glasses succumbed to leg fractures, and even the dinner glasses disappeared one by one like the ten little niggers, the last one ending up, scarred and maimed, as a toothbrush holder among the other shabby genteels on the bathroom shelf. But by the time all this had happened the cut-glass age was over, anyway.

The first episode of the story proper begins in the third paragraph. This prelude reads at first like the whimsical assumption of a stance, as the narrative is put into its historical setting – those crazy, lazy curly-moustached and straw-boatered days of the cut-glass nineties. But it turns out to have rather larger pretensions, in prefiguring the action of a story that extends over several decades, a story with a realistic, 'modern' theme expressed in the form of a fable or fairy-tale. It tells of a wedding-gift, a cut-glass bowl, given in malice by a disappointed suitor who tells the bride-to-be, 'it's as hard as you are and as beautiful and as empty and as easy to see through'. The bowl indeed becomes an accursed object, seemingly endowed with a malevolent power, a significant presence in every catastrophe afflicting the lives of the heroine and her family, and ultimately instrumental in her death. It is both the symbol and the executant of a malign will that transcends the human struggle to be free and successful and happy:

> 'You see, I am fate,' it shouted, 'and stronger than your puny plans; and I am how-things-turn-out and I am different from your little dreams, and I am the flight of time and the end of beauty and unfulfilled desire; all the accidents and imperceptions and the little minutes that shape the crucial hours are mine.'

This passage from the end of the story, when the distraught heroine has the delusion that the bowl is speaking to her, recalls a significant phrase from the opening paragraphs: 'and then the struggle for existence began'. The bowl itself ('the big bowl in the centre') is one of the *existences* that tenant the sideboard and the china-closet. Others are the bonbon dish, the wine-glasses, the dinner-glasses, time's victim's awaiting their fractures and maimings, their exile to a shabbier life. In mythographic mime they foretell human destinies in which there will also be casual accident, maiming and a sad lapse into despairing gentility. These opening paragraphs predispose the reader to an interpretation of the story as a fairy-tale form with realistic reference. They announce a rhetorical strategy and at the same time anticipate the shaping of the plot.

THE RHETORIC OF EPISODES

Narrative openings are an important aspect of the rhetoric of fiction. The author faces a challenge that complicates the ordinary need for a *captatio benevolentiae*, an appeal to goodwill, with a further appeal to the curiosity of the reader, who must feel not only a willingness to read the story but also the stimulus of wanting to know, or at least to guess – even, at length, to be proved wrong – what is going to happen. It would be very difficult to meet this challenge with complete, sovereign, devil-may-care originality. Readers like to be orientated to the story; they want at least a little information about time and place and person. The writer is consequently obliged to draw to some extent on the established conventions which satisfy this contract with the reader, but all conventions permit some originality of handling, as the opening to 'The Cut-Glass Bowl' demonstrates.

All narrative episodes tend to be conditioned in this way, as, on the one hand, specimens of a convention recognized and often enjoyed for its own sake by the reader, and on the other hand as instruments of an original authorial purpose. The frank enjoyment of narrative conventions is something we all know from our cinematic experiences, particularly of certain genres, like the Western. When the louvred half-doors of the saloon swing back and the man in the white hat and clean neckerchief enters, we expect at least a wild fist-fight involving all bystanders (including the town drunk) and culminating in the reduction to matchwood of the entire establishment (the combatants finger mild bruises and grin ruefully), or if not that, a quick shoot-out and the satisfactory demise of the unshaven villain in the black hat and sweaty brown shirt. We expect the crooked lawyer to wear a dove-grey double-breasted waistcoat and madam at the saloon, who sings and has a good heart and will die in White Hat's arms, to have swept-up hair, a brazen *décolleté*, black net stockings and a frilly garter. These are all ingredients in the customary rhetoric of a type of narrative. They can be naively employed, or they can be used with a difference. They can even be mocked. There are Westerns in which conventions are handled with great originality and a serious questioning of the assumptions that underlie them. The classic *High Noon*, for example, turns on a typical piece of Western narrative rhetoric: the episode in which the criminal returns to take his revenge on the lawman who has jailed him. In popular convention, loyal townspeople, strong in civic virtue, would rally to the support of the fearless, foeless, faultless sheriff. 'I say we run them varmints out of town!' somebody would have cried. 'I say we put 'em right back on that train.' But in the film the townsfolk are cynics, self-seekers or poltroons, and the sheriff, who is brave but not fearless, discovers that he is surrounded by people who do not wish him well. The implications of the conventional episode are subverted; nevertheless it remains a conventional episode, an option in the narrative rhetoric of the Western.

Literature at all times, art-literature as well as folk-literature, has structural rhetorics of this kind. Medieval narrative is, like the Western film, a complex of conventions that can be naively paraded or explored with great sophistication. There is the framing device of the dream, which allows the narrator to give free rein to allegory and fantasy; dreamers owe no debt to probability, and can tell the truthful lies of art without incurring an ecclesiastical frown. There all kinds of optional episode: descriptions of the warrior, his arms, his good steed; descriptions of the lady he serves, and his first sight of her; descriptions of castles and forests; catalogues of heroes, horses, swords, trees, flowers; descriptions of the *locus amoenus*, the good place, and the bad place, the *locus malus*; apostrophes and complaints of various kinds; tributes to the chastening and refining power of love; meditations on woman as temptress and saint; accusations; curses; debates on moral and theological issues. Some of these constituents recur, in transmuted forms, in later literature, but as every age has a different social constituency and a different climate of attitudes and suppositions, so the episodic rhetoric of narrative gradually changes and accommodates new or modified elements. One of the recurrent options of Victorian and early-twentieth-century fiction, for example, is the description of a meal – not a royal feast or a civic banquet, but the domestic meal that expresses the bonds of family, the ties of friendship, the civilities and convivialities of a period when to share a good table was one of the principal forms of entertainment.

Here is the account of what is possibly the best-remembered meal in Victorian literature – Dickens's description, in *A Christmas Carol*, of Christmas dinner in the Cratchit household. The wonder of the feast is a goose:

> There never was such a goose. Bob said he didn't believe there ever was such a goose cooked. Its tenderness and flavour, size and cheapness, were the themes of universal admiration. Eked out by apple-sauce and mashed potatoes, it was a sufficient dinner for the whole family; indeed, as Mrs Cratchit said with great delight (surveying one small atom of a bone upon the dish), they hadn't ate

it all at last! Yet every one had had enough, and the youngest Cratchits in particular, were steeped in sage and onion to the eyebrows! But now, the plates being changed by Miss Belinda, Mrs. Cratchit left the room alone – too nervous to bear witnesses – to take the pudding up and bring it in.

Suppose it should not be done enough! Suppose it should break in turning out! Suppose somebody should have got over the wall of the back-yard and stolen it, while they were merry with the goose – a supposition at which the two young Cratchits became livid! All sorts of horrors were supposed.

Hallo! A great deal of steam! The pudding was out of the copper. A smell like a washing-day! That was the cloth. A smell like an eating-house and a pastrycook's next door to each other, with a laundress's next door to that! That was the pudding! In half a minute Mrs Cratchit entered – flushed, but smiling proudly – with the pudding, like a speckled cannon-ball, so hard and firm, blazing in half of half-a-quartern of ignited brandy, and bedight with Christmas holly stuck into the top.

Oh, what a wonderful pudding! Bob Cratchit said, and calmly too, that he regarded it as the greatest success achieved by Mrs Cratchit since their marriage. Mrs Cratchit said that now the weight was off her mind, she would confess she had had her doubts about the quantity of flour. Everybody had something to say about it, but nobody said or thought it was at all a small pudding for a large family. It would have been flat heresy to do so. Any Cratchit would have blushed to hint at such a thing.

At last the dinner was all done, the cloth was cleared, the hearth swept, and the fire made up. The compound in the jug being tasted, and considered perfect, apples and oranges were put upon the table, and a shovel-full of chestnuts on the fire. Then all the Cratchit family drew round the hearth, in what Bob Cratchit called a circle, meaning half a one; and at Bob Cratchit's elbow stood the family display of glass. Two tumblers, and a custard-cup without a handle.

These held the hot stuff from the jug, however, as well as golden goblets would have done; and Bob served it out with beaming looks, while the chestnuts on the fire sputtered and cracked noisily. Then Bob proposed:

'A merry Christmas to us all, my dears. God bless us!

Which all the family re-echoed.

'God bless us every one!' said Tiny Tim, the last of all.

We are at liberty to read this celebrated passage, with its quotable conclusion, as an affectionate, humorous, benevolent account of a good Christmas tuck-in, enjoyed by a poor, decent, loving family that deserves its hour of pleasure. It is certainly that; but this meal at the Cratchits,' (observed by the penitent Scrooge and his tutelary Spirit) is also in the nature of a sacrament of fellowship, and its imagery and incidental turns of phrase suggest, particularly towards the end, religious parallels. The Cratchit family in its half-circle round the hearth, where Bob officiates with hot punch in a custard cup, strikingly resemble communicants at some domestic altar-rail. The very name of Cratchit is used as though, *mutatis mutandis*, it might be the name of a sect: 'Everybody had something to say about it, nobody said or thought it was at all a small pudding for a large family. It would have been flat heresy to do so. Any Cratchit would have blushed to hint at such a thing.'

Too solemnly pursued, these quasi-religious semblances might seem far-fetched and even blasphemous, but Dickens circumvents his own essential seriousness with a stylistic play that offsets the affectionately realistic reporting of banal utterances ('Mrs Cratchit said now the weight was off her mind, she would confess she had had her doubts about the quantity of flour') with passages of theatrical demonstration, rhetorically figured:

> Suppose it should not be done enough!
> Suppose it should break in turning out!
> Suppose somebody should have got over the wall of the back-yard
>   and stolen it, while they were merry with the goose . . .

> A great deal of steam!
>   The pudding was out of the copper.
> A smell like a washing-day!
>   That was the cloth.
> A smell like an eating-house and a pastrycook's next door to each
>   other, with a laundress's next door to that!
>   That was the pudding.

Dickens amuses himself (and his readers) by fooling with the customary tidiness of rhetorical schemes. In the first of the passages cited above, he uses anaphora (repetition of the first word in successive constructions) and parison, but in the third sentence volubly overruns – shouts down, as it were – the parisonic limit requiring a construction of a length roughly equal to that of its predecessors (for example 'Suppose somebody should have stolen it!'). The second passage plays a similar game of comically frustrated figures. There is a neat dialogic match of 'That was the cloth' and 'That was the pudding', but the counter to 'A smell like a washing day' is the serial exuberance of 'A smell like an eating-house and a pastrycook's next door to each other, with a laundress's next door to that.' He assumes the posture of the orator, only to mock at the rhetorical habits of that posture; and his sense of the figurative as a ever-present potential in language is recurrently brought to terms with an even keener sense of what ordinary, intimate, banal, domestic talk is like. This stylistic admixture is precisely adapted to the description of Christmas dinner in a poor family, the Cratchits; it is a realistic feast, but it is also a ritual celebration of the cheerful power of a selfless love.

Another description of a meal – a rather long description, making up a substantial portion of the narrative – is found in James Joyce's story, 'The Dead'. It, too, begins with a goose:

> At the moment Aunt Kate came toddling out of the supper-room, almost wringing her hands in despair
>
> 'Where is Gabriel?' she cried. 'Where on earth is Gabriel? There's everyone waiting in there, stage to let, and nobody to carve the goose!'
>
> 'Here I am, Aunt Kate!' cried Gabriel, with sudden animation, 'ready to carve a flock of geese, if necessary.'
>
> A fat brown goose lay at one end of the table, and at the other end, on a bed of creased paper strewn with sprigs of parsley, lay a great ham, stripped of its outer skin and peppered over with crust crumbs, a neat paper frill round its shin, and beside this was a round of spiced beef. Between these rival ends, ran parallel lines of side-dishes: two little monsters of jelly, red and yellow; a shallow dish full of blocks of blancmange and red ham, a large green leaf-shaped dish with a stalk-shaped handle, on which lay bunches of purple raisins and peeled almonds, a companion dish on which lay a solid rectangle of Smyrna figs, a dish of custard topped with grated nutmeg, a small bowl full of chocolates and sweets wrapped in gold and silver papers and a glass vase in which stood some tall celery stalks. In the centre of the table there stood, as sentries to a fruit-stand which upheld a pyramid of oranges and American apples, two squat old-fashioned decanters of cut glass, one containing port and the other dark sherry. On the closed square piano a pudding in a huge yellow dish lay in waiting, and behind it were three squads of bottles of stout and ale and minerals drawn up according to the colours of their uniforms, the first two black, with brown and red labels, the third and smallest squad white, with transverse green sashes.
>
> Gabriel took his seat boldly at the head of the table and, having

looked to the edge of the carver, plunged his fork firmly into the goose. He felt quite at ease now, for he was an expert carver and liked nothing better than to find himself at the head of a well-laden table.

So begins the account of the supper-party at the Misses Morkan's annual dance. ('It was always a great affair. . . Everybody who knew them came to it. . . Never once had it fallen flat. . . For years and years it had gone off in splendid style, as long as anyone could remember.') The description of the well-laden supper table, almost Dickensian in its lyrically sensuous relish of good cheer, is one of the highlights of the story; and yet it is puzzling. Why is it there? Why does Joyce go to such lengths, and in such detail, almost meditating on his object, as a painter meditates on a still life? The story, after all, is not a simple description of a delightful musical evening and lavish hospitality. Most of it is concerned with persons, with little actions and exchanges, with things said and remembered, with the ordinariness that contains our human anguish. It is busy with small events, chattering along until the last page comes, with Gabriel's silent thoughts and the soundless fall of the snow. Why, then, this extraordinary interpolation, this narra-tive-halting page, this intricately motionless *nature morte*? Are we meant to stop asking pointless questions, and enjoy a nice piece of descriptive prose? Or docs the rhetoric have its reasons?

This passage has its place in a pattern of episodes commenting directly or obliquely on the central character, Gabriel Conroy, and also developing a major theme in the story, the sense of the past and of time passing. There is something very attractive about the silent orderliness of a well-prepared table before the casual onslaughts of appetite reduce it to a debris of dishes and left-overs. It is almost an emblem of urbanity and civilization – a perception which, indeed, informs Joyce's style. The display of food acquires an architecture of sorts – so that, for example, the jellies turned out of their moulds make 'little minsters', cathedral-like forms, and the fruit-stand upholds a 'pyramid' of oranges. This silent comestible city has its silent comestible (and potable) citizenry, thanks to a simple fact of language: that the verbs *lie* and *stand* imply both the non-animate and the animate. The goose and the ham, which 'lie' on the table, are clearly non-animates (though the ham has 'a paper frill *round its shin*'), as are the tall celery stalks (but then again, why not 'long' celery stalks?) which 'stand' in a glass vase. But when we come to the decanters and the bottles of ale and stout, animate subjects are clearly indicated: these are sentries on duty, squads of soldiers on parade. And *lie*, too, has in the end connotations of the animate, as the 'pudding on the huge yellow dish' is said to 'lie in waiting'; not to lie at hand, or lie ready, but to lie in waiting, in attendance, like some strange new species of courtier. It cannot be an accident that the whole description of the supper-table tends to suggest a prospect of a wholly agreeable, uncontradictable, uncontradicted social order. This, the onlooker thinks, is exactly how things should be in a good place in a good world. This, indeed, is traditionally how things should be; this is what it was like in the good old days.

And this is exactly how Gabriel thinks they should be. The supper-table's implication of order, authority, respect for traditional things in their traditional place, soothes him after some disturbing exchanges, almost a quarrel, with his Irish nationalist friend, Miss Ivors. Gabriel does not like to be unsettled, or his way of life to be questioned. His equanimity is only restored when he sits down, at the head of the table, in the role of paterfamilias, to carve the goose. Then, we are told, 'he felt quite at ease', and 'liked nothing better than to find himself at the head of a well-laden table'. His precarious feelings of self-respect and self-assurance are restored, as people defer to him in this familiar role. But our acceptance of that restoration of confidence really depends on the long preceding description of the 'well-laden table'. It is the correlate of the traditional urbanity, the bourgeois sense of well-being and self-evident status, that Gabriel really admires; and it is incidentally one of the partition-walls of the story, one of the passages that mark out the divisions of the interior structure.

WHERE THE AUTHOR STANDS

One of the difficulties (paradoxically, therefore, one of the pleasures) of reading a story like 'The Dead' is to know just where the author stands; how he would like us to interpret these events, what attitudes he would encourage us to take, what, indeed, his own attitude is. As we seek to come to terms with the rhetoric of narrative, the authorial stance is a factor we may have to take into account. Some authors define their role for the benefit if not always the enlightenment of their readers. Chaucer pretends to

have got the story of *Troilus and Criseyde* from an author called
Lollius – a pretence which absolves him from moral responsibility
for the narrative – and at the end of the story piously deplores the
damnable passions of his misguided hero. In *Vanity Fair*, Thack-
eray repeatedly addresses the reader with observations upon the
characters and the action, and compares himself with a puppet-
master managing a theatre of make-believe. John Fowles, in his
novel *The French Lieutenant's Woman*, also intervenes repeatedly
and in a rather more complicated way, with comments not only on
character and action, but also on the techniques and options of
story-telling. Such cases are deceptive, because while the author
puts up a platform, we can never be quite sure where he stands;
indeed we may fairly guess that the posture of detachment is
insincere. It is often harder for the reader to accommodate a
designedly visible author than it is to read stories from which the
sense of an author as external controller of the tale has been
virtually eliminated. (In William Faulkner's *As I Lay Dying*, for
example, there is no intrusive author, and therefore no authorial
stance to take into account; the characters tell the story.)

In nineteenth-century fiction particularly, there are numerous
instances of narrative governed not only by the 'visible author',
but also by the intrusions of a recognizable authorial style. A note
is struck, a manner established, and whenever the note or the
manner recur, the reader senses the author's presence, which,
however, may be 'visibly' asserted when the writer insists on
directly controlling responses to the narrative. There is a familiar
piece of fiction that opens thus:

> No one who had ever seen Catherine Morland in her infancy, would
> have supposed her born to be an heroine. Her situation in life, the
> character of her father and mother, her own person and disposi-
> tion, were all equally against her. Her father was a clergyman,
> without being neglected, or poor, and a very respectable man,
> though his name was Richard – and he had never been handsome.
> He had a considerable independence, besides two good livings –
> and he was not in the least addicted to locking up his daughters. Her
> mother was a woman of useful plain sense, with a good temper, and
> what is more remarkable, with a good constitution. She had three
> sons before Catherine was born, and instead of dying in bringing
> the latter into the world, as any body might expect, she still lived on
> – lived to have six children more – to see them growing up around
> her, and to enjoy excellent health herself. A family of ten children
> will always be called a fine family, where there are heads and arms

and legs enough for the number; but the Morlands had little other right to the word, for they were in general very plain, and Catherine, for many years of her life, as plain as any. She had a thin awkward figure, a sallow skin without colour, dark lank hair, and strong features – so much for her person – and not less unpropitious for heroism seemed her mind.

Within three sentences, Jane Austen (for of course this is the beginning of her *Northanger Abbey*) is teasing her readers outrageously with a humour that a later generation would have called 'scatty' and a later one still 'zany'. The sign of scattiness is the gifted irrelevance and the inspired *non sequitur*, the happy leap from the odd juxtaposition to the false conclusion: 'Her father was a clergyman, without being neglected, or poor, and a very respectable man, though his name was Richard – and he had never been handsome.' In this playful *concordia discors* there is a purpose which the reader is not long in guessing; Jane Austen is clearly mocking the conventions of the kind of popular fiction – the circulating library fiction of her time – in which heroines are beautiful and virtuous, parents penurious, and mothers wont to die wanly in childbirth. The detached, whimsical, mocking style, this *knowing* manner of the novelist addressing novel-readers, persists throughout the first chapter, so that with the advent of the story proper in the second chapter, the reader is prepared to adopt Jane Austen's own stance, and read the book as a fiction affectionately smiling at fictions, a novel about Catherine Morland as heroine of a novel. And indeed, at the end of the fifth chapter, the author intrudes on the action – by now developing nicely – with a declaration of policy, a proclamation defending the status of fiction and justifying, as educative of the imagination and taste, the practice of reading novels:

> Yes, novels – for I will not adopt that ungenerous and impolitic custom so common with novel writers, of degrading by their contemptuous censure the very performances, to the number of which they are themselves adding – joining with their greatest enemies in bestowing the harshest epithets on such works, and scarcely ever permitting them to be read by their own heroine, who, if she accidentally take up a novel, is sure to turn over its insipid pages with disgust. Alas! if the heroine of one novel be not patronized by the heroine of another, from whom can she expect protection and regard? I cannot approve of it. Let us leave it to the Reviewers to abuse such effusions of fancy at their leisure, and over

every new novel to talk in threadbare strains of the trash with which
the press now groans. Let us not desert one another; we are an
injured body. Although our productions have afforded more
extensive and unaffected pleasure than those of any other literary
corporation in the world, no species of composition has been so
much decried. From pride, ignorance, or fashion, our foes are
almost as many as our readers. And while the abilities of the nine-
hundredth abridger of the History of England, or of the man who
collects and publishes in a volume some dozen lines of Milton, Pope,
and Prior, with a paper from the Spectator, and a chapter from
Sterne, are eulogized by a thousand pens – there seems almost a
general wish of decrying the capacity and undervaluing the labour
of the novelist, and of slighting the performances which have only
genius, wit, and taste to recommend them. 'I am no novel reader – I
seldom look into novels – Do not imagine that *I* often read novels –
It is really very well for a novel.' – Such is the common cant. – 'And
what are you reading, Miss – ?' 'Oh! it is only a novel!' replies the
young lady, while she lays down her book with affected indiffer-
ence, or momentary shame. – 'It is only Cecilia, or Camilla, or
Belinda;' or, in short, only some work in which the greatest powers
of the mind are displayed, in which the most thorough knowledge
of human nature, the happiest delineation of its varieties, the
liveliest effusions of wit and humour are conveyed to the world in
the best chosen language. Now, had the same young lady been
engaged with a volume of the Spectator, instead of such a work,
how proudly would she have produced the book, and told its name;
though the chances must be against her being occupied with any
part of that voluminous publication, of which either the matter or
manner would not disgust a young person of taste: the substance of
its papers so often consisting in the statement of improbable
circumstances, unnatural characters, and topics of conversation,
which no longer concern any one living; and their language, too,
frequently so coarse as to give no very favourable idea of the age
that could endure it.

Now this quite lengthy digressive passage, in which Jane Austen
begins by cajoling and ends in haranguing her readers, is
structurally necessary because it has to be established that Catherine and her bosom friend Isabella are united by a strong interest in
dances, millinery and spine-tingling novels. Indeed we find them
at the beginning of the next chapter almost squealing with
anticipatory rapture over the titles of terrors in store: Castle of
Wolfenbach, Clermont, Mysterious Warnings, Necromancer of
the Black Forest, Midnight Bell, Orphan of the Rhine, and Horrid

Mysteries. ('Yes', says Catherine, 'but are they all horrid, are you sure they are all horrid?') In immediate juxtaposition with this, the author's apology for her profession seems coloured with the irony so characteristic of Jane Austen, the amiable shrewdness of one always too wise to take herself and the world too seriously. But such an impression cannot really survive a rereading of this passionate excursus at the end of the fifth chapter. There comes a point, about half-way through her declamation, perhaps at the words 'Let us not desert one another . . .', when we must begin to suspect that our author is in solemn earnest; when it appears that she is saying to us, with some force, 'Very well, let us have a little parodic fun, but let us not have any nonsense about the novel being a shamefully inferior species of literature.' It adds to the force of her address that, for the first time in the book, she speaks in the first person: '*I* will not adopt . . .' Whether her outburst is a transient fit of pique, or the expression of a long-harboured sense of grievance, or a realization that the story on which she has embarked cannot be all parodic mockery, but will touch on serious questions of conduct and relationship; for whatever reason Jane Austen may have written this passage, it signals a change of stance. It warns us that while the mockery of Catherine-as-heroine may well continue, the author reserves her right to be interested in Catherine-as-person; in fact, to write a novel about Catherine which will not involve 'improbable circumstances' or matters 'which no longer concern any one living'.

By the time the closing pages of the book are reached, the author has persuaded us, and herself, to look at her characters as real people in a real world. The parodic mockery of the 'heroine' and her perils has given place to expressions of satisfaction on the occasion of Catherine's marriage to Henry Tilney, and Eleanor Tilney's to 'the man of her choice'. The distance between author and characters no longer exists; she writes of them as personal acquaintances, and invites the reader to think of the conclusion of the story as a satisfactory outcome to the social season:

> The marriage of Eleanor Tilney, her removal from all the evils of such a home as Northanger had been made by Henry's banishment, to the home of her choice, and the man of her choice, is an event which I expect to give general satisfaction among all her acquaintance. My own joy on the occasion is very sincere. I know no one more entitled, by unpretending merit, or better prepared by habitual suffering, to receive and enjoy felicity. Her partiality for

this gentleman was not of recent origin; and he had long been withheld only by inferiority of situation from addressing her. His unexpected accession to title and fortune had removed all his difficulties, and never had the General loved his daughter so well in all her hours of companionship, utility, and patient endurance, as when he first hailed her 'Your Ladyship!'

At the close, it is social comedy (with this reminder of General Tilney's inveterate snobbery) that has displaced the literary spoof of the opening. The writer, going without concealment about the business of settling her creatures into comfortable prospects, declares in the last sentence that hers has been a social and moral purpose, though quite what the moral is, the reader must decide: 'I leave it to be settled by whomsoever it may concern', she says, 'whether the tendency of this work be altogether to recommend parental tyranny, or reward filial disobedience.' Thus, even at the end, when all is made plain and we seem to know what our position should be, the subtlety of her rhetoric, its capacity for evading what might have been the issue, is such that we can never be wholly sure where this author stands.

7

The Humours of Rhetoric

'But Kevin,' says Sharon, 'I just don't, you know, know where I stand with you, do I? You know? I mean, you know, do you love me, or what?' 'Sure I love you, doll,' says Kevin, who knows that in moments of tenderness you call your chick 'doll', even in Liverpool. 'You're aces with me, kid.' 'Why do you love me, Kevin?' asks Sharon, pushing her luck just a little. 'Why does anyone love anyone?' muses Kevin, and a look of profound philosophical anxiety ravages his homely features. 'I mean,' says Sharon, 'it's not just, you know, for my *body*, is it?' 'Doll, you got a great body,' says Kevin. 'But is that why you love me?' says Sharon. 'Don't you love anything else about me?' 'Oh sure,' says Kevin. It is beginning to dawn on him that some unusual effort of articulation is required. 'You're kind, know what I mean? I mean, you know, you're a kind person. And very clean in your habits. I like that.' 'But will you always love me?' begs Sharon. And now, if Kev has anything at all about him, if there is one drop of amorous blood in his veins, one spark of gallantry in his skull, he will surely leap to his feet and declaim:

> Will I always love you? Will I always love you?
> Until Hell freezes over, dear, I will love you,
> Until fish whistle in the trees, my darling, I will love you,
> Until orchids grow on the municipal rubbish tip, I will love you,
> Until the Bank of England hands out free samples, I will love you,
> Until Liverpool Football Club sinks into the Fourth Division, I will
>   most dearly love you,
> Until the Conservative Party annual conference in plenary session
>   rises to a rousing rendition of the *Internationale*, my doll,
>   my chickadee, my, like, you know, pusscat, you will be mine.

That should do the trick quite as well as a chorus or 'You'll Never Walk Alone'. If Sharon is not utterly mollified and bowled over, she may at least laugh, because rhetoric turns up in some funny places and tickles some funny bones. It has its humours, relished in general by those with a verbal gift of hamming it up and camping it up, and studied in particular by writers with a disposition to make sophisticated fun of literary conventions.

Rhetoric in its humour is learned, elaborate, sly, often delightfully subtle; but its first requirement is a happy flouting of the rules of measure and decorum that sober practice imposes. It willingly assumes what Puttenham calls 'the vice of surplusage'. It does nothing by halves, or discreetly; at refinement's tea-table, where cucumber sandwiches and a Victoria sponge should elegantly suffice, it offers great slabs of figgy pudding with peanut butter to follow. Its excesses are matched only by its impertinences. It wears the right suit on the wrong occasion; it takes its harp to the harmonica players' party; it stands up at funerals and welcomes everyone to the Senior Citizens' Keep Fit Classes. There are people who cannot stomach it. But there are also many who delight in it, because, without ever feeling got at, they see what the rhetorician is getting at. In rhetorical humour, as in all other aspects of rhetoric, there is a compact, a presuppositional understanding, between the beguiler and the beguiled.

Often it is a quite learned compact. You cannot, as a writer, make rhetorical sport of a convention or a style unless you are very well acquainted with it; and correspondingly, you cannot, as a reader, wholly appreciate the sport if you have a poor knowledge of literary language and conventions. Writers and readers make up a literary club, and the jokes are for the initiated who have passed the entrance test. This might describe the conditions of parody, and, indeed, the rhetorician's humour is basically parodic. There are three discernible kinds. There is parody in the most usual sense, as the mocking imitation of a particular work or a well-known style; there is a travesty of general rhetoric, a sort of 'rhetoricizing' not derived from or aimed at any particular work (for an example, see above, in the paragraph beginning 'Rhetoric in its humour is learned . . .' and ending '. . . the beguiler and the beguiled'.); and there is a pastiche, a 'pasting up' of diverse styles, when humorous effects are derived from juxtapositions of the grand and the vulgar, the sublime and the pedestrian, or from the application of a high style to a lowly theme. These 'humours' of rhetoric often co-exist, as variant aspects of one rhetorical act. In the opening paragraph of this chapter, for example, there is some parody, of the kind of romantic rhetoric exemplified by Burns's 'O My Luve is Like a Red, Red Rose' ('And I will luve thee still, my dear, / Till a' the seas gang dry'); there is a travesty of a rhetorical device, in the increasing absurdity and long-windedness of some of the *untils*; and there is pastiche in the marked juxtaposition of 'low' and 'high' styles, and in the attribution of a 'high' style to a 'low' character (or as an eighteenth-century writer might have put it, 'a person of the meaner sort'). Rhetoric may thus take different, convergent, routes to humour. Its habits of mockery are in some ways unchanging, in others mutable, inasmuch as rhetoric, like other institutions, addresses itself to transient fashions and particular kinds of cultural phenomenon. To see what has changed in the last six hundred years, and to understand that some things never change, we must take a few chronological soundings.

FIRST SOUNDING: THE FOURTEENTH CENTURY

To say that Chaucer used rhetoric would be a little like saying that Billy the Kid used a gun. We may say that he used it a lot. He also laughed at it a lot (whereas Billy the Kid probably regarded his own propensities with some seriousness). One of his most engaging comic characters, the Eagle in *The House of Fame*, is a high-flying, fast-talking, super-pedantic bird of ingenious brain, the very model of a donnish rhetorician. In the *Tale of Sir Thopas*, with its 'drasty ryming' and its laborious trudge through the narratological conventions of medieval romance, Chaucer – the teller of the tale – cheerfully offers himself as victim of his own satire. His finest essay in parodic rhetoric, however, is undoubtedly *The Nun's Priest's Tale*, that impishly inspired marital comedy, a ludicrously learned reworking of the fable of the Cock and the Fox, and a story which ends, like all good myths, with a pointer to the moral, or *anagogical* interpretation (see p. 90):

> Lo, swich it is for to be reccheless
> And necligent, and truste on flaterye.
>   But ye that holden this tale a folye,
> As of a fox, or of a cok and hen,
> Taketh the moralite, goode men.
> For seint Paul seith that al that writen is,
> To oure doctrine it is ywrite, ywis;
> Taketh the fruit, and lat the chaf be stille.

(See, now, what it means to be careless and negligent and put your trust in flattery. But all you who think that this is just a stupid tale about a fox or about a cock and hen – look for the moral, my friends. For St Paul says that everything that is written is written for our instruction; so take the fruit and forget about the chaff.)

This is the bookish conclusion of a bookish narrator, who leads his hearers a merry dance through medieval scholarship, including medicine and the theory of the humours, dream lore, classical and modern examples of supernatural monitions, incidental allusions to astrology, the doctrine of predestination, the singing of mermaids and other things beside. And here is that part of the tale in which the cock, Chauntecleer, succumbs to the flattery of Russell the fox and tries to show how well he can sing:

This Chauntecleer stood hye upon his toos,
Strecchynge his nekke, and heeld his eyen cloos,
And gan to crowe loude for the nones.
And daun Russell the fox stirte up atones,
And by the gargat hente Chauntecleer,
And on his bak toward the wode hym beer,
For yet ne was ther no man that hym sewed.

(Chauntecleer stood on tip-toe, stretching out his neck and closing his eyes, and started to crow as loud as he could. And straight away Mr Russell the fox jumped up and grabbed Chauntecleer by the throat, and carried him off on his back towards the wood, for as yet there was no pursuit.)

One might expect to hear about that 'pursuit', and hear about it immediately; but thirty-seven lines are to elapse before the account of the chase begins. Seventeen of those intervening lines are devoted to this:

O destinee, that mayst nat been eschewed!
Allas, that Chauntecleer fleigh fro the bemes!
Allas, his wyf ne roghte nat of dremes!
And on a Friday fil al this meschaunce.
O Venus, that art goddesse of plesaunce,
Syn that thy servant was this Chauntecleer,
And in thy servyce dide al his poweer,
Moore for delit than world to multiplye,
Why woldestow suffre hym on thy day to dye?
O Gaufred, deere maister soverayn,
That whan thy worthy kyng Richard was slayn

With shot, compleynedest his deeth so soore,
Why ne hadde I now thy sentence and thy loore,
The Friday for to chide, as diden ye?
Thanne wolde I shewe yow how that I koude pleyne
For Chauntecleres drede and for his peyne.

(O destiny, that may not be avoided! Alas, that Chauntecleer flew
down from the beams! Alas, that his wife thought dreams unimportant! And all this misfortune came on a Friday. O Venus, goddess of
pleasure, since this Chauntecleer was your servant and exerted
himself to the utmost in your service – more for the delight than for
the multiplication of the species – why were you willing to let him
die on *your* day? O Geoffrey, dear unsurpassable master, who made
such bitter lamentation for your good King Richard when he was
killed, why couldn't I have your wit and learning, to denounce
Friday as you did? Then I would show you how I could bewail
Chauntecleer's fear and suffering.)

What is going on here may remind opera-lovers of those moments
when the stage action is halted while the singers ask themselves,
and each other, and the *numi* and the *cieli*, about the turmoil in
their minds, about the beating of their hearts, about the stupefac-
tion in their souls, about scarce knowing what to do, scarce finding
words to say. They continue thus, scarce finding words to say, for
ten minutes, until swords are drawn or a chorus of happy peasants
invades the stage. Medieval narrative also had conventional 'arias',
or set pieces, of various kinds. The kind Chaucer is laughing at in
this passage from *The Nun's Priest's Tale* is the *lamentatio*, or
comploratio, or 'complaint'; which might be about the death of a
hero, or the loss of a lover, or the loneliness of exile, or, in general,
the blind injustices of fickle fortune. A complaint could draw
stylistically on various devices: the apostrophe of supernatural
powers ('Oh, ye gods!'), reproaching them for inattention or
neglect of a deserving case ('Where were you when my Tommy
crossed the road?'); the accusation or commination of an accursed
object ('Vile omnibus! Depraved banana skin!'); the invocation of
learned authority ('Ah, use the crossing, says the Highway Code');
the passage of self-reproach ('Why did I send him for a dozen
eggs?'); the disconsolate conclusion ('Now all the eggs are broken!
What a shame!')

  Elements of this kind are present in the Nun's Priest's lamentation which has three apostrophic levels – the address to destiny,
the complaint to Venus, and the appeal to 'Gaufred' – meaning

Geoffrey de Vinsauf, author of the *Poetria Nova*, a manual of poetics published a decade after the death, in 1199, of Richard I. The first apostrophe, to Destiny, is a cry of 'I told you so', the Nun's Priest being a firm believer in predestination. Even the day was predestined – a Friday. This brings on the second apostrophe, to Venus, whose day (*dies Veneris, vendredi*) Friday is. Now the tone is accusatory – 'Where were you? Why did you let this happen to your devoted servant, and on that day of all days?' The humour of having a Christian priest make theological representations to a pagan goddess is compounded by the additional joke of having him earnestly commend Chauntecleer's sexual activities as 'more for the delight than for the multiplication of the species'. The reproach to Venus for her lamentable absence on her very own day brings in Geoffrey de Vinsauf, and his *lamentatio* for Richard I, who received his fatal wound on a Friday:

> O Veneris lacrimosa dies! O sidus amarum!
> Illa dies tua nox fuit et Venus illa venenum.

> (O piteous day of Venus! O bitter constellation! That day was thy night, that Venus thy bane.)

(There is a pun, of the type 'person'/'poison', on 'Venus'/ 'venenum'; the pun involves meaning as well as sound, since *venenum* in Latin can mean both 'poison' and 'love-potion'.)

This is indeed learned stuff – almost grotesquely learned, if we consider that the priest's story is nothing more ambitious than a good old folk-tale. But he has not done with his lament. Before the peasants can rush on to the stage, we must have another twenty lines of declamatory rhetoric:

> Certes, swich cry ne lamentacion,
> Was nevere of ladyes maad whan Ylion
> Was wonne, and Pirrus with his streite swerd,
> Whan he hadde hent kyng Priam by the berd,
> And slayn hym, as seith us *Eneydos*,
> As maden alle the hennes in the clos,
> Whan they had seyn of Chauntecleer the sighte.
> But sovereynly dame Pertelote shrighte
> Ful louder than dide Hasdrubales wyf,
> Whan that hir housbonde hadde lost his lyf,
> And that the Romayns hadde brend Cartage.
> She was so ful of torment and of rage

That wilfully into the fyr she sterte,
And brende hirselven with a stedefaste herte.
   O woful hennes, right so criden ye,
As, whan that Nero brende the citee
Of Rome, cryden senatoures wyves
For that hir husbondes losten alle hir lyves –
Withouten gilt this Nero hath hem slayn.
Now wole I turne to my tale agayn.

(Indeed, when Troy was won, the ladies never made such outcry
and lament – after Pyrrhus, with drawn sword, had seized King
Priam by the beard and slain him, as the *Aeneid* tells us – as did all
the hens in the yard when they had seen what was happening to
Chauntecleer. But most of all, Dame Pertelote shrieked, much
louder than Hasdrubal's wife did when her husband lost his life and
the Romans had burned Carthage. She [Hasdrubal's wife] was so
consumed by torment and rage that she leaped willingly into the
fire and with a resolute heart burned herself to death. O, woeful
hens, you cried out just as the wives of senators cried when Nero
burned the city and their husbands lost their lives. That Nero killed
them, guiltless though they were. But now – back to my tale.)

Our learned narrator now makes the standard move of alluding to
appropriate examples, or paradigms (*exempla*, *paradigmata*) of
distressed females on distressful occasions. What is also standard is
the negative comparison, the rhetorician's way of saying 'you
never saw the like of it': the great occasion is made incomparable
by comparisons. The occasion here is the invasion of a cottage
garden, but the comparisons tell of the fall of cities; thus
hyperbolically does the narrator dwell on his theme until, having
made up his tidy threesome of examples, he briskly announces
'But now – back to my tale.'

What follows is indeed a brisk recital, a hectic account of the
chase, as the cottagers, shouting 'Out! harrow! and weylaway! Ha!
ha! the fox!' pursue the delinquent with much noise and bustle. We
are in fact plunged into another style appropriate to a different
kind of stock element in narrative. (The chase of the fox was a
common theme in medieval popular literature and art; much as
the car-chase is a standard ingredient in some modern films.)
Surely nothing could be more marked than the transition, at an
abrupt signal ('back to my tale'), from the learned style of the
lamentation and the *paradigmata* to the bucolic vigour of this:

Ran Colle our dogge, and Talbot and Gerlonde,
And Malkyn, wyth a dystaf in hir hand;
Ran cow and calf, and eek the verray hogges,
So fered for the berkyng of the dogges
And shoutyng of the men and wommen eke,
They ronne so hem thought hir herte breeke.
They yolleden as feendes doon in helle;
The dokes cryden as men wolde hem quelle;
The gees for feere flowen over the trees;
Out of the hyve cam the swarm of bees.

Of bras they broghten bemes, and of box,
Of horn, of boon, in which they blewe and powped,
And therwithal they skriked and they howped.
It seemed as that hevene sholde falle.

(Away they ran, the dogs Coll and Talbot and Garland, and Molly
with a distaff in her hand – the cow ran, the calf ran, the very hogs
ran, so frightened by the barking of the dogs and also by the
shouting of the men and women, they ran till they thought their
hearts would burst. They yelled like fiends in hell. The ducks
squawked as though someone was going to kill them. The geese
took fright and flew away over the trees. The bees came out of the
hives. . . . They brought trumpets made of brass, and of boxwood,
of horn, of bone, in which they blew and tooted, and all the while
they shrieked and whooped. It seemed as if the sky would fall in.)

Although this passage of verse is ruled by its own not-so-homely figurative rhetoric – the schemes of anaphora, parison, asyndeton
and polysyndeton all get a peep-in here – the effect, by comparison with the preceding extracts, is one of rollicking popular
recital. One symptom of the shift in style is the observable change
in sentence-length and structure. The verse-sentences of the
preceding passages, particularly of the *paradigmata*, tend towards
length and complex subordination; for instance, the example of
the ladies of Troy and 'Pirrus with his streite swerde' is a single
sentence running through seven lines of verse and containing
several embedded subordinate clauses. By contrast, the sentences
in the 'chase' extract are simple and short, clauses are juxtaposed
asyndetically or simply co-ordinated, and there is not such a great
use of subordination. This syntactic shift is accompanied by
obvious differences in the character of the vocabulary. The
lexicon of the complaint passages is learned, Frenchified, bookish,

tending to express concepts and abstractions: 'destinee', 'eschewed', 'plesaunce', 'servyce', 'multiplye', 'soverayn', 'sovereynly', '(com)pleyne', 'lamentacion', 'torment', 'senatoures'. When the chase begins, we find, by contrast, a profusion of everyday. Saxon, concrete terms: 'dogge', 'cow', 'calf', 'hogges', 'dokes', 'gees', 'bees', 'bras', 'box', 'horn', 'boon', 'ran', 'yolleden', 'powped', 'shriked', 'howped'. In general tendency this vocabulary is monosyllabic, and thus productive of a distinctive verse-rhythm. Compare this:

> And in thy service did al his poweer
> Moore for delit than world to multiplye

with this:

> Of bras they broghten bemes, and of box,
> Of horn, of boon, in whiche they blewe and powped

The rhetorical texture has changed, in a way that illustrates the primary sense of *pastiche*. Contrasting styles are brought together in a collage which is funny in its total effect, but which also derives humour from the highlighting of each style in juxtaposition with its neighbour. The 'lamentation' episode stands out against the contrasting colour of the 'chase' narrative, and vice versa.

Anyone studying *The Nun's Priest's Tale* must be struck with the reflection that this is a learned joke looking for a learned audience. The modern reader is obliged to work rather solemnly at the text, boning up on Geoffrey de Vinsauf, dream-lore, the pattern and conventions of the medieval sermon and so on. But Chaucer among his contemporaries surely had his eye on people who would know their literary stuff without benefit of the scholiast; just as the present-day film-maker relies on the supposition that his audience will be well enough versed in the culture of the film to recognize, of their own accord, a typical episode, a device, a parodic allusion. Chaucer's joke is to have a highly educated priest (and one with enough sap in him to be a little sexy) tell an old knockabout tale with an old knockabout moral, but tell it in just the way a learned yet lively ecclesiast might be expected to tell it, as a fable dressed up in a romance garbed in a homily. This is a very good joke, but we cannot begin to understand it without appreciating a fact of literary humour in general and rhetorical humour in particular: that it asks for a quite a lot of knowledge, and that the bond between the humorist and his audience is only as durable as the information they share.

SECOND SOUNDING: THE SIXTEENTH CENTURY

With that we pass to Shakespeare, one of whose characters (the shepherd Corin, in *As You Like It*) observes that 'he that hath no wit by nature nor art may complain of a good breeding, or comes of a very dull kindred' – meaning that if people are blockheads it is either because it runs in the family or because they are of noble blood and never had to go to school. Shakespeare had his 'wit', his mental gifts, both by nature and by art, having attended a grammar school in Stratford-upon-Avon, where no doubt the curriculum included the elements of rhetoric.[1] He has always been praised, and rightly so, for his insight into human nature, and for his power, particularly in the great tragedies, to make his characters speak in language which, however elevated, always rings true to human feelings and responses, and to the individuality of the speaker. It is possible, though, that in praising what seems to us to be his supreme gift, the expression of 'nature', we undervalue the 'art' in his dramas, the rhetorical mastery that informs some of the great scenes and speeches in his histories and Roman plays and that creates passages of stylish humour in the comedies, where characters are often seen in rhetorical power-manoeuvres, or where the play of language allows the dramatist to proceed entertainingly through some necessary business of the plot. (Much of the fifth act of *As You Like It*, for example, consists of the patter, the patterning, the repeated tit-for-tat of rhetorical fun and games.)

One of the best, and probably the best known, of Shakespeare's jokes at rhetoric's expense is a passage in the first part of *King Henry the Fourth* (Act II, Scene iv), in which Prince Henry and Falstaff humorously rehearse what the Prince will say when he attends court and is required by the King to answer for his irregular conduct. Falstaff at first plays the part of the King (overplaying outrageously, to the tearful amusement of the Hostess), and begins with a wickedly accurate parody of the Euphuistic rhetoric mentioned here in our previous chapter (see p 136). The first sentence might have been written by Lyly himself:

Falstaff:	Harry, I do not only marvel where thou spendest thy time, but also how thou art accompanied: for though the camomile, the more it is trodden on, the faster it grows, yet youth, the more it is wasted, the sooner it wears. That thou art my son, I have partly thy mother's word, partly my own opinion; but chiefly a villainous trick of thine eye, and a foolish hanging of the nether lip, that doth warrant me. If, then, thou be son to me, here lies the point; – why, being son to me, art thou so pointed at? Shall the blessed sun of heaven prove a micher, and eat blackberries? a question not to be ask'd. Shall the son of England prove a thief, and take purses? a question to be ask'd. There is a thing, Harry, which thou hast often heard of, and it is known to many in our land by the name of pitch: this pitch, as ancient writers report, doth defile; so doth the company thou keepest; for, Harry, now I do not speak to thee in drink, but in tears; not in pleasure, but in passion; not in words only, but in woes also: – and yet there is a virtuous man whom I have often noted in thy company, but I know not his name.
Prince Henry:	What manner of man, an it like your majesty?
Falstaff:	A goodly portly man, i'faith, and a corpulent; of a cheerful look, a pleasing eye, and a most noble carriage; and, as I think, his age is some fifty, or, by'r lady, inclining to three-score; and now I remember me, his name is Falstaff: if that man should be lewdly given, he deceiveth me; for, Harry, I see virtue in his looks. If, then, the tree may be known by the fruit, as the fruit by the tree, then, peremptorily I speak it, there is virtue in that Falstaff: him keep with, banish the rest. And tell me now, thou naughty varlet, tell me where hast thou been this month?

What gives Falstaff's oratory its mirthful point is the skilled unskilfulness, observable in the best parodies, that mixes the plausible imitation with the implausible invention. The 'camomile' similitude, for example, is pure Lyly; but the trope of the 'micher', the blackberry-eating truant, is pure Falstaff, or overgrown schoolboy. The 'King's' measured, parisonic turns of phrase expound lunatic meanings: 'That thou art my son, I have *partly thy mother's word, partly my own opinion.*' Worse (or better still), they generate lunatic expansions: 'but chiefly a villainous trick of thine eye, and a foolish hanging of thy nether lip, that doth warrant me'. The Euphuistic constructions, elegantly alliterated and bound up in matching sets of three, are blotched with happy vulgarities: 'I do not speak in drink, but in tears; not in pleasure, but in passion; not in words only but in woes also.' The last two *cola* in that example are thoroughly acceptable specimens of Lylyan vacuity; it is the first, with its hilarious intimation that the King of England, on a court occasion, might *speak in drink* that gives the parodic game away. (Significantly, this is the non-alliterating *colon*; Lyly, had he been responsible for such a sentence, would have written something like 'I speak not in *teen* (= anger) but in (*tears*'.) The punning play on *sun/son* is a commonplace of Elizabethan rhetoric, and the antanaclasis of *point/pointed at* is certainly not untypical, but both have the air of being dragged in and heavily laboured. This is Falstaff's comic concept of the language of the court: Euphuistic sonorities slipping into sniggers, the grand lurching into the gorblimey. It is not surprising that even he cannot sustain this unique style, but lapses into affectionate Eastcheap: 'And tell me now, thou naughty varlet, tell me where thou hast been this month?'

Here the Prince is moved to protest that this is nothing like the language of a King, and that he will demonstrate the royal style. The roles are accordingly reversed, and Prince Henry, playing his father, begins the game again:

Prince Henry:	Now, Harry, whence come you?
Falstaff:	My noble lord, from Eastcheap.
Prince Henry:	The complaints I hear of thee are grievous.
Falstaff:	'Sblood, my lord, they are false: – nay, I'll tickle ye for a young prince, i' faith.
Prince Henry:	Swearest thou, ungracious boy? henceforth ne'er look on me. Thou art violently carried away from grace: there is a devil haunts thee, in the likeness of an old fat man – a tun of man is thy companion. Why dost thou converse with that trunk of humours, that bolting-hutch of beastliness, that swoll'n parcel of dropsies, that huge bombard of sack, that stuff'd cloakbag of guts, that roasted Manningtree ox with the pudding in his belly, that vanity in years? Wherein is he good, but to taste

> sack and drink it? wherein neat and cleanly, but to
> carve a capon and eat it? wherein cunning, but in
> craft? wherein crafty, but in villainy? wherein
> villainous but in all things? wherein worthy, but in
> nothing?

The Prince has his own version of the royal rhetoric, as par-
odically inspired as Falstaff's, as comically distinguished by the
personal waywardness with the objective model. The model is that
of moral/religious homily, as indicated by this 'King's' vocabulary
at the beginning of his admonitions: *ungracious*, *grace*, *devil*, point
to the homiletic strain which no doubt the Prince intends to spoof.
But, like Falstaff, he is carried away by his own invention. The end
of this speech is certainly a splendid burlesque of sermonizing
rhetoric; as one born to the manner of a figurative pulpit, the
Prince parades schemes of *parison*, *anaphora* (constructions successively linked by the first word), *erotema* (the appeal by questioning),
polyptoton (in 'craft'/'crafty', 'villainy'/'villainous'), *anadiplosis*
(the last word of one construction becoming the first word of the
next) and, in consequence of the anadiplosis, *climax*, which
Puttenham calls 'the marching figure' and also 'the *clyming* figure,
for *Clymax* is as much as to say a ladder'. This would normally
imply an ascent, but in Prince Henry's burlesque the 'ladder' goes
downward step by step through the recital of Falstaff's irredeema-
ble defects.

   This is a shrewd parodic conclusion, a climax indeed, but before
these final clauses, with their obvious indication of an oratorical
control or harnessing of the theme, the Prince has seemingly
allowed himself the quite uncourtly pleasure of an unharnessed
gallop of abuse. From 'that trunk of humours' to 'that vanity in
years' there is a cultivated *cacemphaton*, or bad language, which
according to Puttenham is 'in some cases tollerable, and chiefly to
the intent to mooue laughter, and to make sport, or to give it some
pretty strange grace'. The 'grace' of this outburst appears with the
realization that the apparent runaway does, after all, have reins. It
is the protracted *asyndeton* that conveys the effect of excited
speech running out of restraint, but asyndeton is accompanied by
anaphora (in 'that . . . that . . . that') suggesting a kind of calculation of the successive surges of insult, and the insults are in some
instances rather deliberately impelled by the figure of *oxymoron*
('that reverend vice, that gray iniquity, that father ruffian, that

vanity in years'). The Prince's rhetorical essay is thus doubly humorous: humorous in the first instance because the intended homily apparently gets out of hand and charges away into abuse, albeit inspired abuse, and in the second instance humorous because it turns out that the abuse itself is under quite firm rhetorical control. It is as though a modern dramatist should represent Her Majesty the Queen, or the Prime Minister, or the Archbishop of Canterbury as ceremoniously reproving the British nation for its sins, but digressing in quite methodical heat to scold the citizens all in choice back-street style ('you rotten stinkers, you mouldy packets of last year's cheese, you dirty dregs of the dustbin, you fruity smells, you soggy sensations . . .') Prince Henry, indeed, has the honour of inventing a new rhetorical genre, the Eastcheap Homily. But Falstaff is about to go one better. With a delicate respect for the proprieties of grammar, he demurely enquires:

Falstaff:	I would your Grace would take me with you: whom means your Grace?
Prince Henry:	That villainous abominable misleader of youth, Falstaff, that old white-bearded Satan.
Falstaff:	My lord, the man I know.
Prince Henry:	I know thou dost.
Falstaff:	But to say I know more harm in him than in myself, were to say more than I know. That he is old – the more the pity, – his white hairs do witness it; but that he is – saving your reverence – a whoremaster, that I utterly deny. If sack and sugar be a fault, God help the wicked! if to be old and merry be a sin, then many an old host I know is damn'd: if to be fat to be hated, then Pharoah's lean kine are to be loved. No my good lord; banish Peto, banish Bardolph, banish Pointz: but for sweet Jack Falstaff, kind Jack Falstaff, true Jack Falstaff, valiant Jack Falstaff, and therefore more valiant, being, as he is, old Jack Falstaff, banish him not thy Harry's company, banish him not thy Harry's company: – banish plump Jack, and banish all the world.

Falstaff has once more shifted the ground of the rhetorical contest; we have moved to the *genus iudicium*, to forensic rhetoric, and this is the *peroratio* of the speech for the defence ('My lord, members of the jury, I know my client, I know him, I may venture to say, as well as I know myself, and I can assure the court of his impeccable character . . .'). Like any good courtroom practitioner, Falstaff willingly imputes to his client (that is, to himself) a crime of which he has not been accused, in order to deny it emphatically: 'That he is old – the more the pity – his white hairs do witness it; but that he is – saving your reverence – a whoremaster, that I utterly deny.' This is a combination of *procatalepsis* (anticipating an objection or a charge) and *antanagoge* (making an admission but adding a compensatory claim: 'It is true that my client has extravagant tastes, but he has never in his life stolen from Harrods'). In general, Falstaff exploits the discursive modes of *paromologia* – he admits or concedes – and *dichologia* – he excuses; and this alternation of 'admittedly' and 'on the other hand' produces the solemn parisonic ding-dong of the first half of the speech. Then, with 'no, my good lord', comes the closing apostrophe, or appeal to the judge, a sonorous compound of *anaphora* ('banish Peto, banish Bardolph, banish Pointz'), *antistrophe* ('sweet Jack Falstaff, kind Jack Falstaff, true Jack Falstaff'), *auxesis* ('and therefore more valiant, being as he is old Jack Falstaff'), culminating in the pathetic reiteration of 'banish not him thy Harry's company'. It is a superb evocation of the eloquent counsel making the hopeful utmost of a hopeless case.

Shakespeare must have enjoyed writing this scene, but his enjoyment had to depend, after all, on the anticipation that his linguistic liveliness would be appreciated by an equally lively and well-informed audience. This comic encounter could only be relished to the full by theatregoers who could recgnize the mockery of forensic and hortatory styles and had some acquaintance with current literary fashion. They would also need to have some sense of the difference between a truly courtly style and the Falstaffian spoof; but for their benefit and for ours, the 'real' confrontation of Prince and King follows within two or three scenes, in Act III, Scene ii, where Shakespeare portrays in all seriousness the royal father upbraiding his delinquent son. That scene also is the occasion for much rhetoric, as King Henry expounds the burdens and the policies of kingship, but with no sense of a supervising author laughing at and relishing the exaggerations of style. We are back to the sober drama of the world after the public house pantomime. The tavern scene does, however, serve a dramatic purpose in characterizing the bond that holds Prince Henry and Falstaff. Their friendship is that of worthy adversaries in wit; only Falstaff can get the better of Prince

Henry and only Prince Henry can hold a candle to Falstaff. Observing the scene or reading it, we of the audience feel in our turn an admiring affection for these personages, and for their creator who so hugely enjoys, and needs us to enjoy, the rampage of rhetoric on the loose.

THIRD SOUNDING: THE EIGHTEENTH CENTURY

'Rhetoric on the loose' is perhaps not the first phrase one might choose to characterize the century of Johnathan Swift and Samuel Johnson; it sounds altogether too unbuttoned, unleashed and licentious for that rational age. Yet from the examples of our eighteenth-century writers a textbook of rhetoric might be compiled, and the examples would not in all cases be quite serious. There is an Augustan smile, which sometimes has a dangerously quarrelsome glitter but which is commonly a clubbable, sociable thing. The club is the urbane company of the literate; the funny rhetoric is the civilized mockery of literariness.

We meet this mocking spirit in, for example, Pope's *The Rape of the Lock*, a work which Pope himself characterized as 'an heroi-comical poem'. It laughs at the 'little unguarded Follies' of feminity, in a style which burlesques both the 'machinery' (the activities and interventions of supernatural beings) and the language of classical epic poetry as the eighteenth century understood it. The classics were sedulously translated, para-phrased or 'Englished' into decasyllabic couplets, an industry in which Pope himself was prominent. Here, for instance, is a part of 'The Episode of Sarpedon', 'translated from the twelfth and sixteenth books of Homer's Iliads'. Sarpedon, an ally of the Trojans, incites Glaucus to join him in attacking the fortification that defends the Greek fleet:

> Resolved alike, Divine *Sarpedon* glows
> With gen'rous rage, that drives him on the Foes.
> He views the Tow'rs, and meditates their Fall;
> To sure Destruction dooms the *Grecian* Wall;
> Then casting on his Friends an ardent Look,
> Fir'd with the Thirst of Glory, thus he spoke.
> Why boast we, *Glaucus*, our extended Reign
> Where *Xanthus*' streams enrich the *Lycian* plain?
> Our num'rous Herds that range each fruitful Field,

And Hills where Vines their Purple Harvest yield?
Our foaming Bowls with gen'rous *Nectar* crown'd,
Our Feasts enhanc'd with Musick's sprightly Sound?
Why on those Shores are we with Joy survey'd,
Admir'd as Heroes, and as Gods obey'd?
Unless great Acts superior Merit prove,
And vindicate the bounteous Powr's above:
'Tis ours, the Dignity They give, to grace;
The first in Valour, as the first in Place;
That while with wondring Eyes our Martial Bands
Behold our Deeds transcending our Commands,
Such, they may cry, deserve the Sov'reign State,
Whom those that Envy dare not Imitate!
Could all our Care elude the greedy Grave,
Which claims no less the Fearful than the Brave,
For Lust of Fame I should not vainly dare
In fighting Fields, nor urge thy Soul to War.
But since, alas, ignoble Age must come,
Disease, and Death's inexorable Doom;
The Life which others pay, let Us bestow,
And give to Fame what we to Nature owe;
Brave, tho' we fall; and honour'd if we live;
Or let us Glory gain, or Glory give!

We need not linger on this, except to note its content: it is the speech of the warrior counselling war, and its argument is that as leaders enjoy privileges they must set examples, for virtue's sake risking the death that must in any case come to all, the coward as well as the hero. Sarpedon's speech – heavily figured, incidentally – has its persuasive effect; he and Glaucus rush off to battle, and, as Pope puts it, 'The Troops pursue their leaders with Delight'. Now here is another speaker, at a different council, in *The Rape of the Lock*. The ladies, inflamed by the Baron's impertinent theft of a lock of Belinda's hair, urge war on men, but Clarissa calls for restraint, good humour, and self-knowledge:

Then grave *Clarissa* graceful wav'd her Fan;
Silence ensu'd, and thus the Nymph began.
Say, why are Beauties prais'd and honour'd most,
The wise Man's Passion, and the vain Man's Toast?
Why deck'd with all that Land and Sea afford,
Why Angels call'd, and Angel-like ador'd?
Why round our Coaches crowd the white-glov'd Beaus,
Why bows the Side-box from its inmost Rows?

How vain are all these Glories, all our Pains,
Unless good Sense preserve what Beauty gains:
That Men may say, when we the Front-box grace,
Behold the first in Virtue, as in Face!
Oh! if to dance all Night, and dress all Day,
Charm'd the Small-pox, or chas'd old Age away;
Who would not scorn what Huswife's Cares produce,
Or who would learn one earthly Thing of Use?
To patch, nay ogle, might become a Saint,
Nor could it sure be such a Sin to paint.
But since, alas! frail Beauty must decay,
Curl'd or uncurl'd, since Locks will turn to grey,
Since painted, or not painted, all shall fade,
And she who scorns a Man, must die a Maid;
What then remains, but well our Pow'r to use,
And keep good Humour still whate'er we lose?
And trust me, Dear! good Humour can prevail,
When Airs, and Flights, and Screams, and Scolding fail.
Beauties in vain their pretty Eyes may roll;
Charms strike the Sight, but Merit wins the Soul.

If the passages are now compared, this speech of Clarissa may be seen as the mirror image of Sarpedon's address to Glaucus. Sarpedon is a man, indeed a demigod; Clarissa is a woman, or, in the convention of Pope's fable, a nymph. Sarpedon's is the rural world of herds, harvests and vines; Clarissa's the urban ambience of coaches, dances and the theatre. Sarpedon speaks for war as the only option for honour; Clarissa pleads for peace as the only option for sense. (She pleads in vain, as it turns out; to the feminists of her day, her rhetoric is the defeatist propaganda of an Auntie Tom.)

The serious rhetoric thus undergoes a comic transmutation. There are, furthermore, significant echoes of one passage in the other. Compare this:

Why on these Shores are we with Joy survey'd,
Admir'd as Heroes, and as Gods obey'd?

with this:

Why round our Coaches crowd the white-glov'd Beaus,
Why bows the Side-box from its inmost Rows?

And this:

'Tis ours, the Dignity They give, to grace;

The first in Valour, as the first in Place;

with this:

That Men may say, when we the Front-box grace,
Behold the first in Virtue, as in Face!

And this:

But since, alas, ignoble Age must come,
Disease, and Death's inexorable Doom;

with this:

But since, alas! frail Beauty must decay,
Curl'd or uncurl'd, since Locks will turn to grey

And this:

The Life which others pay, let Us bestow,
And give to Fame what we to Nature owe;

with this:

What then remains, but well our Pow'r to use,
And keep good Humour still whate'er we lose?

These clear parallels alone illustrate the parodic debt of the *Rape* passage to the *Sarpedon* speech. In figurative rhetoric the derived passage outdoes its model. There is a schematic structure in line after line, couplet after couplet: 'The wise Man's Passion and the vain Man's Toast'; 'Why Angels called, and Angel-like ador'd?'; 'Unless good Sense preserve what Beauty gains'; 'Oh! if to dance all Night, and dress all Day, / Charm'd the Small-pox, or chas'd old Age away'; 'To patch, nay ogle, might become a saint' (a case of *epanorthesis*); 'And she who scorns a Man, must die a maid'; 'Charms strike the Sight, but Merit wins the Soul.'

But what is it, after all, that makes Pope smile his Augustan smile? His is quite a complex act of mockery. The fun is inspired by an actual event, the impolitic snipping-off of a lock of Miss Arabella Fermor's hair by one Lord Petrie; the satire is directed at social manners and the characters of women; the fable is humorously given a supernatural turn, through the introduction of 'machinery' derived from Rosicrucianism; and the parody is couched in the mock-epic language suggested to Pope by a French poem, Nicholas Boileau-Despreaux's *Le Lutrin*. His immediate linguistic source, however, is his own 'Englishing' of Homer, and his parodic targets can therefore be said to include his own style. The Augustan smile mocks the world, mocks writing, but also mocks the smiler. This runs through eighteenth-century letters, almost as a moral principle; good humour and self-knowledge are the aims of the well bred, though sometimes breeding is lost in the snarl of satire or the bitterness of irony.

FOURTH SOUNDING: THE NINETEENTH CENTURY

With the nineteenth century, however, humorous rhetoric becomes less urbane. Voices are raised, the grand manner becomes a little flashy and theatrical, the mocking face owes less to raillery and more to desperation. The great comic rhetoricians of nine-teenth-century literature laugh in theatres that echo loneliness and melancholy. Byron has the gift of humorous rhetoric. So does Dickens. Here, first, is Byron, in a typical virtuoso performance from the first canto of *Don Juan*:

> 'Tis sweet to hear
> At midnight on the blue and moonlit deep
> The song and oar of Adria's gondolier,
> By distance mellow'd, o'er the waters sweep;
> 'Tis sweet to see the evening star appear;
> 'Tis sweet to listen as the night-winds creep
> From leaf to leaf: 'tis sweet to view on high
> The rainbow, based on ocean, span the sky.
>
> 'Tis sweet to hear the watch-dog's honest bark
> Bay deep-mouth'd welcome as we draw near home;
> 'Tis sweet to know there is an eye will mark
> Our coming, and look brighter when we come;
> 'Tis sweet to be awaken'd by the lark,
> Or lull'd by falling waters; sweet the hum
> Of bees, the voice of girls, the song of birds,
> The lisp of children, and their earliest words.
>
> Sweet is the vintage, when the showering grapes
> In Bacchanal profusion reel to earth,
> Purple and gushing; sweet are our escapes
> From civic revelry to rural mirth;
> Sweet to the miser are his glittering heaps,
> Sweet to the father is his first-born's birth,
> Sweet is revenge – especially to women,
> Pillage to soldiers, prize-money to seamen.

Sweet is a legacy, and passing sweet
    The unexpected death of some old lady
Or gentlemen of seventy years complete,
    Who've made 'us youth' wait too – too long already
For an estate, or cash, or country seat,
    Still breaking, but with stamina so steady
That all the Israelites are fit to mob its
Next owner for their double-damn'd post-obits.

'Tis sweet to win, no matter how, one's laurels,
    By blood or ink; 'tis sweet to put an end
To strife: 'tis sometimes sweet to have our quarrels,
    Particularly with a tiresome friend:
Sweet is old wine in bottles, ale in barrels;
    Dear is the helpless creature we defend
Against the world; and dear the schoolboy spot
We ne'er forget, though there we are forgot.

But sweeter still than this, than these, than all,
    Is first and passionate love – it stands alone,
Like Adam's recollection of his fall;
    The tree of knowledge has been pluck'd – all's known –
And life yields nothing further to recall
    Worthy of this ambrosial sin, so shown,
No doubt in fable, as the unforgiven
Fire which Prometheus filch'd for us from heaven.

(Byron uses the word *stamina* in the historical sense of 'the original elements constituting any organism'; by *Israelites* he means (Jewish) moneylenders. A *post obit* was a loan repayable upon the death of the borrower, out of the latter's estate. The sense of the lines in which these expressions occur is that although the 'estate' on which money has been borrowed is gradually diminishing in value, it is still so sound, basically, that the impatient money-lenders are ready to rush in and demand their repayments from the new owners.)

This is a grandly self-indulgent exercise in the sublime; more particularly, in the artifice called *merismus*, which, according to Puttenham, occurs 'when we may conveniently utter a matter in one entire speach or proposition, and will rather do it piecemeal and by distribution of every part for amplification sake'. The 'entire speech or proposition' here is that there is nothing as sweet as first love, but the proposition is 'distributed' over the long tally of examples. The master-figure, connecting the items in the tally, is *anaphora*; other figures occur within the unifying scheme, notably at the ends of stanzas. The whole rigmarole is a theatrical pretence of passion, and the poet knows it; and yet in his literary nods and becks there is something disturbing, a jarring undertone of distaste. The phrase 'us youth', for example, set in quotation marks, is a reference to Falstaff – the Falstaff who, enthusiastically robbing a band of travelling merchants, rushes upon his victims with the cry 'Strike; down with them; cut the villain's throats; – ah, whoreson caterpillars! bacon-fed knaves! they hate us youth: – down with them; fleece them.'[9] *Us youth* comes funnily from Falstaff, because he is old and fat, but not so funnily from Byron at slim-and-thirty, unless we read the quotation as a sardonic reminder of the larger context – 'Strike; down with them; fleece them'; elderly and inconveniently long-lived kinsfolk, like Falstaff's 'bacon-fed knaves', are fit only to be 'fleeced'. But the joke, that the old are the enemies of the young and ought to get out of the way or be put out, is an uneasy one; we might almost suspect Byron of meaning what he half-says. Nor is his apparently light-hearted reconstruction of the Prometheus legend, at the climax of the passage, altogether innocent of a darker sense. 'No doubt', says Byron, 'the fire which Prometheus stole from heaven was the passion of first love.' To read the legend in this pleasantly perverse way is to poke fun at the paradigm-hunting rhetoricians. Even in fun, however, it remains a paradigm, from which the mythic consequence must be drawn. For his action Prometheus was made to suffer cruel and everlasting torment; are we to assume, analogically, that lifelong suffering will be visited on those who commit the sin of first love? And a further point occurs: that although Prometheus stole the fire, in reading his myth we are not primarily concerned with the deed of theft, any more than in reading the Eden story we interpret the taking of the apple first and foremost as an act of petty larceny. It is disobedience, *hubris*, prideful defiance of the order from on high, that we see in these stories. But Byron with one altered word, the word *filch*, a word taken from the canting vocabulary of thieves, reduces the tragically noble Prometheus to a mere paradigm of thievery. There are no heroes; Prometheus is a thief, as Falstaff was a thief. And what this deconstructionist reading further suggests is that we are all thieves in our pursuit of life's pleasures. Sweets, to be sweet, are necessarily stolen sweets, the sweetness of love being the greatest theft of all. But it is a theft that may be mercilessly punished.

These tensions in meaning, between the jovial proposition and the uneasy implication, are matched by tensions in style. The linguistic comedy of *Don Juan* is notoriously macaronic, a medley of styles after the fashion of Byron's principal exemplar, Luigi Pulci's *Morgante Maggiore*. Byron is never at rest in one style, but changes stance all the time, in case we should find him guilty of sincerity. As the quoted extract may suggest, he shifts back and forth between genuine poetry and adroit versifying; between the high style, the 'sublime', and the common chat of the knowing chap; between true *pathos* and deep-diving *bathos*; between warm ingenuous feeling and cold cynicism. The total effect of all this is to invite attention to the stylist, rather than to the style or to characters expounding the style. Chaucer's rhetorical mockery, in *The Nun's Priest's Tale*, is laid on as thick as Byron's; Shakespeare riots in rhetoric; Pope tailors his rhetoric to his elegantly merry puppets; but in none of these cases does the joke-rhetoric invite us to look at Chaucer, look at Shakespeare, look at Pope, as Byron's humour never stops proclaiming, 'look at *me*'. His style fluently assumes one posture after another, but in every posture there is some unease, some anguish even; the smile on that affable countenance might be mistaken for a grimace.

Now consider Charles Dickens, who certainly comes too late in the textbook scheme of things to be properly called a 'Romantic', but who none the less revelled in that climate of language that Byron helped to create. Dickens is not a *poseur*, yet he poses; every one of his books is a theatre in which humorous rhetoric adorns one role or another. It may be the rhetoric of a character – for example, Mr Micawber; or it may be the rhetoric of the author himself, in his role of impresario. For instance, there is the opening of *A Tale of Two Cities*:

> It was the best of times, it was the worst of times, it was the age of wisdom, it was the age of foolishness, it was the epoch of belief, it was the epoch of incredulity, it was the season of Light, it was the season of Darkness, it was the spring of hope, it was the winter of despair, we had everything before us, we had nothing before us, we were all going direct to Heaven, we were all going direct the other way – in short, the period was so far like the present period, that some of its noisiest authorities insisted on its being received, for good or for evil, in the superlative degree of comparison only.
>
> There were a king with a large jaw and a queen with a plain face, on the throne of England; there were a king with a large jaw and a queen with a fair face, on the throne of France. In both countries it

was clearer than crystal to the lords of the State preserves of loaves and fishes, that things in general were settled for ever.

This opening promises well; it is certainly rhetorical in its tit-for-tat figuration, certainly humorous in its *periergia*, that rather pompous labouring with words that Dickens made into a comic virtue: for example, 'in short, the period was so far like the present period, that some of its noisiest authorities insisted on its being received, for good or for evil, in the superlative degree of comparison only'. (Note the joke, that 'in short' is rather long; note the further joke that the taste for superlatives is mocked in the superlative – not 'some noisy authorities insisted', but 'some of its noisiest authorities insisted'.) The manner of narration seems detached and witty, and we might be at the beginning of a comic or satirical tale, did not the biblical allusion at the end of the second paragraph give a preparatory hint of what is to follow almost immediately, a savage irony, a horrified unwillingness to believe in things that are done in the name of Christianity, civilization, law and the State. It is a kind of grimacing that lures the reader into *A Tale of Two Cities*; Dickens pulls a funny face, and before we know it we are staring at a tragic mask.

The opening of this novel is best understood in comparison with its closing paragraphs. There is a shift of stance, taking place quite gradually through the book, from that of the commentator on 'things in general' – compassionately ironic, but none the less impersonal – to a concern with the affairs of a few people, and ultimately to an identification with the point of view of one person, Sydney Carton. The story ends with Carton's thoughts as he awaits execution and thinks of those for whose sake he is about to lay down his life. It is affective rhetoric in the richest Dickensian strain, uninhibited Victorian theatre:

'I see that child who lay upon her bosom and who bore my name, a man winning his way up that path in life which once was mine. I see him winning it so well, that my name is made illustrious there by the light of his. I see the blots I threw upon it, faded away. I see him, foremost of just judges and honoured men, bringing a boy of my name, with a forehead that I know and golden hair, to this place – then fair to look upon, with not a trace of this day's disfigurement – and I hear him tell the child my story, with a tender and faltering voice.

'It is a far, far better thing that I do, than I have ever done; it is a far, far better rest that I go to than I have ever known.'

If you cannot smile at the big-jawed kings, the chances are that you will not feel a catch in the throat for Sydney Carton, because the same creative spirit informs the ironic rhetoric of the book's opening and the affective rhetoric of its close. The irony is levelled at states and systems; the sentiment is for individuals who are victims of systems. An incidental oddity is that the book begins with a joke about the superlative degrees of *best* and *worst*, and ends with a grave pronouncement on *better*. The 'times' are pronounced best or worst; what individuals hope for is only a better way of behaving. It is perhaps stretching a point beyond stretchable bounds to suggest that Dickens did this designedly; though it is certainly not beyond the creative capacity of his rhetoric.

FIFTH SOUNDING: MODERN TIMES

Byron's postures are superb, and Dickens is sovereign in his bold theatrical style; but the history of post-Victorian letters shows an increasing embarrassment with big rhetoric, demonstrative rhetoric, self-confident, look-at-me-and-enjoy-the-show rhetoric. Even when its purpose is clearly humorous, grandiloquent rhetoric of the Byronic or Dickensian kind is held suspect, and is characterized in words like 'pompous' or 'turgid'. The language of the comic sublime, that full-figured hamming style, loses its creative status and is gradually displaced, from a central position in literature, to a more marginal role, in the work of columnists, essayists, scholars at play, and others whose purpose is wholly facetious and parodic. Thus happily housed in its funny farm or laughing academy, spoof rhetoric becomes a game for the initiated who have read all the books and seen all the acts.

Yet the humours of rhetoric persist in literature and have their functions there. Figurative rhetoric may have lost some of its appeal, but there is a humour of discursive modes, in writings that appear to be increasingly self-aware, at times almost obsessively concerned with the nature of the literary process and the fact that a story is only a story. This discourse humour often takes the form of turning conventions in upon themselves. The text is seen for what it ostensibly is and does; at the same time the text sees itself, so to speak, reflected in a distorting mirror – that is to say, in the author's consciousness of performing a literary act. This is not calculated to provoke a belly-laugh, or a companionable smile, or even the self-congratulatory smirk of the scholarly; what it does incite is something more like the nervous leer with which we confront the absurd.

It might not be thought that a mere stage-direction could function as a looking-glass for literary lunacy. The business of a stage-direction is fairly straightforward. Presented at the beginning of the text of a play, it gives to the prospective producer the author's directions for the staging of the set – and that it is why it is called a stage-direction. It follows certain linguistic conventions: for example, its component sentences are unlikely to have main verbs, and many of them will begin with an adverbial element, in the form of a prepositional phrase ('to the left', 'down right', 'above the door', 'near it' and so on). The description of the set and its furnishings or other properties will systematically take the reader in a certain direction or circuit – from 'up stage' to 'down stage', 'stage left' to 'stage right' and so on. The stage-direction, in short, is a commonplace sample of functional prose, not forming part of the text of the play and hence not entering into the verbal experience which the playwright shares with his public in the theatre. The direction tells the producer and the stage-crew where the fireplace is, where to put the sofa and where the maid is standing when the action begins. It is an extra-curricular document; readers might pass it over, and very often do.

A reader who passed over the following, however, might miss a taste of the pleasurably absurd. It prefaces Harold Pinter's *The Caretaker*:

> A room. A window in the back wall, the bottom half covered by a sack. An iron bed along the left wall. Above it a small cupboard, paint buckets, boxes containing nuts, screws, etc. More boxes, vases, by the side of the bed. A door, up right. To the right of the window, a mound: a kitchen sink, a step-ladder, a coal bucket, a lawn-mower, a shopping trolley, boxes, sideboard drawers. Under this mound on an iron bed. In front of it a gas stove. On the gas stove a statue of Buddha. Down right, a fireplace. Around it a couple of suitcases, a rolled carpet, a blow-lamp, a wooden chair on its side, boxes, a number of ornaments, a clothes horse, a few short planks of wood, a small electric fire and a very old electric toaster. Below this a pile of old newspapers. Under ASTON's bed by the left wall, is an electrolux, which is not seen till used. A bucket hangs from the ceiling.

This is at a basic level quite a sensible and ordinary stage-direction, since it performs the necessary function of telling the stage-manager how to construct the set: where the window and the door are located, where the fireplace is, where the two beds are to stand. Beyond such basic instructions, however, it is frankly anarchic, as though the writer were playing a cruel practical joke on the busy workers backstage; we can only imagine the trouble of hunting out every object in that bizarre miscellany, and of placing it exactly as the playwright indicates. To do so would be an act of faith, based on the assumption that there is a reason, a potential textual significance, for the presence of these diverse properties. Only, perhaps, between periodic checks of the listed items, ticking off the blow-lamp, querying the Buddha, arranging the 'mound', making sure there are nuts and screws in the boxes (never mind what for), might it occur to the stage-manager that someone is making game of his labours. The suspicion might be aroused by the repeated occurrence of the word *boxes*: 'boxes containing nuts and screws, etc.', 'More boxes, vases, by the side of the bed', 'a kitchen sink, a step-ladder, a coal bucket, a lawn-mower, a shopping trolley, boxes, sideboard drawers', 'a rolled carpet, a blow lamp, a wooden chair on its side, boxes, a number of ornaments'. Whenever the writer makes a list, the boxes, it seems, are mischievously thrown in for good measure. This joke (for surely it is intended as such) is perceived in different ways by readers of the text and by spectators in the theatre. For readers it grows subtly, unobtrusively, by repetitions that gradually claim notice. Spectators may not see the joke at all as a discrete item; for them, it may be that the boxes are only a part of the big joke, the appalling comic disorder of the room. They are also unaware, initially, of another joke immediately revealed to the reader: the fact that among this chaotic spillage of unstored objects there is one, the electrolux, which is tidily stowed away under a bed.

And what, after all, is the status of the stage-direction? Is it an immutable *directive*, to be obeyed to the elaborate letter? Why could not the author have been content to show the disposition of the main features of the room, and add a general direction to the effect that there is everywhere a clutter of objects, including boxes, ornaments, furnishings, tools and various household appliances? Why the scrupulous particulars that specify, among other things, that the planks of wood shall be few and short, and that the toaster shall be very old? Clearly this exuberantly realistic stage-direction is a form of near-surrealistic joke. The joke is partly visual, a joke for the audience and on the audience, who will chuckle when the curtain goes up on this amazing clutter, but who will spend a good deal of the play waiting for the lawn-mower to be used or the shopping trolley to be explained (in accordance with Chekhov's recommendation that if you have a gun on the wall in Act I it must go off by Act III). But there are aspects of the joke which spectators cannot immediately share, a humour realized and cultivated textually, and in its absurdity prefiguring the absurdity and unreason, the fractured communication, of the play itself. For the reader, the stage-direction is no longer an extra-curricular document; it is something to be taken into account with the rest of the text.

A comparable act of playfulness with the framing conventions of literary discourse is seen at the beginning of Malcolm Bradbury's novel, *The History Man*. Here the extra-curricular text is the Author's Note, that prefatory paragraph in which the novelist dedicates his work to X, acknowledges the services of Y, and explains the circumstances of composition ('My closing chapters were written in Transylvania, while I was a guest in the charmingly secluded house of Count and Countess Alucard. ... I have to thank them for their warm interest in my work . . . resemblance to persons living or dead is quite accidental'). Like the stage-direction, the Author's Note usually contains information of no more than peripheral relevance to the text; but some notes are more interesting than others. Mr Bradbury begins his by telling us that his fiction is dedicated to one Beamish – who happens to be a character in his fiction:

> This fiction is for Beamish, whom, while on route for some conference or other, I last saw at Frankfurt airport, enquiring from desk to desk about his luggage, unhappily not loaded onto the same plane as he. It is a total invention with delusory approximations to historical reality, just as is history itself. Not only does the University of Watermouth, which appears here, bear no relation to the real University of Watermouth (which does not exist) or to any other university; the year 1972, which also appears, bears no relation to the real 1972, which was a fiction anyway; and so on. As for the characters, so-called, no one but they are pure inventions, as is the plot in which they more than participate, Nor did I fly to a

conference the other day; and if I did, there was no one on the plane named Beamish, who certainly did not lose his luggage. The rest, of course, is true.

If there is a figurative name for this, it may be *aporia*, which Puttenham calls 'the *doubtfull*, because oftentimes we will seeme to cast perils, and make doubt of things when by a plaine manner of speech wee might affirme or deny him'.[3] Bradbury might, indeed, 'by a plaine manner of speech' have affirmed that his story and his characters were wholly fictitious. But he mischievously goes a little farther than that, not only denying that fiction has a basis in real experience, but also questioning the real credentials of experience itself. The story does not exist in history, because even history does not exist in history; the only location for this story's existence is here, on this page, and this sentence is the only voucher for its truth. The next sentence may change matters. We may be reminded a little of Lewis Carroll, or of Kafka, or perhaps of Sterne in *Tristram Shandy* – there are certainly distinguished precedents for what Bradbury does, which is to stake fiction's claim to fictionality, and thus to warn readers that they are not to interpret his story naively, with reference to 'real' places and times ('Malcolm Bradbury and the Intellectual Climate of the 1970s; An Essay in Socio-Political Criticism'), or even with reference to its formal and aesthetic properties ('Character over Plot? A Note on the Structure of *The History Man*'). There is warning, a humorous, rhetorical warning, to leave such things alone; otherwise we may be like Beamish, and lose all our luggage. As indeed did the Baker in Carroll's *The Hunting of the Snark*. He lost his luggage because he left it on the beach, and he lost his name because it was on his luggage; and his uncle warned him 'oh, beamish nephew, beware of the day, / If your Snark be a Boojum! For then / You will softly and suddenly vanish away, / And never be met with again!' Just like Mr Bradbury's Beamish character, in fact.[4]

By questioning conventions of style and discourse-structure, and by drawing the attention of their readers to the processes of writing, modern authors often comically subvert the time-honoured principles of decorum. Those principles distinguish between what is appropriate for writing or for speech, between rhetorics appropriate to different occasions, between styles considered seemly in personages enacting diverse roles. The King may be kingly in the council-chamber, but his pillow-talk ought not to sound like a Speech from the Throne; when the Professor buys the groceries he should not seem to be writing his address to the shop-assistant ('My immediate object in presenting this bank-note may be defined as the purchase of a can of peaches . . .'). There is therefore something comically indecorous about the personage who is so possessed by a style that it becomes an automatic response, overriding social and situational stimuli. This is one of the rhetorical jokes in Tom Stoppard's *The Real Inspector Hound*, a play about a play within a play, in the satirical and parodic tradition of Sheridan's *The Critic*. The principal characters, Moon and Birdboot, are theatre reviewers who from time to time interrupt their 'ordinary' conversations in order to slip, at the drop of an epithet, into effortless reviewerese:

> *Moon*: By the way, congratulations, Birdboot.
> *Birdboot*: What?
> *Moon*: At the Theatre Royal. Your entire review reproduced in neon!
> *Birdboot* (pleased): Oh . . . that old thing.
> *Moon*: You've seen it, of course.
> *Birdboot* (vaguely): Well, I was passing . . .
> *Moon*: I definitely intend to take a second look when it has settled down.
> *Birdboot*: As a matter of fact I have a few colour transparencies – I don't know whether you'd care to . . .?
> *Moon*: Please, please – love to, love to . . .
> (*Birdboot hands over a few colour slides and a battery-powered viewer which Moon holds upto his eyes as he speaks*)
> Yes . . . yes . . . lovely . . . awfully sound. It has scale, it has colour, it is, in the best sense of the word, electric. Large as it is, it is a small masterpiece – I would go so far as to say – kinetic without being pop, and having said that, I think it must be said that here we have a review that adds a new dimension to the critical scene. I urge you to make haste to the Theatre Royal, for this is the stuff of life itself.
> (*Handing back the slides, morosely*) All I ever got was 'Unforgettable' on the posters for . . . What was it?
> *Birdboot*: Oh – yes – I know. Was that you? I thought it was Higgs.

Here is a merry exercise in stylistic misappropriation, or the art of suiting the solemn word to the silly reference. Moon is looking at colour slides, but he does not use the language most of us obligingly use when our friends invite us to look at a their family snapshots: 'Very nice . . . that's a good one . . . haven't they come out well?. . .' He speaks as a reviewer, in the language of reviewing, about a review – not as it appears in print, but as it is seen in coloured lights on the outside of a theatre. There is humour in the use of words like 'scale' and 'colour', which are conventional metaphors of praise in reviewerese but which can be read literally here – the neon display is large and the lights are coloured. There is humour in the fits and misfits of the theatre columnist's stock language – for example in the incongruous suggestion that the neon display might 'settle down' like a dramatic production which improves with several performances. There is humour in Moon's inability to remember the name of the play that brought him his little moment of public notice as a reviewer, although he can remember the word – 'unforgettable' – with which he reviewed it. There is humour in his apparent obliviousness, by the end of his 'review', of Birdboot as the familiar and friend with whom he is supposedly engaged in conversation. Birdboot becomes, for a moment, the readership, the punter at tomorrow's breakfast table: 'I urge you to make haste to the Theatre Royal.' The biggest compliment Moon can pay to Birdboot is to make an oral draft of a review, in language a fellow-reviewer will appreciate. This obliges him, however, to ignore any social sense of a distinction between the way people speak and the way they write. Moon, at this point in the play, as both he and Birdboot at others, 'talks writing'. The play is full of such devices, calculated to make the audience laugh at language used about the language people use, Such, indeed, is the modern rhetorical mirror, which invites us to reflect on the reflection of reflections, to consider how saying implicates saying and how writing is involve in its own processes. Perhaps the humours of rhetoric in all ages are engendered by currently dominant social and intellectual interests. Linguistics and the philosophy of language have seized the twentieth-century imagination even in a popular way, so that the jokes people tell each other, the comedy shows that acquire cult status, the catchy copy written for advertisements and videos, depend on that interlocutory contract which acknowledges that language is the customary referent of language. Perceiving this, the rhetoric-hater will be more than ever convinced that the art is at best a plaything for the fatuous, in general a delusion, and at worst profoundly immoral. So let us finally consider what the prosecution has to say, and what defences may be offered.

8

The Defences of Rhetoric

When Viscount St Albans, Lord Chancellor, was impeached for accepting bribes, his principal defence was that he had taken the money – of course – everybody did – but that he had never allowed it to influence the course of justice. This tactic of bravely owning up then boldly following up (called *antanagoge*: see p. 180) seems to have made little impression on his political contemporaries, who were determined to convict him anyway; but it has served him fairly well at what is often called the bar of history. Textbooks and manuals of reference quote the case in terms ranging from compassionate understanding through benevolent impartiality to something not far short of approval.[1] To judge every case strictly on its merits, even while you have the defendant's silver in your strongbox, can be seen as a mark of peculiar virtue. Francis Bacon took in the bribes, we tell ourselves, but the bribes never took in Francis Bacon.

Note, 'we tell ourselves'. There comes a point in any rhetorical proceeding when the silent partners in the dialogue – the listeners, the readers – are no longer being told; they start to tell themselves, and in doing so help to shape the rhetoric that persuades them. If you are not by now disposed to think that Francis Bacon, good old Francis Bacon, our friend the essayist, cannot be held responsible for the mistakes of that cold jurist, Viscount St Albans; if you do not incline to the belief that the mistakes were in any case attributable to the customs of an age rather than the malignity of an individual; if you have not taken firmly hold of the thought that these were indeed 'mistakes', not *crimes*; if you are not prepared to argue that Bacon actually demonstrated his own moral superiority by withholding the favours for which he had been paid; then it is more than possible that you yourself have no creative grasp of rhetoric. If, on the other hand, you have taken the hint of a shadow of a figure – that antanagogic plea, 'I am a sinner, but as sinners go I am a good one' – and are ready to elaborate that into an eloquent and convincing defence, then you are an apt student, fit to make *chriae* out of all sorts of topics, and thus (in Falstaff's phrase) little better than one of the wicked.[2]

That rhetorical adepts are impostors who tell lies and twist the facts, we know from the frequent testimony of the daily newspapers, in which rhetoric is both castigated and manifested. Rhetoric has what is known as 'a bad press', and this is almost certainly because it thrives on something the Press regards as its own particular sustenance: a perception of the limitations of the human mind, an exploitation of predictable responses, a grasp of the ideas that rule races, classes and individuals. What is in your mind at this moment? It is my business, as a rhetorician, to guess at that, and make something of my guess. If I am wrong, you will despise me. If I am right – come, confess – you will resent me just a little; you will wonder how I got round you; you will be inclined to think that no one could possibly know so much about the complex secret play of your heart and brain; and you may conclude that it is all a windbagging illusion and a cardsharping cheat. But let me here protest that I only know about you what you know about me, which is perhaps very little; what I do know about are the idols that haunt us both.

'Idol' is from the Greek *eidolon*, not meaning a graven image, but a spectre, a phantasm. Francis Bacon wrote about *eidola* in his *Novum Organum*, in a set of aphorisms which are in effect prolegomena to the methods of empirical science.[3] Bacon's 'idols' are the ingrained habits of mind, the fixed ideas, the superstitions, the unquestioning concessions to authority, the aberrant ways of language, that prevent us from knowing the world as it truly is. He distinguished four sorts of idol. The Idols of the Tribe are the fictions which the human brain readily entertains in its eagerness to perceive order and symmetry, create consistent models of experience, discover abstract principles, satisfy emotional cravings. An old idol of the tribe, long since exorcized, is the belief that the Earth stands at the centre of a symmetrical, clockwork universe. It took some time to displace that idol because it had become emotionally necessary; even today, although we do not believe and cannot think that the Earth is at the centre of creation, we often prefer to *feel* that it is.

The Idols of the Cave, in Bacon's own (translated) words 'take their rise in the peculiar constitution, mental or bodily, of each individual, and also in education, habit, and accident'. He is referring to the bias and predispositions which particular studies and professions impart. A logician, for example, will tend to suppose that all experience and observation must be validated by the test of logic ('It's impossible – it's not logical'); a parson may ascribe a flood or a firestorm to the secret purposes of a loving God; a soldier may judge the world in terms of military honour; a near-sighted person may experience the relative largeness of things, a long-sighted person their relative smallness. In some respects the Idols of the Cave appear to be akin to the Idols of the Theatre, which, Bacon explains, are not innate, like the Idols of the Tribe, but take their power over the mind from the authority of philosophical systems or canonized writings. He calls them Idols of the Theatre because it seems to him that systems and theories and what we nowadays will sometimes call 'models' are just like the plots of stage plays, representing worlds that may be complete in themselves but are quite unreal. In general, any study that deals in categories, to such a degree that category becomes more impor-tant than substance, is beset by Idols of the Theatre; the categories are roles in a mental drama, perhaps satisfying in itself but not necessarily a reliable explanation of experience.

Bacon reserves his greatest mistrust for what he calls the Idols of the Market Place, by which he means the common, unscientific uses and abuses of language, which seem to him to be especially pernicious in disposing the unwary mind to error. In short, he mistrusts words, and for two reasons in particular. One reason is that words often bear a specious appearance of signifying some-thing, but are in effect devoid of substance; words like *fortune* and *luck*, for example, may have no real content but be used as convenient tokens in explanation of events and phenomena. (Thus to say that 'Mudville Wanderers have had no luck this season' is to offer a quasi-explanation of the Wanderers' failure to win any games). The other reason is the scientist's grouse, that words are polysemic, accommodating various meanings deter-mined by the context of usage. Bacon chooses for particular illustration the word *humid*, which, he says 'we shall find to be nothing else than a mark loosely and confusedly applied to denote a variety of actions which will not bear to be reduced to any constant meaning'. It is clear that what Bacon hankers after is what came to be called, later in the seventeenth century, 'a

philosophical language' – meaning a vocabulary purged of ambi-
valences by specific definition, or a set of unambiguous symbols
like those used in logical demonstrations.[4] He refers explicitly to
'the use and wisdom of the mathematicians', meaning that terms
in mathematics are strictly defined, are unambiguously symbo-
lized, and are not context-dependent). This view of words must of
a necessity reject the personifications, metaphors, word-play,
ambiguity, that we commonly associate with literary language.

Indeed, Bacon is not addressing himself to matters of literary
style or rhetoric. His concern is to identify the habits of mind that
hinder the advance of experimental science; the idols distort our
perception of the facts and imprison us in our own self-construct-
ing and self-deceiving natures. For better or for worse, however,
those are the habits of mind to which rhetoric appeals in its work
of persuasion. To just such a habit of mind did Bacon make his
own rhetorical appeal when he pleaded, in mitigation of his
offence, that he had taken bribes but had never perverted the
course of justice. This is an application of the *topos* which Aristotle
in his *Art of Rhetoric* calls 'the more and less'. Bacon's argument in
this instance is that the 'less' (that is, the offence of taking bribes)
does not imply the 'more' (the crime of denying justice); so that
while we may say 'He who is willing to pervert justice must
therefore be willing to take bribes', we do not necessarily say 'He
who is willing to take bribes must therefore be willing to pervert
justice' – because while the more contains the less, the less cannot
wholly contain the more. But this way of arguing is characteristic
of the Idols of the Tribe, concerning which Bacon observes that
'what a man had rather were true he more readily believes'. His
view of language, in short, is scientific where science is concerned;
less so where more personal things are at stake. His *Essays* show
him ready enough to appeal, through his knowledge of the world,
of human nature, of the dispositions of various sorts and conditions of men, to the *eidola* which in his capacity as a scientific
thinker he deplores. Indeed, to know the world, to know one's
neighbours, one's townsfolk, one's compatriots, and to *use* one's
knowledge as a skilled rhetorician uses it – turning it into language
and looking for a response to that language – may be said to
depend on one's familiarity with the *eidola* in their social and
ethical manifestations.

Does this mean, then, that rhetoric must exploit potentially fallacious tendencies in the human mind, that it catches us where we are most fanciful and corrupt? Or shall we rather say that the rhetorician accepts the world as it is, takes people for what they are, by and large, and offers us ways of debating what is no more than possible, ways of representing matters in the light of preference, ways of entering into limited contracts with those among whom we talk and struggle? Zeno of Citium distinguished between two styles of communication, which he represented in the images of the closed fist and the open hand. The closed fist is dialectic reasoning, operating in the intimate world of the mind, insisting on the necessary consequences of necessary premises. The open hand is rhetoric, operating in the social world, dealing with the probable or negotiable outcome of generally agreed conditions. Zeno's imagery is very concrete and vivid; we can see the logician's fist as he clinches point after inescapable point, and the orator's palm, turned outward to his audience, as he appeals to them to agree that such-and-such a thing might arguably be the case in this particular social or ethical instance. It is interesting to apply Zeno's distinction to the communicative methods of the two most distinguished thinkers in the Greek world; there is Plato's style, in which mind singly engages mind, and there is Aristotle's, in which, it seems, the lecturer is always addressing an audience. In the *Art of Rhetoric*, for example, he makes repeated appeal to common experience and observation in phrases like 'it is obvious', 'it is evident', 'it is clear'. This apparent open-handedness, however, does not imply sycophancy to his hearers, or a want of discursive rigour, but rather a propensity to come to terms with things as they are, with the imperfections of people as they are, with experience, with the 'common sense' view of matters. This should make him easy to read, but in fact he is often puzzling, commonly pedantic and nearly always prosaic. Plato's close-fistedness does not reflect a lack of generosity, tolerance and social sense, but rather the conviction that knowledge of the truth is the one worthy end of existence, and that rigorous dialectic, according to the educational method of his master Socrates, is the one path to that knowledge. This should render him dogged and forbidding, but in fact he is often poetic and passionate and has considerable literary powers. His doggedness is in his devotion to the principle of deductive interlocution that has nothing to do with the characters of interlocutors, the circumstances of the moment, or the desirability of a particular solution. For all his concern with matters like justice and right government, we feel in him an other-worldliness, by comparison with which Aristotle has the diplomatic *pondus* of a senior civil servant. The common perception is expressed effectively, if a little crudely, by W. B. Yeats:

> Plato thought nature but a spume that plays
> Upon a ghostly paradigm of things;
> Solider Aristotle played the taws
> Upon the bottom of a king of kings.[5]

The second distich refers to the fact that for several years Aristotle was tutor to the young Alexander of Macedon; though what 'solid' influence this may have had on the affairs of the world is open to speculation. Bertrand Russell conjectures that Aristotle had very little intellectual influence on Alexander (despite, one presumes, the posterior applications of the tawse), and expresses surprise that Alexander had so little influence on Aristotle, 'whose speculations on politics were blandly oblivious of the fact that the era of City States had given away to the era of empires'.[6]

Plato's general attitude to rhetoric was that it does in fact tend to corrupt the corruptible and seduce the fanciful with fancies; because its object is not knowledge but belief, and then not belief so much as the possibility of believing or not believing something – in effect, of finding reasons to justify inclinations. His position is set out in the *Phaedrus* and also in his *Gorgias*, where he attacks with particular bitterness the sophists' venal capacity for arguing that black is white, that the weaker case may be the stronger, that the worse is demonstrably the better. He is not wholly ill-disposed towards rhetoricians – he is courteous to Gorgias, and in the *Phaedrus* speaks benevolently of Isocrates – but he is not prepared to accord to rhetoric any pretensions greater than those of a propaedeutic study. Certainly he will not allow it to be an 'art', or as we should now say, a 'science'; the Greek work is *tekhne*. He speaks rather dismissively of the rhetorical practitioner as *logodai-dalos*, a 'speech-rigger' whose art is no more than a political *eidolon*. In the *Gorgias*, he defines the status of rhetoric as being to the soul what cookery is to the body. This striking comparison forms part of a larger framework of antitheses, in which real health of mind and body is contrasted with the mere appearance of well-being. The contrasts may be summarized thus:

	True health	Specious well-being
	|	|
Of *mind* is expressed in	*legislation*	*sophistry*
	|	|
	justice	*rhetoric*
Of *body* is expressed in	*physical training*	*cosmetic treatment*
	|	|
	medicine	*cookery*

The framing of laws, the pursuit of justice, the training of the body and the practice of medicine are, says Plato, true 'arts' which 'have for their object the highest well-being of body and soul respectively'; whereas the sophists, the speechifiers, the beauticians, the restaurateurs, all practice 'arts' which are not arts at all, but ways of flattery or pandering, because they set pleasurable self-indulgence and self-deception above the knowledge of what is true and good. Rhetoric is *kolakeia*, 'pandering'; Plato calls it 'a pursuit which has nothing to do with art, but which calls for a lively, shrewd spirit and a natural aptitude for dealing with people'.[7] To understand his concern and the vigour of his onslaught we have to consider the place routinely held by oratory in the affairs of the Athenian state. In our society, a political speech is only a speech by a politican, and not too much depends on it; and with us, eloquence in the law-court, however effective, still needs to be backed by reliable testimony and solid evidence. In the Athens of Socrates and Plato, by contrast, anything and everything might turn on one man's public performance as an orator – the determination of policy, the election of officials, the decision to reprieve or condemn to death. Men might profess to reverence knowledge, but their real respect was for the power of speech. One can understand Plato's restiveness, and his wish that the affairs of the State might be in the control of philosophers. All the same, it is amusing and oddly touching to find him denouncing rhetoric as a pursuit 'which calls for a lively, shrewd spirit and a natural aptitude for dealing with people', since these qualifications are eminently his own. His dialogues are full of humour, banter, a turn for parody, a knowledge of how people react and interact, where they are vulnerable, where they are strong. His insistence, through the character of Socrates, that answers should be short and to the point, does not prevent him, when it suits him, from allowing Socrates to speak at graceful or forceful length. He is also prepared to abandon strict dialectic in favour of myth and parable; and he is willing to charm his leaders with beautiful descriptions of the settings in which his conversations take place. The *Phaedrus*, memorably beautiful from beginning to end, is a fine example of his literary genius, and is thereby a paradox; for to the modern reader at least it must seem that here rhetoric's professed enemy displays an assured command of the resources of rhetoric. Plato may have mistrusted what we now call 'creative writing', but nothing in the world, not even his own philosophical demon, could prevent him from writing creatively.

ARISTOTLE AND THE CRAFT OF LIKELIHOOD

You could not say quite as much for Aristotle; and yet it was Aristotle who was to attempt, and on the whole to achieve, the rehabilitation of rhetoric, its rescue from the sophists and beauticians. An ill-disposed reader might call the *Art of Rhetoric* wearisome, or at best intermittently engaging; no barefoot Socrates here, reclining under the plane trees and ogling his companion – and hence the reader – with his *O philotes*, 'my dear friend'. Aristotle comes to his theme like a dutiful professor parcelling out his course in a three-term plod, and there is not much in the way of literary pleasure to be had from him; and yet he has a claim to be regarded as one of the founders, *the* founder even, of Western literary theory. He presents an analysis of discourse which is accepted by Cicero, elaborated by Quintilian and adopted by the theologians and publicists of the Middle Ages and Renaissance; the materials and pattern of the speech on the Areopagus become the stuff and shape of the address from the pulpit; and the design and content of the sermon suggest the method and conventional episodes of narrative. The classical connection is not as strong now as it once was, but for a long time the general concept of storytelling followed in tandem the general concept of exposition which we have from Aristotle, whether originally or as a digest and systematic development of earlier ideas and teachings on compositional technique.

In his *Rhetoric* he is not primarily concerned with style and composition (*lexis* and *taxis*), even though these matters are treated at some length. What concerns him above all is the psychological claim of rhetoric, the nature of the proofs it can offer in argument, and the kind of material that may legitimately be used in support of those proofs. Plato thought that rhetoric could prove nothing, not least because it could be unscrupulously used to prove anything. For him this totally invalidated its claims in serious discussion and reduced it to a cosmetic art. Aristotle's endeavour was to show how a rhetorician might in all honesty offer a methodologically defensible kind of proof. The word he uses, however, is *pistis*, which does not mean 'proof' in the scientific sense – that would be *apodeixis*; it means, rather, a demonstration of what, in a given set of circumstances, a reasonable person might take to be probable. Pythagoras, engaged in showing that the square on the hypotenuse of a right-angled triangle is equal to the sum of the squares on the other two sides, is committed to *apodeixis*; Mark Anthony, arguing that the demonstrable generosity and benevolence of Caesar towards the people of Rome showed him to be a most unlikely candidate for the character of an ambitious tyrant, resorts to *pistis*, argument on the grounds of probability.

There are two kinds of *pistis*: the *paradeigma*, or example, and the *enthymeme*, a procedure somewhat resembling the philosophical syllogism, but not requiring as its major premise a factual or logically unassailable proposition.[8] Samuel Johnson has given us a nice example of a doggerel enthymeme:

> If the man who turnips cries
> Cry not when his father dies,
> 'Tis a proof that he had rather
> Have a turnip than his father.

The 'proof' turns absurdly on two meanings of the word *cry*, but the argument is nevertheless genuinely and typically enthymemic. Its implied syllogistic structure is something like this:

1　All men mourn for the things they love.
2　John mourns for X.
3　John does not mourn for his father.
4　Thus John loves X more than he loves his father.

This ostensibly tight little argument needs, of course, to be modified a good deal before it can be offered in the hope of persuading a critical audience. We should have to say, perhaps, that 'Since *it is usual* for *most* men to show *some sign* of mourning for things they love, if John *apparently* mourns for X, but *apparently does not* mourn for his father, it *seems likely* that John loves his father less than he loves X.' The enthymemic argument is not a close-fisted logical process; it is open-handed plausibility, the reasonable case which readers or listeners must judge for themselves. With not very much ingenuity we might construct a rival enthymeme:

1 Wise men regard death as a happy release.
2 No one mourns for a happy occurrence.
3 John does not mourn for his father.
4 John therefore considers his father happy.

This might then be constructed in doggerel form:

> That the man who turnips cried
> Cried not when his father died,
> Demonstrates at least that pappy
> In the last resort was happy.

Many literary inventions are of this kind: enthymemes in which a major premise (here 'Wise men regard death as a happy release') is suppressed and has to be retrieved by the understanding reader. To be sure, a good deal of critical activity, from old-fashioned *explication de texte* to new-fangled deconstruction, consists in discovering the premises that underlie the enthymemic representation.

The enthymeme is a form of thought (etymologically the word means 'consideration') rather than a form of composition, and hence does not require a particular linguistic frame. A common representation, however, consists of a maxim (in Greek, *gnome*; the *sententia* of the Roman and medieval rhetoricians), from which the syllogistic argument is drawn: 'It is prudent to repay your debts promptly – for if you neglect your financial obligations to others, they in turn will feel less obliged to consider what they owe to you. . . .'. Such maxims are drawn from the great fund of common wisdoms and agreed perceptions called the *topoi*, which supply the 'materials', the evidential support, for the rhetorical 'proofs'. Aristotle devotes a considerable part of the first two books of his *Rhetoric* to this question of 'materials'. The *topoi* are of two kinds.

Some, called *idia*, are propositions germane to particular subjects, for example, physics or ethics. Others, the larger mass, are called *koinoi topoi* (the 'loci communes' or 'commonplaces' mentioned in chapter 1) because they are common to all branches of rhetoric and exposition. Of these, Aristotle declares that 'they will not make a man practically wise about any particular class of things, because they do not deal with any particular subject matter'. They deal, one might say, with things in general as perceived by people in general. Strictly speaking, the *koinoi topoi* establish frameworks for argument; one argues as to whether a thing is possible or impossible, whether it has happened or will happen, whether it is greater or lesser, good or bad and so on. Closely associated with this notion of the 'common place', however, are those 'materials' which Aristotle outlines as essential to the speaker's stance of sincere and confident authority (his *ethos*) and his ability to play on the emotions of an audience (*pathos*). It is here that the *Rhetoric* comes into its own, for in discussing the materials of proof Aristotle gives us an insight into the Greek mind and a picture of Greek society such as perhaps no history of the time could give. Here we find a catalogue of moral, social and political attitudes and judgements, a comprehensive view of what the common man commonly supposes. Here are what Bacon was to call the Idols of the Tribe. Here, too, are little essays on human nature, such as this rather unflattering portrait of old age:

> Older men and those who have passed their prime have in most cases characters opposite to those of the young. For, owing to their having lived many years and having been more often deceived by others or made more mistakes themselves, and since most human things turn out badly, they are positive about nothing, and in everything they show an excessive lack of energy. They always 'think', but 'know' nothing; and in their hesitation they always add 'perhaps', or 'maybe'; all their statements are of this kind, never unqualified. They are malicious; for malice consists in looking upon the worst side of everything. Further, they are always suspicious owing to mistrust, and mistrustful owing to experience. And neither their love nor their hatred is strong for the same reasons; but, according to the precept of Bias, they love as if they would one day hate, and hate as if they would one day love. And they are little-minded, because they have been humbled by life; for they desire nothing great or uncommon, but only the necessaries of life. They are not generous, for property is one of these necessaries, and at the same time, they know from experience how hard it is to get and how

easy to lose. And they are cowardly and inclined to anticipate evil, for their state of mind is the opposite of that of the young; they are chilled, whereas the young are hot, so that old age paves the way for cowardice, for fear is a kind of chill. And they are fond of life, especially in their last days, because desire is directed towards that which is absent and men especially desire what they lack. And they are unduly selfish ['self-loving', *philautoi*], for this also is littleness of mind. And they live not for the noble, but for the useful, more than they ought, because they are selfish; for the useful is a good for the individual, whereas the noble is good absolutely.

This brutally frank perception of the aged (which continues for a further page) is preceded by a corresponding *aperçu* of the qualities of the young and is followed by a laudatory account of the prime of life. Aristotle's reason for furnishing these 'materials' smacks of expediency or downright cunning. A wise and well-trained orator will know what old men are like, so that he may know how to appeal to an audience of old men: 'since all men are willing to listen to speeches which harmonize with their own character . . . it is easy to see what language we must employ'.[9] However, what Aristotle has also done here, intentionally or otherwise, is to provide an essay in a literary genre, that of the 'character', as it was subsequently to appear in, for example, the writings of Theophrastus, or at a much later date in the works of seventeenth-century English worthies like Joseph Hall and John Earle. He has also thereby contributed fundamentally to the general theory of 'character' in literature.

Another piece of Aristotelian matter that was destined for literary transmutations is the *paradeigma*, the example, used in corroborative support of the enthymeme. Examples, Aristotle suggests, may either precede the argument, in which case their function is one of *epagoge*, 'induction', or they may come at the end, when they will resemble, he proposes, the testimony given by witnesses in court (*corroborative evidence*; this is exactly how the Nun's Priest uses examples in his narrative – see chapter 7, p. **172**). Most interesting is his comment on the possible sources of the orator's examples. They may, he says, consist of reference to things that have actually happened; but where necessary, the orator may invent them for himself.[10] Fiction, providing it be plausible fiction in accordance with the communality of human experience and behaviour, is thus accepted as a legitimate constituent of the *pistis*, the general 'proof'. You may make your own mythograms; you may practise the craft of likelihood.

THE CORRUPTION OF THE HEARER

Aristotle may well have supposed that in his writings on rhetoric he was laying the foundations of an intellectually respectable *tekhne*, based on the enthymeme. The enthymeme is, however, only a part of the rhetorical procedure, associated with the matter of the speech, rather than the emotions it is intended to arouse (*pathos*), or the stance (*ethos*) it sets out to convey. Indeed, Aristotle expressly warns his readers not to attempt enthymemes in conjunction with any effort to play on the emotions, 'for it will either drive out the emotion or it will be useless'.[11] Some degree of emotional appeal he finds necessary. It must not be such as will lead to the undermining of virtue or the perversion of justice, but all the same, for better or for worse, people are inclined to be per-suaded when they are pleased; and therefore some cultivation of style is necessary to accommodate what Aristotle calls 'the corruption of the hearer'.[12]

The further we pursue Aristotle in his framing of rhetorical theory, the more we recognize in his presentation a plotting of that middle ground between philosophy and literary art, in which the principles of reasoning blend with the elements of fiction. As soon as the sage, abandoning the austerity of close reasoning, attempts in the slightest way to charm or divert his audience, he exploits the 'corruption of the hearer' which is also the amiable goal of the story-teller. Among modern writers, who could be more respectful of legitimate argument than Bertrand Russell? Yet here, from his essay 'The Modern Midas', is a piece of enthymemic demonstration, in the course of which we find him making a claim, not on the emotions but on the ordinary humanity of his readers:

> In almost every transaction, the seller is more pleased than the buyer. If you buy a pair of shoes, the whole apparatus of salesmanship is brought to bear upon you, and the seller of the shoes feels as if he had won a little victory. You, on the other hand, do not say to yourself: 'How nice to have got rid of those nasty dirty bits of paper, which I could neither eat nor use as clothing, and to

have got instead a lovely new pair of shoes.' We regard our buying as unimportant in comparison with our selling.

This has all the earmarks of the enthymeme: the opening proposition, the syllogistic statement of contraries or incompatibles (here, 'how the seller sees it' – 'how the buyer sees it'), the conclusion which is in effect a reformulation of the opening proposition. The argument is attended, however, by a certain charm of personality, attributable in the first instance to the author's direct pronominal address to the reader. The proposition in the first sentence is impersonally couched in the passive. In the second sentence, where he begins to elaborate his argument, Russell immediately enlists his reader's co-operation with the appeal of the second person pronoun, *you*. When the original proposition re-emerges in a slightly different form, the assumption that author and reader are by now completely at one is expressed in the pronoun *we*.

Something is added, however, to what is after all a routine business of making friends by discreetly manipulating pronouns. Russell imputes speech to his readers – or rather, suggests that they *might* speak in such-and-such a way; and it is not the way of prunes and pedants, but of warm, ordinary folk who use warm, ordinary words like *nice*, *nasty* and *lovely*. He thus undertakes a simple exercise in fiction: he creates his readers as characters, and in a guise which he presumably supposes that they will find acceptable. It is part of my 'corruption' as a reader, that I like to suppose that the author would like me if he knew me; here Russell offers me that assurance.

About a page further on from the passage quoted above, this follows:

> There was once a butcher in a small town who was infuriated by the other butchers who took away his custom. In order to ruin them, he converted the whole town to vegetarianism, and was surprised to find that as a result he was ruined too. The folly of this man seems incredible, yet if is no greater than that of all the Powers. All have observed that foreign trade enriches other nations, and all have erected tariffs to destroy foreign trade. All have been astonished to find that they were as much injured as their competitors. Not one has remembered that trade is reciprocal, and that a foreign nation which sells to one's own nation also buys from it either directly or indirectly. The reason they have not remembered this is that hatred of foreign nations has made them incapable of clear thinking where foreign trade is concerned.

The particular interest of this lies in its representation of the Aristotelian dictum concerning examples: 'There are two kinds of examples, namely one which consists in relating things that have happened before, and another in inventing them oneself.' We surely cannot believe in Russell's example of the mad butcher as something that actually happened. It is palpably an invention, and yet one that serves plausibly to give concrete effect to the argument urged in the remainder of the passage. Russell is working with the *topoi* of the lesser and the greater (the lesser folly of tradesmen, the greater folly of governments), and of 'could happen – has happened' (what the butcher is alleged to have done *could* happen, because in the actions of governments it *has already* happened).[13] The fiction conveniently lends itself to a strategy of argument. This must remind us, however, that there is argument in all fiction, and that what we as readers do when we discern themes, implications and morals in stories is not very different from the act of discerning the role of propositions, maxims and examples in rhetorical display. The more we understand what is involved in the art of rhetoric, the more keenly aware do we become of what is artfully rhetorical in literature.

THE TALENTS OF THE SPEAKER

As hearers and readers we have our sensibility, our 'corruption' as Aristotle severely calls it, which is arguably a gift of receptiveness corresponding to the productive talent we exercise as speakers. The ancients were in no doubt that an orator must be a person of considerable creative talent; it is one of the insistent themes of the first book of Cicero's *De Oratore*, which takes the form of a discussion fictionally set in the house and garden of Lucius Crassus, Cicero's tutor in rhetoric, at Tusculum. Crassus, one of the friendly disputants, states the requirements of good oratory: *Nam et animi atque ingenii celeres quidam motus esse debent, qui et ad excogitandum acuti, et ad explicandum ornandumque sint uberes, et ad memoriam firmi atque diuturni.* ('For there should be certain lively activities of mind and spirit, shrewd in invention, prolific in exposition and illustration, exact and unfailing in memory.')[14] The word *ingenium*, here loosely translated as 'spirit', might be more fully rendered by our word 'creativeness'. The orator – and by extension the writer – must have a certain intellectual capacity (*animus*) which is inventively exploited by the positive, dynamic

gifts is the virtue of each kind; the particular gift of humankind is the power of speech; therefore the cultivation of the power of speech is highly virtuous. It looks suspiciously like an Idol of the Cave, if not an Idol of the Tribe. Quintilian is on much more convincing ground when he is discussing educational methods and when, in doing so, he illustrates the potentially creative value of a humane and imaginative study of rhetoric. He is always more persuasive as classroom teacher than as theoretician, and some of his general pronouncements on such matters as the study of composition could hardly be bettered. Here he is, for instance, on the art of writing:

> Sit primo vel tardus dum diligens stilus, quaeramus optima nec protinus offerentibus se gaudeamus, adhibeatur iudicium inventis, dispositio probatis. Delectus enim rerum verborumque agendus est et pondera singulorum examinanda. Post subeat ratio collocandi versenturque omni modo numeri, non ut quodque se profert verbum occupet locum. Quae quidem ut diligentius exsequamur, repentenda saepius erunt scriptorum proxima. Nam praeter id quod sic melius iunguntur prioribus sequentia, calor quoque ille cogitationis, qui scribendi mora refrixit, recipit ex integro vires et velut repetito spatio sumit impetum.

> (At first the pen must move slowly but surely. We must make choice of what is best, and not be carried away by things that come on the spur of the moment; we must bring judgement to bear on our ideas, and if they pass muster we must present them with care. For we must indeed *choose* both ideas and words, and each choice is to be separately weighed in our minds. Then we need to work out the order of composition, bearing in mind all the rhythmical possibilities and not putting the words down just as they come to us. To do this as carefully as possible, we shall often have to revise what we have just written. For apart from the fact that in this way we ensure better cohesion between what follows and what precedes, the warmth of thought, which has cooled a little during our writing, is kindled afresh, and takes new impetus as though by repeating its course.)

These observations, set down nearly two thousand years ago, are as just and pertinent today as they ever were, and must move the heart of any teacher to affectionate recognition of a colleague patiently coming to grips with perennially familiar problems. It is not the application of rules that Quintilian stresses here, but rather the processes of choosing, evaluating, revising and learning as a result of revision; his excellent account of what happens when we write acknowledges the fact (urged by centuries of professors upon generations of students) that the process is itself heuristic, that the knowing comes from the doing. At the heart of all the effort is what Quintilian calls the *calor cogitationis*, the 'warmth of thought'. It is to the mind's 'warmth' that the pattern and style of discourse must answer, with an artful fastidiousness that awakens a corresponding 'warmth' in the mind of the reader. To over-write, to manufacture expression in elaborate excess of content, is tasteless, and is condemned as 'frigid'. Cicero and Quintilian say *frigidus*; in the Greek writers the corresponding term is *psykhros*. Aristotle traces 'frigidity' of style in Greek prose to four principal causes: the use of too many compound words, the use of strange words, the excessive use of epithets and the injudicious use of metaphors.[18] By these criteria the habitual style of our modern copywriters is, if not 'frigid', at least 'cool'; but we have in some ways lost touch with classical canons of taste and the concepts of creativeness that those canons imply.

CREATIVENESS AND THE REHABILITATION OF RHETORIC

'Creativeness' must be a key word if one is nowadays to mount a convincing defence of rhetoric as a study. Other defences may have their historical interest, but will not convince the modern mind. We have seen too many eloquent demagogues, some of them honest souls, some of them hypocrites, some of them venal jackasses, some of them thoroughly evil men (Hitler was a devastatingly effective orator), to be convinced of the proposition that the rhetorician must by nature be a good man. As to the 'virtue' of rhetoric, we cannot avoid the accusation that this strength may be turned to harmful as well as to good purposes, and the excuse that this is not the art's fault will not altogether mitigate the possible offence. Eloquence is in any case no longer generally regarded as the supreme intellectual gift of humankind, and our societies and politics are no longer principally reliant upon it. If we still accept the notion that knowledge is power, what we mostly respect is not the kind of 'knowledge' that rhetoricians have claimed, a knowledge of human motives, of probabilities in event and behaviour, of common attitudes and habits of thought, of different sorts and conditions of people. Such knowledge ought to be respected, no doubt, but it is rarely thought of as 'real' knowledge; rather as a knack of dealing with people, or as a kind of cunning. In fact, all the charges Plato had to bring against rhetoric and rhetoricians still remain, whether in the reasoning of those who follow Plato, or in the suspicions of those who follow their own noses.

One of the ironies of the history of the subject is that the retreat from rhetoric in modern times, its loss of intellectual and moral credit, seems in retrospect to have been accelerated by the efforts of a reformer who sought to redefine the scope of rhetoric in order to reinvigorate the subject and promote its educational and creative value. Petrus Ramus (Pierre de la Ramée, 1515–72), dissatisfied with the traditional organization that loosely incorporated the dialectic and stylistic elements of composition, proposed a redistribution that would assign the former (that is *heuresis* and *taxis*) to the province of logic, and the latter (*lexis*, *hypocrisis*) to rhetoric proper. A major purpose of this was to enable Ramus to bring literary texts and their structure into the general province of logic. When a writer or speaker conceives and prepares his material, according to Ramus, his mental operations are essentially those of the dialectician; he becomes a rhetorician only in the act of presenting his material to hearers or readers. Ramist doctrines were educationally fruitful, and we can still find traces of them in the modern classroom and in critical theory. They had, however, one consequence which can hardly have been intended by Ramus, of encouraging rhetoricians to elaborate the stylistic aspect of composition and neglect its dialectic foundation. The almost inescapable tendency was the identification of 'rhetoric' with 'figures of speech', and therefore with mere insubstantial linguistic trickery. In its literary manifestations the elevation of style, as exemplified by our sixteenth-century writer Lyly (see p. 136), inevitably provoked a reaction against the ornate, expressed first by Bacon in his *Advancement of Learning*, and subsequently by the scientists of the Royal Society, who considered their business to be with things, not words.

Rhetoric may well look like an art at the end of its tether, and to denounce it has become almost a mark of intellectual and moral respectability. But for all that can be said against it, it will not oblige its detractors by dying out – not just yet. There are two related reasons for this tenacious hold on life, two effects traceable to the single cause of human creativeness. Cicero and Quintilian were perhaps right, after all, to appeal to the *virtus* of the race – except that the 'virtue' of humankind is arguably something other than, and prior to, reason and eloquence. It lies in perceiving relationships, making connections, designing an order, projecting a shape; it lies in the impulse to *create*; something that the Tribe will always strive to do, even when relationship, connection, order, shape are beheld nowhere except in the mind of the beholder. The art of rhetoric is in one sense a mere technology, but a valuable one because it provides us with the means of creating. It provides the patterns and procedures that enable us to frame and train our perceptions; it gives the templates, so to speak, that enable us to construct our views and know what we think. It does not matter whether the art is demonstrated by an instructor, or whether it is self-taught; whether it is articulated in a classroom or worked out in the silence of the study; whether it is learned in terms that have not changed for two thousand years or acquired on a system that someone cobbled up last week. 'Rhetoric' in this important sense is just another name for 'technique', and technique is something that students of any accomplishment must acquire. If you cannot find someone to teach you a technique, you must make your own; and if you teach yourself a technique for writing, you have made yourself a rhetoric.

The 'related reason' for rhetoric's continued life is that in studying it we in fact study the thing that fascinates us most, our primary human *virtus*, our creativeness, the nature, causes and forms of which can never cease to engage the enquiring mind. All matters presented in works on rhetoric as resources and procedures for the practising orator – the *topoi*, the enthymeme, the materials of 'proofs', the directions concerning *inventio* and *dispositio* – are at bottom attempts to understand how the mind works as it goes about its creative business. There are of course forms of creativeness that are non-verbal, and almost certainly there is nothing that a rhetorician could say that would begin to explain the *heuresis* of painting, music or mathematics. But as long as we present arguments, tell stories, write poems, make jokes, we shall be interested in how these things come into being, what each verbal activity involves and how such activities are related to each other. We shall investigate, and in doing so may elect to give our investigations some preferred academic name – aesthetics, literary criticism, deconstruction, textology; but we shall be practising nothing other than a form of rhetoric, if our enquiries lead us beneath the surface and into the origin of texts.

This defence of rhetoric, as something that both manifests a primary creative impulse and promotes our understanding of it, does not imply an Olympian pastime that has lost its mundane uses. Rhetoric continues to be the social practice Aristotle and Cicero wanted it to be, because there are always questions to be argued, issues to be debated and cases to be presented. What are the current materials for rhetoric? My newspaper tells me: the national economy; immigration and race relations; apartheid; drug abuse; the spread of AIDS; famine in the Third World. Such are the matters that yield the topics that produce the enthymemes that suggest the examples that fill the columns that journalists make. To say, with a long face of disapproval, that these are questions too important for rhetoric is wholly to miss the point; they simply must be discussed rhetorically if they are to be discussed at all. Without a rhetoric we cannot bring the issue into perspective; even Plato (whose Attic frown I seem to see) might consent to that. That there are 'good' and 'bad' rhetorics needs hardly to be said, but then what is it we evaluate? The general practice of an art of persuasion? The particular case that the rhetorician is trying to demonstrate? Or the writer's skill in choosing, ordering and presenting his argument? These are interesting questions, in which you, *O philotes*, are more deeply involved than you may suppose. You see I have designs on you, as the tattooist said to his girl friend . . . ; but perhaps we should move elsewhere, away from this crowded page and into some sociable corner where we may take a cup of this or a glass of that, and continue at our leisure our discussion of this entrancing subject.

Notes

Chapter 1 'If I Might Claim Your Attention for a Moment...'

1 Horace, *Odes*, IV, 7, 'Diffugere nives'; James Michie translates, 'No blue blood, no good deeds done, no eloquent pleading / Ever shall conjure you back.' See *The Odes of Horace*, tr. James Michie (Harmondsworth, 1967, repr. 1973), pp. 230–1.

2 Aristotle (*Rhetoric*, II. xviii, 2) indicates that the *koinoi* are the topics common to the three kinds of rhetoric: the forensic, the deliberative and the epideictic (demonstrative). In the course of a long discursive life, however, *koinos topos – locus communis – commonplace* has gradually shifted its meaning towards the sense of 'matter or formulation of common experience'. *Topos/locus* in the older literature has at least three senses: (1) a 'place', ie. a 'heading' or category, to which a given kind of argument may be assigned, and under which arguments may be mnemonically 'stored'; (2) a 'position' from which to develop an argument, demonstration or train of discourse; and (3) a theme drawn from general experience – an expression of conventional wisdom.

3 'Five sequent elements'. Corax of Syracuse, author (in the fifth century B.C.) of the earliest known of the Greek systems of forensic rhetoric, divided the argument into three parts, the exordium (*prooimion*), the confirmation and refutation (*agones*) and the epilogue (*epilogos*), a scheme which could be expanded into five parts by adding the 'narration', or statement of case (*diegesis*) after the exordium, and by developing the 'confirmation' with supporting arguments (*parekbaseis*). Cicero (*De Oratore*, I.xxxi, 143) outlines the parts of the oration as; the initial appeal to the goodwill of the audience, followed by the

statement of the case, followed by the definition of the matters essentially at issue, followed by arguments in confirmation and refutation, leading to the peroration. Quintilian (*Institutio*, III.ix, 1) states that 'most authorities divide the forensic speech into four parts: the exordium, the statement of facts (*narratio*), the proof (*probatio*) and the peroration'. To this he adds that some would complicate the scheme by adding further categories. He himself is critical of rigid models (see *Institutio*, II.xiii, 1). The author of the *Ad Herennium* (III.i) states that a discourse has six parts, which he calls *exordium*, *narratio*, *divisio*, *confirmatio*, *confutatio*, *conclusio*. This is the source for most subsequent representations of the matter. The *divisio* corresponds to the Ciceronian 'definition of the matters essentially at issue'.

4   But Anthony's 'plain man' approach is after all just a little stylish, with its 'lend me your ears' for 'listen'. Shakespeare echoes Latin literary idiom: cf. Livy, *praebere aures conviciis adulescentium*, 'to lend ears to the grumbles of the young'.

5   On style levels, see, for example, Cicero, *De Oratore*, III.li, 199.

6   James Boswell, *Life of Johnson* (Oxford, repr. 1983) p. 524.

7   Geoffrey Chaucer, *The Clerk's Tale*, 'Prologue', l. 15–18.

8   Roman rhetoricians used the term *color*, and also *lumen* ('light', i.e. 'illustration'). See *Rhetorica ad Herennium*, IV.xi, 16 and IV.xxiii, 32: *quae si rarae disponentur, distinctam sicuti coloribus . . . reddunt orationem* ('which, if they [i.e. the figures] are sparingly used, set off the style like colours') and *si raro interseremus has exornationes . . . commode luminibus distinctis inlustrabimus orationem* ('if we introduce these ornaments infrequently . . . we shall brighten our style agreeably with distinctive highlights').

9   The roof of the car may seem an odd place for the 'spoiler'. In this case, however, the car is of the so-called 'hatchback' design, and the spoiler – just a little one – is mounted above the tailgate.

References

p.1   *The Holy Bible* (Authorized Version, 1611), Genesis,III, 1–6.

p.10   Shakespeare, *Julius Caesar*, Act III, Scene ii.

p.14 Thomas Sprat, *History of the Royal Society* (1667).
p.16 James Boswell, *Life of Johnson*, ed. R.W.Chapman (Oxford, repr. 1983).
p.19 *The Independent*, Tuesday 12 January 1988.
p.23 Advertisement for *Peugeot 205*; in the *Radio Times*, B–15 January 1988.

Chapter 2   Rhetoric as Emotion

1   The 'directives' are, in fact, pluridirectional; they address both the maker and the occupant of the grave.
2   Shakespeare, *Sonnets*, 146: 'Poor soul, the centre of my sinful earth'.

References

p.29 Shakespeare, *The Tempest*, Act IV, Scene i.
p.32 St Paul, Corinthians I, 15, 51–4.
p.34 John Donne, *Holy Sonnets, IV; in Poems*, ed. H.J.C. Grierson (Oxford, 1912). (Spelling here modernized.)
p.38 Abraham Lincoln, 'Address at the Dedication of the National Cemetery at Gettysburg', 19 November 1863.
p.41 'Lugete, o veneres', in *Catulli Carmina*, ed. Robinson Ellis (Oxford, 1937), III.
p.42 Emily Dickinson, 'A Country Burial', in *Poems, First and Second Series*, ed. Mabel Loomis Todd and T. W. Higginson (Cleveland & New York, 1948; 2nd ser. IV.xxiii.
p.44 Dylan Thomas, 'A Refusal to Mourn . . .', in *Collected Poems, 1934–1952* (London, 1952).

Chapter 3   Rhetoric as Distraction

1   'Simplicity',: John Hollander and Frank Kermode (*The Literature of Renaissance England*, Oxford, 1973, p. 432) gloss this as 'stillness', which may well be a misprint for 'silliness'. 'Stillness' vitiates the sense of the line, which rather pointedly contrasts two meanings of 'simple', i.e. 'straightforward' and 'stupid' (as in *simpleton* or *Simple Simon*). The latter sense of 'simple' persists in regional English.
2   '1st September 1939' in W. H. Auden, *Collected Shorter Poems, 1930–1944* (London, 1950), p. 74.

References

p.54   Chaucer, *Troilus and Criseyde*, I, 218–31, in *The Works of Geoffrey Chaucer*, ed. F. N. Robinson (2nd edn, London, 1957).

p.56   Tennyson, 'The Last Tournament', ll. 457–67 in *The Poems of Tennyson*, ed. Christopher Ricks (London, 1969).

p.57   Milton, *Paradise Lost*, I, 192–210, in *The Literature of Renaissance England*, ed. John Hollander and Frank Kermode (New York, London and Toronto, 1973). (Text with modernized spelling.)

p.60   C. Day Lewis, 'As One Who Wanders...', in *Collected Poems 1954* (London 1954).

p.64   Shakespeare, *Sonnets*, 66.

p.66   Wordsworth, *The Prelude (1850), III, 598–611*, in *William Wordsworth, The Prelude, A Parallel Text*, J.C.Maxwell (Harmondsworth, 1971).

p.67   Wordsworth, *Prelude*, III, 582–97.

p.68   W.H.Auden, 'Birthday Poem (to Christopher Isherwood)' in *Collected Shorter Poems, 1930–1944* (London, 1950).

p.70   Trader's 'pitch' in a street market, Loughborough, Leicestershire (*c*. 1980); my transcription from tape recording.

p.71   'Ads' from the personal columns, *The Weekly*, Seattle, 20–6 August 1986.

Chapter 4   Images of Argument

1   Among Shakespeare's own inkhornisms in this play are *tortive*, *protractive* and *persistive* – all from Agamemnon's address to the Greek commanders (I.iii. 1ff.). The *OED* cites this context and records no earlier instances.

2   In the aphorisms of his *Novum Organum*, tr. R.J.Ellis and James Spedding, in *Collected Works of Francis Bacon*, ed. J.Spedding, R.L. Ellis and D.D.Heath (7 vols, London, 1857–9). On the *Idols*, see chapter 8 below.

3   'Tropodrome', on the model of *syndrome*, a pattern of symptoms or signs; thus a *tropodrome* would mean a pattern of thematically related tropes. A joke-word, perhaps; yet there is a need for some such term to distinguish the incidental flourish of metaphor from the careful organization of mythic narrative.

References

p.78   Shakespeare, *Troilus and Cressida*, Act I, Scene iii.
p.90   The Gospel According to St Luke, 8, 11–15.
p.91   St Paul, Euphesians 6, 11–17.
p.92   G.K.Chesterton, 'The Wind and the Trees' in *Chesterton's Stories, Essays and Poems* (London, repr. 1965).
p.99   Article in the *Observer* newspaper, 7 August 1988.

Chapter 5   Figures of Speech, Facts of Language

1   'Whose woods these are . . .' is the first line of Frost's 'Stopping by Woods on a Snowy Evening', from the volume called *New Hampshire* (1923); see *Robert Frost, Selected Poems* (London, 1955), p. 145.

2   George Puttenham, *The Arte of English Poesie* (1589), ed. Gladys D.Willcock and Alice Walker (Cambridge, 1936), pp. 163, 178, 186.

3   Demetrius, *On Style*, tr. W. Rhys Roberts (London, 1927), IV, 196 (p. 423).

4   Puttenham, *English Poesie*, p.201. Puttenham calls *antanaclasis* 'the *Rebound*, alluding to the tennis ball which being smitten with the racket reboundes back againe'.

5   Quintilian, *Institutio Oratoria*, Viii.vi. 8. Cicero notes in *De Oratore*, III.xxxix, 157: *Similitudinis est ad verbum unum contracta brevitas, quod verbum in alieno loco tanquam in suo positum si agnoscitur, delectat, si simile nihil habet, repudiatur*, ('[A metaphor] is a contraction of a simile into one word, which occupies an alien context as though it really belonged there; if its applicability is recognized it gives pleasure, but if it offers no resemblance it is rejected.') On the whole, Quintilian's is the more cogent explanation.

6   The traditional concept of metonymy is expounded in the *Rhetorica ad Herennium*, IV.xxxii, where it is called *denominatio*. For broader views of the term in modern critical and semiotic theory, see Kenneth Burke, *A Grammar of Motives* (1945); and Roman Jakobson, 'Closing Statements: Linguistics and Poetics', in *Style in Language* ed. T.A.Sebeok (Cambridge, Mass., 1960).

7   Jakobson, 'Closing Statement', pp. 369–70.

8   The point of Cicero's pun is that in the course of his general

depredations Verres had pillaged the temple of Hercules, thus giving the god more trouble than did the Erymanthine boar, which Hercules slew as one of his labours. Elsewhere in the Verrines, Cicero suggests that Verres will make a clean sweep of everything (*verres* being the second person singular of the future tense of *verrere*, to sweep). He also puns on the name of Verres' predecessor in office, one Sacerdos. The word *sacerdos* signifies a sacrificing priest, and the pig was a sacrificial animal; it was a bad priest, says Cicero, who left behind him a worthless pig like Verres. Quintilian is uncomfortable about jokes on names, which seem to him to border on bad taste, but defends Cicero in this instance on the grounds that the witticisms are *ab aliis dicta*, quoted from others.

9   In Sonnet 135, 'Whoever hath her wish, thou hast thy *Will*', Shakespeare puns on his own given name in three senses, i,e, 'volition', 'desire', and 'sexual organ'.

References

p.109 Samuel Johnson, *The Vanity of Human Wishes* 291ff., in *Poems*, ed. David Nichol Smith and Edward L.MacAdam (Oxford, 1941).

p.110 St Paul, Corinthians I, 13, 11–12.

p.118 Swift, 'An Argument to prove that the Abolishing of Cristianity in England may . . . be attended with some inconveniences . . . in *Swift: Gulliver's Travels and Selected Writings in Prose and Verse*, ed. John Hayward (London and New York, 1944).

p.120 W.H. Auden, *Collected Shorter Poems, 1930–1933* (London, 1950); for the various lines quoted here, see respectively pp. 99, 288, 189, 122, 100, 21.

p.121 W. H. Auden, *Collected Shorter Poems*, p. 160.

p.124 Shakespeare, *Macbeth*, Act V, Scene iii.

p.129 Shakespeare, *King Henry IV, Part I* Act V, Scene i.

Chapter 6   Patterns of Writing, Processes of Art

1   Aristotle, *Poetics*, VII. 2ff.

2   William Labov, 'The Transformation of Experience in Narrative Syntax' in *Language in the Inner City: Studies in the Black*

English Vernacular (Philadelphia, 1984) pp. 354–96. The narrative framework here cited is described on pp. 363ff.

3　In the Introduction to their edition of *Euphues* (New York and London, 1916), Morris W.Croll and H. Clemens provide an excellent analysis of the stylistic elements of Euphuism.

4　The pattern, in fact, incorporates two figures: that of *chiasmus*, and that of *epanodos*, which Puttenham (*English Poesie* p. 221) calls 'the *retire*'.

5　Quintilian (*Institutio*, X.i, 79) says of Isocrates that he was *in compositione adeo diligens, ut cura eius reprehendatur* ('so studious in composition that his care is reprehensible') – in other words, finicky to a fault, This description applies very well to Lyly, whose pursuit of compositional rhythms may owe something to Isocrates: see William A. Ringler Jr., 'The Immediate Source of Euphuism', *PMLA*, LIII (1938), pp. 678–86.

References

p.131 Samuel Johnson, *The Vanity of Human Wishes*, 291–322, in *poems*, ed. David Nichol Smith and Edward L. MacAdam (oxford, 1941).

p.136 John Lyly, *Euphues: The Anatomy of Wit* (1578), ed. Morris W. Croll and H.Clemens (New York and London, 1916).

p.139 Francis Bacon, 'Of Studies'; *Essays*, in *Works*, ed. James Spedding, R,L. Ellis, and D.D.Health (7 vols, London, 1857–9).

p.143 John Donne, *Holy Sonnets*, IV in *Poems*, ed. H.J.C. Grierson (Oxford 1912). (Spelling here modernized.)

p.145 Wordsworth, 'Composed upon Westminster Bridge, September 3, 1802: Miscellaneous Sonnets, XXXVI', in *Poetical Works of William Wordsworth*, ed. Thomas Hutchinson (London, 1913).

p.147 Browning, 'Memorabilia', in *Browning: A Selection*, ed. W.E.Williams (Harmondsworth, 1954, repr, 1981).

p.149 Browning, 'Two In the Campagna' ibid.

p.152 F.Scott Fitzgerald, 'The Cut-Glass Bowl', in *The Stories of F. Scott Fitzgerald, vol I: The Diamond as Big as the Ritz and other Stories* (Harmondsworth, 1962).

p.155 Dickens, *A Christmas Carol*, in *Christmas Books*, intr. Eleanor Farjeon (London, 1954) (*The New Oxford Illustrated Dickens*).

p.158 James Joyce, 'The Dead' in *Dubliners* (London, 1914; repr. Harmondsworth, 1976).

p.161 Jane Austen, *Northanger Abbey*, ed. R.W. Chapman (Oxford, 1923).

Chapter 7   The Humours of Rhetoric

1   On Shakespeare's education, see Thomas W. Baldwin, *William Shakspere's Small Latine and Lesse Greeke* 2 vols (Urbana, Ill, 1944).

2   *Henry IV, Part I*; Act II, Scene ii, 84f.

3   Puttenham, *English Poesie*, p.226.

4   *The Hunting of the Snark*, in *The Penguin Complete Lewis Carroll* (Harmondsworth, repr. 1984), pp.677–99. The Baker's loss of his luggage and his name is recorded in Fit the First; and the uncle's warning to his 'beamish nephew' in Fit the Third.

References

p.168 Chaucer, *The Nun's Priest's Tale*, in *The Works of Geoffrey Chaucer*, ed. F.N.Robinson (2nd edn, London, 1957).

p.176 Shakespeare, *King Henry IV, Part I*, Act II, Scene iv.

p.181 Alexander Pope, 'The Episode of Sarpedon', and *The Rape of the Lock*, Canto V in *The Poems of Alexander Pope* ed. John Butt (London, 1963).

p.185 Byron, *Don Juan*, Canto I, in *Lord Byron: Don Juan*, ed. T.G, Steffan, W.W.Pratt and E. Steffan (Harmondsworth, 1900).

p.188 Dickens, *A Tale of Two Cities*; intr. Sir John Shuckburg (London, 1949) (*The New Oxford Illustrated Dickens*)

p.191 Harold Pinter, *The Caretaker* (London,1960)

p.193 Malcolm Bradbury, *The History Man* (London, 1975)

p.195 Tom Stoppard, *The Real Inspector Hound* (London, 1968).

Chapter 8   The Defences of Rhetoric

1   One of the cooler judgements on Bacon's plea that gifts never influenced his decisions has been pronounced by Bertrand Russell, in *History of Western Philosophy* (London, 1946), p. 563: 'As to that, anyone may form his own opinion, since there can be no evidence as to the decisions that Bacon would

have come to in other circumstances.'

2   *Chriae*, 'moral essays', are mentioned by Quintilian as part of the training of the young student of rhetoric (*Institutio*, I.ix, 3ff.). A *chria* is roughly equivalent to a 'homework essay' – and in the form *kria* is still bears that meaning among Swedish schoolchildren.

3   See note 2, chapter 4 above.

4   See, for example, *An Essay towards the Establishment of a Real Character and a Philosophical Language* (1668), by John Wilkins, Bishop of Chester. Wilkins's aim was the elimination of ambiguity, in the writing system ('character') and in the lexicon; he remarks on the 'many wild errors that shelter themselves under the guise of affected phrases; which being philosophically unfolded and rendered according to the genuine and natural importance [= 'import', 'sense'] of words, will appear to be inconsistence and contradictions'. His views on language are strikingly similar to those expressed by his contemporary, Thomas Sprat; here cited in Chapter 1, p. 14.

5   W.B.Yeats, 'Among Schoolchildren', in *Collected Poems* (London, 1900), p.244.

6   Bertrand Russell, *A History of Western Philosophy*, p. 183.

7   Plato's account of rhetoric as 'cookery' and so on is to be found in the *Gorgias*, sections 462–5.

8   In *Rhetoric*, II.ii, 8, Aristotle draws analogies between the procedures of dialectic, with its inductions and syllogisms, and those of rhetoric, with its examples and enthymemes; the example (*paradeigma*), he says, is a kind of induction, and the enthymeme is a kind of syllogism.

9   Aristotle, *Rhetoric*, II.xiii, 16.

10   Aristotle, *Rhetoric*, II.xx, 2.

11   Aristotle, *Rhetoric*, III.xvii, 8.

12   Aristotle, *Rhetoric*. III. i, 6.

13   These *topoi* are mentioned by Aristotle (*Rhetoric* II. xviii, xix) in a list of the standard resources of the orator.

14   Cicero, *De Oratore*, I.xxv, 113.

15   Cicero, *De Oratore*, I.xx, 91.

16   Cicero, *De Oratore*, I.xxii, 102 ff.; Quintilian, *Institutio*, II.xvii, 1ff.

17   Quintilian, *Institutio*, II.xx, 9.

18   Aristotle, *Rhetoric*, III.iii, 1–4.

References

p.205   Samuel Johnson: '*BURLESQUE* of the following lines of Lopez de Vega. An *IMPROMPTU*:Se acquien los leones vence / Vence una muger hermosa / O el de flaco avergence / O ella di ser mas furiosa.' Here cited from *Miscellaneous Poems* in *The Works of Samuel Johnson*, vol.XI (London, 1787).

p.207   Aristotle, *Rhetoric*, II.xiii.

p.209   Bertrand Russell, 'The Modern Midas' in *In Praise of Idleness* (London 1935, repr. 1976).

p.214   Quintilian, *Institutio Oratoria*, X.iii, 5 (My translation).

Bibliography

General

Corbett, Edward P. J., *Classical Rhetoric for the Modern Student (New York, 1965)*.

Dixon, Peter, *Rhetoric* (London, 1971).

Lanham, Richard A., *A Handlist of Rhetorical Terms: A Guide for Students of English Literature* (Berkeley and Los Angeles, 1968).

Vickers, Brian, *Classical Rhetoric in English Poetry (London, 1970)*.

Vickers, Brian (ed.), *Rhetoric Revalued: Papers from the International Society for the History of Rhetoric* (New York, 1982).

Weinberg, Bernard, 'Rhetoric after Plato', in *Dictionary of the History of Ideas*, ed. in chief Philip P. Werner, (vol. IV, pp.00). (New York, 1973).

Classical Rhetoric

Texts

(LCL- Loeb Classical Library, London. Dates cited are of the first printing and of the reprint consulted.)

Greek

Aristotle, *The 'Art' of Rhetoric*, tr. J. H. Freese (LCL, 1926; repr. 1947).

Aristotle, *The Poetics*, tr. W. Hamilton Fyfe (LCL, 1927; repr. 1965).

Demetrius (called 'Demetrius of Phalerum') *On Style*, tr. W. Rhys Roberts. With Aristotle, *The Poetics* (LCL, 1927; repr. 1965).

Isocrates, 'Against the Sophists' and 'Antidosis', in *Works*, tr. G. Norlin and L. van Hook (3 vols, LCL, 1928–45), see vol. II.

Longinus, *On the Sublime*, tr. W. Hamilton Fyfe. With Aristotle, *The Poetics* (LCL, 1927; repr. 1965).

Lucian, 'A Professor of Public Speaking', in *Works*, vol. IV, tr. A. M. Harmon (LCL, 1925).

Plato, *Gorgias*, in *Works*, vol.V, tr. W. M. R. Lamb (LCL 1925; repr. 1975). (See also the excellent translation of the *Gorgias* by Walter Hamilton, Penguin Classics, 1960).

Plato, *Phaedrus*, in *Works*, vol. I, tr. H. N. Fowler (LCL, 1914; repr. 1947).

Latin

Cicero, *De Inventione* and *De Optimo Genere Oratorum*, tr. H. M. Hubbell (LCL, 1949).

Cicero, *De Oratore* (Books I and II), tr. E. W. Sutton and H. Rackham (LCL, 1942).

Cicero, *De Oratore* (Book III) and *De Partitione Oratoria*, tr. H. Rackham (LCL, 1942).

Cicero *Brutus*, tr. G. L. Hendrickson, and *Orator*, tr. H. M. Hubbell (rev. edn., LCL, 1962).

Anon., formerly attributed to Cicero, *Rhetorica ad Herennium*, tr. H. Caplan (LCL, 1954).

Quintilian, *Institutio Oratoria*, tr. H. E. Butler (4 vols, LCL 1920–2).

Commentaries and Studies

Benner, Margareta, *The Emperor Says: Studies in the Edicts of the Early Empire* (Gothenburg, Acta Universitatis Gothoburgensis, 1975).

Bolgar, R. R., *The Classical Heritage and its Beneficiaries* (Cambridge 1954).

Clark, M. L. *Rhetoric at Rome: A Historical Survey* (London, 0000).

Kennedy, George, *The Art of Persuasion in Greece* (Princeton, 1963).

Kennedy, George, *The Art of Rhetoric in the Roman World* (Princeton, 1972).

Leeman, A. D., *Orationis Ratio: The Stylistic Theories and Practice of the Roman Orators, Historians and Philosophers* (Amsterdam, 1963).

Medieval Rhetoric

Atkins, J. W. H., *English Literary Criticism: The Medieval Phase* (Cambridge, 1943).

Curtius, Ernst Robert, *European Literature and the Latin Middle Ages*, tr. Willard R. Trask (New York and London, 1953, first publ. 1948).

Howell, Wilbur Samuel (ed. and tr.), *The Rhetoric of Alcuin and Charlemagne* (New York, 1965).

Murphy, James J. (ed.), *Three Medieval Rhetorical Arts* (Berkeley, Los Angeles and London, 1971). [The 'arts' are treatises: on letter-writing (Anon., 1135); on poetics (Geoffrey de Vinsauf, 1210); and on preaching (Robert de Basevoin, 1322).]

Murphy, James J., *Rhetoric in the Middle Ages: A History of Rhetorical Theory from St Augustine to the Renaissance* (Berkeley and Los Angeles, 1974).

Murphy, James J., *Medieval Eloquence* (Berkeley and Los Angeles, 1978).

Payne, Robert O., 'Chaucer and the Art of Rhetoric', in *Companion to Chaucer Studies* ed. Beryl Rowland (Toronto, 1968), pp. 38–57.

Renaissance Rhetoric and English Literature

Texts

Fraunce, Abraham, *The Arcadian Rhetorike* (1588), ed. Ethel Seaton (Oxford, 1950).

Hoskins, John, *Directions for Speech and Style* (c. 1599), ed. Hoyt H. Hudson (Princeton, 1935).

Peacham, Henry, *The Garden of Eloquence* (1577), Scolar Press Facsimiles. (Manston 1971).

Puttenham, George, *The Art of English Poesie* (first publ. 1589), ed. Gladys D. Willcock and Alice Walker (Cambridge, 1936).

Ramus, Petrus, *Dialectique (Dialecticae Libri Duo*, 1555), ed. Critique avec introduction, notes et commentaire de M. Dassonville (Travaux d'Humanisme et Renaissance, Geneva, 1961).

Sidney, Sir Philip, *An Apology for Poetry, or the Defence of Poetry* (1595), ed. Geoffrey Shepherd (London, 1965).

Wilson, Thomas, *The Arte of Rhetorique* (2nd edn., 1560), ed. G.H.Mair (Oxford, 1909).

Studies

Baldwin, Thomas W., *William Shakspere's Small Latine and Lesse Greeke*, 2 vols. (Urbana, Ill., 1944).

Broadbent, J. B., 'Milton's Rhetoric', in *Modern Philology*, LVI (1959), pp. 224–42; reprinted in Alan Rudrum (ed.), *Milton: Modern Judgements* (London, 1968).

Clemen, Wolfgang, *English Tragedy before Shakespeare: The Development of Dramatic Speech*, tr. T.S. Dorsch (London, 1961).

Croll, Morris W. and Clemens, H. (eds.), *Euphues (Euphues: The Anatomy of Wit* and *Euphues his England)* (New York and London 1916).

Croll, Morris W. *Style, Rhetoric, and Rhythm* ed. J. Max Patrick and Robert O.Evans (Princeton, 1966).

Howell, Wilbur S., *Logic and Rhetoric in England, 1500–1700* (Princeton, 1956).

Joseph, Sister Miriam, *Shakespeare's Use of the Arts of Language* (New York, 1947).

Lanham, Richard A., *The Motives of Eloquence: Literary Rhetoric in the Renaissance* (New Haven and London, 1976).

Ringler, William A. Jr., 'The Immediate Source of Euphuism', *PMLa*, LIII (1938), pp. 678–86.

Sandford, William Phillips, *English Theories of Public Address*, 1530–1827. Ohio State University (dissertation, 1965).

Sonnino, Lee A., *A Handbook to Sixteenth Century Rhetoric* (London, 1968).

Tuve, Rosemond, *Elizabethan and Metaphysical Imagery: Renaissance Poetic and Twentieth-Century Critics* (Chicago, 1947).

Vickers, Brian *Francis Bacon and Renaissance Prose* (Cambridge, 1968).

Vickers, Brian, *The Artistry of Shakespeare's Prose* (London, 1968).

Aspects of English Rhetoric from the Restoration to the Nineteenth Century

Texts

Blair, Hugh, *Lectures on Rhetoric and Belles Lettres*, 2 vols (London, 1783); Reprinted with an Introduction by Harold F.Harding (Carbondale and London, 1965).

Golden, James L. and Corbett, E. J. P. (eds), *The Rhetoric of Blair, Campbell and Whately* (New York, 1968).

Smith, Adam, *Lectures on Rhetoric and Belles Lettres* (1762–3; given at Glasgow, text from notes made by a student) ed. John M. Lothian (London, 1963).

Studies

Blakemore, Steven, *Burke and the Fall of Language: The French Revolution as a Linguistic Event* (Hanover NH, 1988).

Boulton, James T., *The Language of Politics in the Age of Wilkes and Burke* (London, 1963).

Feder, Lillian, 'John Dryden's Use of Classical Rhetoric', *PMLA, LXIX (1954), pp. 1258–78.*

Nash, Walter, 'Tennysonian Topography', in *Studies in Honour of Kenneth Cameron*, Leeds Studies in English, XVIII (1987), pp. 55–69.

Olson, Elder, 'Rhetoric and the Appreciation of Pope', *Modern Philology*, XXXVII (1939–40), pp. 13–35.

Petrie, Graham, 'Rhetoric as Fictional Technique in *Tristram Shandy*', *Philological Quarterly* XLVIII (1969), pp.479–94.

Stone, P. W. K., *The Art of Poetry, 1750–1820* (London, 1967).

Sucksmith, H. P., *The Narrative Art of Charles Dickens: The Rhetoric of Sympathy and Irony in his Novels* (London, 1970).

Modern Studies on Rhetoric, Criticism and the Ideology of Language

Booth, Wayne C., *The Rhetoric of Fiction* (Chicago, 1961).

Bosmajian, Haig A. (ed.), *Readings in Speech* (New York, 1965).

Brooks, Cleanth and Warren, Robert Penn, *Modern Rhetoric* (2nd edn., New York, 1958).

Burke, Kenneth, *The Philosophy of Literary Form* (Baton Rouge, 1941; New York, 1957).

Burke, Kenneth, *A Grammar of Motives* (Eaglewood Cliffs, 1945).

Culler, Jonathan, *Structuralist Poetics* (London, 1975).

Culler, Jonathan, *The Pursuit of Signs* (London, 1981).

de Man, Paul, 'The Rhetoric of Temporality', in Charles S. Singleton (ed.), *Interpretation: Theory and Practice* (Baltimore, 1969), pp. 173–209.

Hawkes, Terence, *Structuralism and Semiotics* (London, 1977; repr. with rev. bibliography, 1983).

Jauss, Hans Robert, *Toward an Aesthetic of Reception*, tr. T. Bahti, intro. Paul de Man (Brighton, 1982).

Labov, William, 'The Transformation of Experience in Narrative Syntax', in *Language in the Inner City: Studies in the Black English Vernacular* (Philadelphia, 1972; 7th printing, 1984).

Leech, Geoffrey N., *A Linguistic Guide to English Poetry* (London, 1969).

Leech, Geoffrey N. and Short, M. H., *Style in Fiction* (London, 1981).

Mohrmann, G. P., Stewart, Charles J. and Ochs, Donovan J., *Explorations in Rhetorical Criticism* (Philadelphia and London, 1973).

Nash, Walter, *Designs in Prose: A Study of Compositional Problems and Methods* (London, 1980).

Nash, Walter, *The Language of Humor: Style and Technique in Comic Discourse* (London, 1985).

Norris, Christopher, *Deconstruction: Theory and Practice* (London and New York, 1982).

Quirk, Randolph, *Words at Work: Lectures on Textual Structure* (London, 1987).

Richards, I. A., *The Philosophy of Rhetoric* (New York and London, 1936).

Ricoeur, Paul, *The Rule of Metaphor: Multi-disciplinary Studies of the Creation of Meaning in Language*, tr. Robert Czerny with Kathleen McLaughlin and John Costello, SJ (London, 1978; first publ. 1975).

Robey, David (ed), *Structuralism: An Introduction*, Wolfson College Lectures, 1972 (London, 1973).

Subject Index

Note: Incidental references to authors, literary works, &c., are in most cases not indexed. The abbreviation *cit* = 'cited'; *cit* and *comm* = 'citation accompanied by commentary'.